AT HOME
with the WORD®
2021
Sunday Scriptures and Scripture Insights

YEAR B

Rebekah Eklund, PhD
Maribeth Howell, PhD, STD
Teresa Marshall-Patterson, MA
Letitia Thornton

ALSO AVAILABLE IN A LARGE PRINT EDITION

LTP
LITURGY
TRAINING
PUBLICATIONS

Nihil Obstat
Rev. Mr. Daniel G. Welter, JD
Chancellor
Archdiocese of Chicago
March 13, 2020

Imprimatur
Most Rev. Ronald A. Hicks
Vicar General
Archdiocese of Chicago
March 13, 2020

The *Nihil Obstat* and *Imprimatur* are declarations that the material is free from doctrinal or moral error, and thus is granted permission to publish in accordance with c. 827. No legal responsibility is assumed by the grant of this permission. No implication is contained herein that those who have granted the *Nihil Obstat* and *Imprimatur* agree with the content, opinions, or statements expressed.

Published by the authority of the Committee on Divine Worship, United States Conference of Catholic Bishops.

Prayers in the introductions to each liturgical time are adapted from *Prayers for Sundays and Seasons, Year B,* by Peter Scagnelli, Chicago: Liturgy Training Publications, 1998.

At Home with the Word® 2021 © 2020 Archdiocese of Chicago: Liturgy Training Publications, 3949 South Racine Avenue, Chicago, IL 60609; 800-933-1800; fax: 800-933-7094; email: orders@ltp.org; website: ltp.org. All rights reserved.

This book was edited by Mary G. Fox. Michael A. Dodd was the production editor, Anna Manhart was the cover designer, Anne Fritzinger was the interior designer, and Kari Nicholls was the production artist.

The cover for this year's *At Home with the Word*® is by James B. Janknegt. The interior art is by Kathy Ann Sullivan.

Printed in the United States of America

ISBN: 978-1-61671-536-6

AHW21

Welcome to At Home with the Word® 2021

THE AUTHORS OF THE INTRODUCTIONS

Marielle Frigge, OSB, taught Scripture and theology for thirty-three years at Mount Marty College in Yankton, South Dakota, and is now formation director for Sacred Heart Monastery. Michael Cameron teaches Scripture and history of Christianity in the theology department at the University of Portland in Oregon.

SCRIPTURE READINGS

For each Sunday, you will find the three readings and Responsorial Psalm from the *Lectionary for Mass*, from which readings are proclaimed in Roman Catholic churches in the United States.

SCRIPTURE INSIGHTS

Two authors have written Scripture Insights for 2021. Rebekah Eklund teaches Christian Scripture, theology, and ethics at Loyola University Maryland in Baltimore. Her doctorate in New Testament is from Duke Divinity School in Durham, North Carolina. She is the author of *Jesus Wept: The Significance of Jesus' Laments in the New Testament* (T&T Clark, 2015) and is writing a book exploring the meaning of the Beatitudes throughout history. She wrote the Scripture Insights from the Seventh Sunday of Easter through the Solemnity of Jesus Christ, King of the Universe.

Maribeth Howell is a Dominican Sister of Adrian, Michigan. She has taught Old Testament at Kenrick Seminary, in St. Louis, Missouri; St. Mary Seminary, in Wickliffe, Ohio; and Aquinas Institute of Theology, in St. Louis, Missouri, where she is professor emerita of biblical studies. Her PHD and STD are from the Catholic University of Leuven, Belgium. She is the translator of the Psalms in *Dominican Praise* and has written a variety of articles and contributed chapters in several academic and pastoral publications. Sr. Howell wrote the Scripture Insights from the First Sunday of Advent through the Solemnity of the Ascension of the Lord.

PRACTICE OF FAITH, HOPE, CHARITY

Two authors wrote the Practice of Faith, Hope, or Charity. Teresa Marshall-Patterson facilitates the Christian initiation process and liturgical ministries at St. Vincent de Paul Catholic Church in Andover, Kansas. She is the author of *We Learn About Our Parish Church* (LTP, 2010). She wrote the practices from the Seventh Sunday of Easter through the Solemnity of Our Lord Jesus Christ, King of the Universe.

Letitia Thornton has been the director of the Office of Worship in the Diocese of Boise, Idaho, for twelve years. She serves as the Region XII representative to the national board of the Federation of Diocesan Liturgical Commissions. She wrote the practices from the First Sunday of Advent through the Solemnity of the Ascension of the Lord.

ADDITIONAL DOWNLOADABLE QUESTIONS AND ACTIVITIES

Download additional questions and activities for three audiences: families, Christian initiation groups, and other adult groups. The link http://www.ltp.org/ahw will take you to the *At Home with the Word®* Extra Content page. Click on the desired audience: Adult Faith-sharing Groups, Christian Initiation Groups, or Families.

WEEKDAY READINGS

See the opening of each liturgical time for a list of Scripture texts read at Mass on weekdays and on feasts falling on weekdays.

ART FOR 2021

On the cover, James B. Janknegt has illustrated the Baptism of the Lord. This is the fifth of several scenes from salvation history to appear on the covers of *At Home with the Word®*. The reading is from John 5:1–9, proclaimed on the Feast of the Baptism of the Lord. In the interior art, Kathy Ann Sullivan uses a scratch-board technique to evoke the liturgical seasons, from our ancestors on the Jesse tree to the oil lamps for Ordinary Time in the fall. She designed the scenes in the baptismal font at St. Mary's Cathedral in Colorado Springs.

Table of Contents

The Lectionary

By Marielle Frigge, OSB

WHAT IS A LECTIONARY?

The word *lectionary* comes from the Latin word *legere*, "to read," and names a collection of Scripture readings from both the Old and New Testaments that are proclaimed throughout the liturgical year in a particular order. Christian lectionaries were in use already in the fourth century, but before the invention of the printing press in the mid-fifteenth century, readings differed from place to place. Printing allowed for a more standardized lectionary, so that Catholics around the world could hear the same Bible readings at Mass on any given day.

However, in the four centuries before the Second Vatican Council (1963–65), the lectionary had a somewhat limited ability to touch the faith lives of Catholics. Most could not understand what was read because Scripture readings as well as the prayers of the Mass were proclaimed in Latin. Further, because the lectionary of that time used only particular selections from the Bible repeated year after year, Catholics received a restricted exposure to the riches of Scripture.

GIFTS OF THE SECOND VATICAN COUNCIL

After the Second Vatican Council, not only were the biblical readings made available in the language of the people, but the structure of the lectionary was expanded as well. These changes resulted from a fresh understanding of the role of Scripture in the liturgy. Returning to the ancient understanding that Christ is present in the Scriptures, the Council Fathers further emphasized that the Eucharist nourishes God's people at two tables: the proclaimed Word of God and the Eucharistic banquet. For this reason, the revised Lectionary includes much more Scripture. Rather than repeating a yearly pattern, it includes a three-year cycle for Sundays and a two-year cycle for weekdays. Through this expanded array of selections, it aims to present the broad sweep of the salvation story, arranged purposefully around the liturgical year with the four major liturgical seasons of Advent, Christmas Time, Lent, and Easter Time punctuating the many weeks of Ordinary Time.

These great liturgical seasons instruct the faithful in the most significant aspects of salvation history. The liturgical year begins with Advent, expressing the ancient longing and hope of God's covenant people for redemption. Christmas Time celebrates the Incarnation of the Lord, God's Word of salvation fully present and active in the world, made flesh in Jesus the Christ. During Lent, the Scripture readings call Christians to deeper conversion: to amend their ways of failing to respond to God's saving Word, to cultivate greater intimacy with God, and to rejoice that he never ceases to offer life-changing mercy. These Scriptures about conversion speak powerfully to those preparing for initiation. Easter Time proclaims the Paschal Mystery, the redeeming death and Resurrection of Jesus Christ. That mystery leads us into life in divine Spirit, poured out upon all the faithful at Pentecost, sending us out to serve. In addition to highlighting the liturgical seasons, the lectionary illuminates other key mysteries of Catholic faith in solemnities such as the Most Holy Trinity, the Most Holy Body and Blood of Christ, the Assumption of the Blessed Virgin Mary, and in feasts such as the Presentation of the Lord and the Exaltation of the Holy Cross.

FOUR SUNDAY SCRIPTURE SELECTIONS

At Home with the Word® provides all four Scripture passages of each Sunday: a selection from the Old Testament (except during Easter Time when we hear from Acts of the Apostles); a Responsorial Psalm or canticle; a New Testament reading from one of the letters, the Acts of the Apostles, or Revelation; and, most important, a Gospel passage. Each year of the three-year cycle draws from a particular Gospel account: Matthew in Year A, Mark in Year B, and Luke in Year C. The Gospel of John, so highly symbolic and profound, is heard in the liturgical seasons. The Lectionary includes readings from John on several Sundays of Lent, during the Sacred Paschal Triduum, and most Sundays of Easter Time. Because Mark is the shortest Gospel account, some

Sundays of Ordinary Time in Year B use passages from John.

The pattern of today's Catholic lectionary has served as a model for lectionaries of several other Christian churches. As a result, Catholics and many Protestants hear the same Scripture passages proclaimed on Sundays. The biblical Word of God thus draws them closer.

Understanding how the four Scripture passages of each Sunday are related can help us appreciate how the lectionary invites Christians to understand, ponder, and integrate the message of God's Word. The First Reading from the Old Testament usually bears some connection to the Gospel passage, often by means of a significant person, event, or image. Rooted in the ancient practice of the Jewish synagogue, the Responsorial, which follows the First Reading, is usually from a psalm and represents the people's response to God's Word in the First Reading. In this way the first two Scripture passages mirror a theme woven throughout the Bible: God always takes the initiative to address humankind, speaking a Word that invites a response from God's people. The Responsorial may also illustrate or clarify what the First Reading proclaims, or may be related to the liturgical season, and thus is intended to foster meditation on the Word of God.

Frequently the Second Reading, always from the New Testament, follows the ancient practice of *lectio continua* (Latin for "continuous reading"), so that on each Sunday we hear important selections in order from a particular book. For example, the Second Reading is often an excerpt from one of the letters of St. Paul, and by continuous reading over several Sundays, the lectionary presents some of his major theological insights in a particular letter.

During Ordinary Time the lectionary presents continuous reading in the Gospels also, allowing us to see each evangelist's distinctive way of unfolding the Gospel story. For example, in Year A, from the Fourteenth Sunday in Ordinary Time to the end of the liturgical year in November, we hear the Gospel of Matthew from chapter 11 through chapter 25. Not every verse of Matthew is included, and occasionally a Sunday solemnity or feast requires a reading from a different Gospel, but continuous reading relates major aspects of Matthew's narrative, just as it does for Mark's in Year B and Luke's in Year C. Over time, through continuous reading, we can become familiar with the particular content and qualities of each Gospel account.

THE LECTIONARY AS A VISUAL SIGN

The lectionary nourishes us with its words proclaimed in the liturgy—the Lord's own voice speaking to his people. It also nourishes us as a visual sign of the Lord's presence among us. The United States Conference of Catholic Bishops reminds Catholics that gestures and physical objects used in liturgy are "signs by which Christians express and deepen their relationship to God" (*Built of Living Stones: Art, Architecture, and Worship,* 23). Although the Lectionary's proper place during the liturgy is on the ambo (the special podium from which readings are proclaimed), a part of the lectionary—the Gospel readings—has been made into a separate Book of the Gospels. That book, often richly decorated, may be carried in the entrance procession on Sundays and holydays. It is placed on the altar at the beginning of Mass and then, when the assembly rises to sing the Alleluia, the Gospel reader may processes with the book to the ambo, accompanied by servers holding candles. In response to the deacon or priest's introduction to the Gospel reading, the people respond, signing their forehead, lips, and heart with a small cross. Observing such signs and ceremonies, one could not miss the special reverence we give to the Word of God—especially in the Gospel.

In the bishops' teaching about the ambo, from which the Scriptures are proclaimed, we find an apt crystallization of the Church's conviction about the role of Scripture in the Mass. Urging that the ambo should be of a size and placement that draws attention to the sacred Word, the document says, "Here the Christian community encounters the living Lord in the word of God and prepares itself for the 'breaking of the bread' and the mission to live the word that will be proclaimed" (*Built of Living Stones,* 61).

Introduction to the Gospel according to Mark

By Michael Cameron

In the late 60s of the first century, nearly forty years since the Resurrection and Ascension of the Lord, he had not yet returned. Jerusalem was under siege by the Romans, and the persecution of Christians in Rome itself was intensifying after the fire of 64. Peter and Paul had died, and few eyewitnesses to Jesus' ministry were left. Christians had told and retold the stories of Jesus' ministry, death, and Resurrection over the years, but Christians began to feel the need for written instruction.

In these years, Mark, leaning on the teachings of Peter and others, wrote his Gospel, the earliest one we have. It is likely that he wrote for his suffering community in the environs of Rome. His main concern was to record the basic facts and stay faithful to the tradition, and Mark wrote with a flair for the dramatic and a rich theological sense.

Suffering had thrown Mark's community into a spiritual crisis. The crisis came not because of weak faith, but through a strong faith too focused on the privileges and glory of being the community of the Resurrection: being disciples meant enjoying the benefits of Jesus' victory (see 10:35–45). As a counterweight to this, Mark refocused on Jesus' death as the foundation of discipleship (8:31–35). Mark's primary themes of the Kingdom of God, the identity of Jesus, and the call to discipleship each undergo dramatic development in the Gospel in light of the cross. For Mark, everything, even Jesus' glorious return, stands in the shadow of his crucifixion. The German New Testament scholar Martin Kähler aptly called the Gospel according to Mark "a passion narrative with an extended introduction."

JESUS PROCLAIMS THE KINGDOM

In Mark's first chapters, Jesus is a messianic figure on the move, proclaiming the nearness of God's Kingdom in his words and works. As the Spirit "drove" Jesus into the wilderness after his baptism (1:12), so Jesus charges the early pages of Mark with divine power and urgency. The synagogue exorcism in 1:21–28 demonstrates Jesus' mastery of the spiritual world; the healings that follow in

1:29—2:10 reveal that the Kingdom's power lies in redemptive service. Jesus never defines the Kingdom of God, but the parables of chapter 4 describe its characteristics. Irresistibly it comes, grows, changes everything, feeds everyone. It heals bodies, repairs hearts, defeats evil, creates community. Nothing stops its relentless coming; not sin (2:7), disease (1:40–45), calamity (4:35–41), or demonic forces (3:22–27). The Kingdom emerges as a result of God's action, not humanity's.

The unfeeling religious leaders fail to receive the message (3:1–6). They lack the spiritual eyes and ears to perceive the new in-breaking of God's love in Jesus' ministry and the new turning to God's love that this requires. Paradoxically, Jesus finds this among tax collectors (2:15–17), the sick (1:29–34), and the wretched (5:1–20).

BECOMING DISCIPLES OF JESUS

Initial faith through the miracles is only a first step. The disciples struggle to fulfill the Master's hopes for them. "Do you not yet have faith?" Jesus asks early on (4:40). After Jesus feeds the five thousand, he cares for the disciples by walking to them on the water during their midnight struggle. They merely become frightened. Mark comments, "They had not understood the incident of the loaves. On the contrary, their hearts were hardened" (6:52). Jesus tries again by feeding the four thousand, but their minds are fixed on literal bread. "Do you still not understand?" Jesus asks (8:21).

Peter confesses that Jesus is the Messiah (8:29). But his awareness is only partial, for he needs Jesus to fit his expectations, which definitively exclude suffering. Jesus calls the idea satanic (8:33). Eventually one disciple betrays him, another denies him, and all desert him. Some readers think that Mark's telling of the disciples' failures is his way of disparaging official Christian leadership. But the disciples were later reconciled to the Lord after his Resurrection and lived to prove their faith. It is more likely that Mark is encouraging Jesus' followers to take heart from the disciples' example of recovery from failure. With Peter's martyrdom still a recent memory, the story of him denying the Lord would have special power.

CHRIST THE SUFFERING SERVANT

The Son of God has a rich, deep humanity in this Gospel. Mark's Greek word for Jesus' reaction to the plight of the leper in 1:41 might be translated "his heart melted with compassion," the same word used for Jesus' compassion on the crowds.

Jesus insists that his divinity should not be made known (1:44; 3:12; 5:43; 7:36; 8:26, 30), a motif known as the messianic secret. He refuses to be the political messiah that people expected. He reinterpreted honors in terms of his mission as suffering servant, processing into Jerusalem on a humble donkey (11:1–10), not a horse, as a conquering king would. He is anointed by an anonymous woman, not for enthronement but for burial (14:3–9). He wears royal attire and receives homage from the Gentiles, but in mockery (15:16–20). Jesus establishes the new covenant of Jeremiah 31 by becoming the Suffering Servant of Isaiah 53: "This is my blood of the covenant poured out for many" (14:24).

From the beginning the reader knows that Jesus is the Son of God (1:1). Throughout the Gospel the only voices to confess his true identity come from God (1:11; 9:7) and demons (1:24; 3:11; 5:7). Meanwhile, religious leaders call him demon-possessed (3:22), his family thinks he's a lunatic (3:21), and village neighbors complain he's pretentious (6:2–3). To their credit the disciples begin to wonder, "Who then is this?" (4:41). But no human lips confess his true identity—until the end. Stripped of his dignity, his disciples, his life, destitute and utterly alone, Jesus draws his last breath. But at this precise moment the long-awaited confession comes from a Roman centurion: "Truly this man was the Son of God!" (15:39). Jesus' death reveals the identity of God's Son, a living tableau of the disciples' calling to live the Way of the Cross. The Resurrection is proclaimed by disciples who have received a new life after they have lost their lives "for my sake and that of the gospel" (8:35).

Introduction to the Gospel according to John

By Michael Cameron

This Gospel has no year of its own in the lectionary's three-year cycle, but it is strongly represented *every* year during Christmas, Lent, and Easter Time; it also appears in Ordinary Time in Mark for Year B, Sundays 17–21. John shares some features of the first three Gospels (called "synoptic" for "seeing together"). Some stories overlap, characters seen in the synoptics reappear, and John clearly voices the evangelistic, instructional purpose of all the Gospels: that you may believe and receive life in Jesus' name (20:31).

But its vision stands majestically apart, like the eagle that became this Gospel's symbol. It is rooted in the teaching of a mysterious unnamed figure, the "disciple whom Jesus loved" (13:23; 19:26; 20:2; 21:7, 20), who authenticates this Gospel's "testimony" (19:35; 21:24). It uniquely portrays the divine Word acting with God and as God to create all things (1:1–5), taking human flesh to reveal the Father's glory (1:1, 14–18).

John communicates in distinctive ways. The Synoptics tell Jesus' story in compact vignettes; John constructs chapter-long dramas (see especially chapters 4, 9, and 11). The first three Gospels contain pithy, memorable sayings about God's Kingdom; John's Jesus speaks hypnotically repetitive discourses focused on eternal life (for example, 6:22–59; 10:1–18; chapters 14–17). The synoptics' homespun parables pique curiosity about Jesus' message; the Johannine Jesus poetically develops elements like water (4:7–15), bread (6:25–35), and light (3:19–21; 9:4–5; 12:35–36) into metaphors for contemplating divine truth.

John tells unique stories about Jesus: he changes water into wine (2:1–11), disputes with Nicodemus (3:1–21), engages the Samaritan woman at the well (4:4–26), heals a man born blind (9:1–41), raises dead Lazarus (11:1–45), chides the doubting Thomas (20:24–29), and cooks post-Easter breakfast for the disciples (21:1–14). John also varies details from some familiar synoptic stories, among which Jesus "cleanses the Temple" early in his ministry rather than late (2:13–22); the synoptics' Passover meal ("the Last Supper") is a meal *before*

Passover where Jesus washes the disciples' feet (13:4–15); the synoptic Jesus anguishes before death, but in John goes to the cross with serenity (12:27; 18:11); and unlike the synoptics, John has Jesus die on the day of preparation for Passover when the Passover lambs are sacrificed. These repeated references to Passover heighten the sacrificial symbolism of Jesus' death. Likewise, a strong liturgical symbolism makes Jesus' death the true Passover lamb sacrifice (1:29), his risen body the true Temple (2:21), and his sacramental Body and Blood the true food and drink of Israel's wilderness journey (6:53–58).

John's hallmark strategies of indirectness and double meanings entice characters to move from surface earthly meanings to encoded heavenly meanings. Some catch on, like the woman at the well (4:4–26), but others miss the point, like Nicodemus, (3:3–10), the crowds (7:32–36), and Pilate (18:33–38). This indirectness separates truly committed disciples from the half-hearted window shoppers (2:23–25). Jesus performs "signs" (not "miracles") that lure people up the new ladder of Jacob arching from earth's pictures to heaven's glory (1:51; Genesis 28:12). This imagery of signs ends in a plain revelation about Jesus' divinity not found in the synoptic Gospels. His seven solemn "I AM" statements (6:35; 8:12; 10:7; 10:11; 11:25; 14:6; 15:1) recall God's revelation to Moses as "I AM" (Exodus 3:14) and testify to Jesus as the only source of life. So the inner truth of the blind man seeing is, "I am the light of the world" (9:5), and of the dead man rising, "I am the resurrection and the life" (11:25).

Jesus' signs hint at his divine glory (2:11) to be fully revealed at his "hour" (2:4; 7:30; 8:20; 13:1). Like the disciples, readers put things together only after the Resurrection (2:22); then we realize that as Jesus was "lifted up" for crucifixion by the Romans, he was lifted up to glory by his Father (3:14; 8:28; 12:32). He mounted his cross like a king ascending his throne, as Pilate's placard unwittingly proclaimed (19:19–22). The Son's mission was to reunite the world to its source of eternal life in God (3:16; 4:34; 17:4). He died with satisfaction that this work was accomplished, and announced, "It is finished!" (19:30).

In the Gospel according to John, God the Father is unseen and mostly silent, but pervasively present. The Father sent the Son, loves him (5:20; 15:9), bears him witness (5:37; 8:18), glorifies him (8:54), and dwells with him (14:11). The Father grants the Son to have life in himself, to judge the world, and to raise the dead (5:19–30). Father and Son together gave life to the world at creation (1:1–2), and continue to do so (5:17). God the Son in human flesh has "explained" the Father, literally "brought God into the open" (1:18). The Son does this so completely that Jesus says, "Whoever has seen me has seen the Father" (14:9; 12:45).

But divine life emanates from a third mysterious presence, "the Spirit of truth" (14:17). The Father and the Son together send the Spirit (15:26), who teaches the disciples about what Jesus said and who he was (14:26; 16:13). By the Spirit's indwelling, divine life flows through them like a river (7:38–39; 14:17).

John depicts the disciples as fruitful vine branches that the Father lovingly tends (15:1–5). Omitting all other ethical instruction, this Gospel says that the only measure of the disciples' fruitfulness is their love for one another (13:34–35; 15:12–17).

True to character, this Gospel is sometimes one-sided. John's sense of Jesus' real humanity is relatively weak; and though teaching that "salvation is from the Jews" (4:22), it can be hostile toward Judaism (8:21–26, 37–59). John must be balanced by the rest of the New Testament and the Church's later teaching. But its profound spiritual theology of the Word made flesh (1:14) has decisively shaped Christian theology, spirituality, and art, ever since it was written in the late first century.

Introduction to St. Paul and His Letters

By Michael Cameron

PAUL'S CONVERSION

Saul of Tarsus was born about the same time as Jesus, to a pious Jewish family in Tarsus, in the Roman province of Cilicia (modern eastern Turkey). Well educated, and extremely religious, this son of Roman citizens was a member of the strict Pharisees (Philippians 3:5–6). In Christianity's earliest days, he says, "I persecuted the church of God beyond measure and even tried to destroy it" (Galatians 1:14–15). But then came the sudden turning point of his life: just outside Damascus, a brilliant flash of light blinded his eyes, buckled his legs, and altered his mind about God's design for human salvation (Acts 9:1–19). Christ's last known post-Resurrection appearance suddenly brought the Pharisee to birth as an Apostle, as "one born abnormally" (1 Corinthians 15:8).

Since Moses had said that anyone hanged on a tree was cursed by God, the crucified Christ had been a stumbling block to Saul, the Jew. But God revealed to Paul (Saul's Greek name) the awesome truth that this crucified man was God's power and wisdom (1 Corinthians 1:24). Christ's death and Resurrection had turned the page of world history and unleashed the powers and blessings of the Age to Come. In that knowledge, Paul discounted everything that went before in his life as "rubbish" in comparison to knowing Christ, even his prized Jewish pedigree. Paul's blockbuster insight was that, for Jews and Gentiles alike, saving faith in Jesus Christ alone, not the works of Moses' Law, made one a part of God's people (Philippians 3:5–10).

PAUL'S MISSION AND TEACHINGS

That insight released a mighty energy in Paul to announce Christ to the whole world. So began Paul's thirty-plus-year missionary ministry. He suffered beatings, imprisonments, and repeated brushes with death, but by the mid-60s of the first century, he had planted a network of vibrant Christian communities throughout the eastern Mediterranean basin. Concerned to stay in touch with his churches, to feed them with sound teaching, and to protect them from poachers, he wrote letters that eventually became part of our New Testament. Their profound theology, breathless style, and stirring imagery have kindled and rekindled Christian faith ever since.

Paul never knew the earthly Jesus, and he speaks little of stories familiar to us from the Gospels (though he knew Peter and the Apostles personally, used their traditions, and quotes Jesus' words at the first Eucharist). Paul's thinking flows almost exclusively from the reality of the Lord's death and Resurrection—the moment when God's power decisively defeated sin and inaugurated the Age to Come.

Paul explains that event with an outpouring of vivid metaphors. His imagery of "justification" imagines a scene at the Judgment Day when Christ's death acquits us of breaking the Law of Mount Sinai (Romans 3:21–31). His liturgical concept of "sanctification" pictures Christ giving believers the holiness needed to approach God in purity (1 Corinthians 6:11). Paul connects to economic imagery when he speaks of "redemption," portraying Christ's costly death buying us back from slavery to sin (Romans 3:24; 1 Corinthians 6:20). His political-military picture envisions humanity's ancient and chronic warfare with God brought to an end in "reconciliation" (Romans 5:10–11). He evokes the family with his "adoption" image, conveying our change of status when Christ made us over from slaves to children of God (Romans 8:14–15; Galatians 4:4–7).

Christians behave not according to external laws, Paul teaches, but by the force of the Holy Spirit, who produces in believers the many fruits of the new life (Galatians 5:22–23), the greatest of which is love (1 Corinthians 13:13). The same love of God displayed in Christ's death pours forth into our hearts through the Holy Spirit (Romans 5:5–8). The Spirit remakes us in the image of Christ: "all of us, gazing with unveiled face on the glory of the Lord, are being transformed into the same image from glory to glory, as from the Lord who is the Spirit" (2 Corinthians 3:18).

Christ somehow joined us to himself at his Cross so that when he died, we died (2 Corinthians 5:14). Christians "baptized into Christ's death" die to their old selves and rise to newness of life (Romans 6:3–4). In this new humanity, which leaves behind old identities, the oneness of Christ knows "neither Jew nor Greek, slave nor free, male nor female" (Galatians 3:28). All drink of the same Spirit who makes them the mystical "Body of Christ" (1 Corinthians 12:12–27), the Church, whose members offer worship to God while humbly serving one another. In Christ we are "the new creation: the old things have passed away; behold, the new things have come" (2 Corinthians 5:17).

But the new life emerging in Christians conflicts with the world as it is. Paul leaves social change to God while urging Christians to live patiently within the structures of society as they stand until the new age takes over. So slaves do not seek freedom, the unmarried do not seek marriage, and Gentiles do not seek circumcision, because "the world in its present form is passing away" (1 Corinthians 7:17–31).

For the time being we see God, the world, and ourselves in a blur, but one day we will understand everything (1 Corinthians 13:12). Bodily death is pure gain: we depart to "be with Christ" (Philippians 1:23)—Paul does not say more—and await the resurrection of the body, when Christ "will change our lowly body to conform with his glorious body" (Philippians 3:21). We will be radically different, but somehow still ourselves, just as wheat stalks are both different from, and the same as, the tiny seeds they come from (1 Corinthians 15:36–49). When that moment comes, Christ's work will be done, and God will be "all in all" (1 Corinthians 15:28).

But for Paul and his readers, including us, the present remains the time for work. With the hope of the Resurrection constantly drawing us on, Paul says, we must "be firm, steadfast, always fully devoted to the work of the Lord, knowing that in the Lord your labor is not in vain" (1 Corinthians 15:58).

Studying and Praying Scripture

By Michael Cameron

A recent study claimed that only 22 percent of American Catholics read the Bible regularly, and just 8 percent are involved in Scripture groups. Not many know how profoundly biblical the Roman Catholic Church has been from her very roots, having "always venerated the divine scriptures as she venerates the Body of the Lord" (*Dei Verbum* [*Dogmatic Constitution on Divine Revelation*], 21). How may Catholics learn to read Scripture? This essay sketches a path for seekers.

PREPARING TO READ

Become an apprentice to the Bible. Ordinary people can reach a good level of understanding, but at a cost: the Bible yields its riches to those who give themselves to the search for understanding. Start by reading daily, even if only for a few minutes. Join a group that reads and discusses Scripture together.

You will need tools. Think of yourself as a prospector for the Bible's gold. Nuggets on the ground are easily picked up, but the really rich veins lie beneath the surface. Digging requires study, commitment, and skills.

Invest in tools that reap the harvest of others' labors. Buy a study Bible with introductions, explanatory notes, and maps. Use another translation for devotional reading and comparison. Get access to a Bible dictionary with detailed information on biblical books, concepts, geography, outlines, customs, and so forth. Bible concordances will help you find all occurrences of particular words. A dictionary of biblical theology will give guidance on major theological ideas. A Bible atlas will give a sense of the locations and movements in the biblical stories. Recent Church documents on the Bible offer rich instruction to seekers.

READING FOR KNOWLEDGE

Get to know historical contexts suggested by a passage. Learn all you can about the Bible's basic story line, its "salvation history," beginning with Israel and continuing in the Church. Salvation by God's grace, obedience to God's will, and judgment on sin are basic to both Old and New Testaments. Learn about the covenants with Abraham and David that emphasize God's grace. The covenant with Moses presumes God's grace and emphasizes obedience. Both covenant traditions reemerge and are fulfilled in the New Covenant in Jesus, who pours out his life to save all people (grace) but is extremely demanding of his disciples (obedience).

Read entire books of the Bible in order to gain a sense of the "whole cloth" from which the snippets of the Sunday lectionary are cut. Try to imagine what the books meant for their original authors and audiences. Ask how and why a book was put together: What is its structure, outline, main themes, literary forms, overall purpose?

Get to know the Old Testament narratives and psalms, but learn the Gospel accounts especially. The lectionary's yearly focus on Matthew, Mark, or Luke offers an opportunity to learn each one. John is the focus during the Church's special seasons.

Reading for Wisdom

Read as one who seeks God, like the writer of Psalm 119. Ask what the text is requesting you to believe, do, or hope. Jesus' powerful proclamation in Mark 1:15 gives a strong framework: "This is the time of fulfillment" (now is the time to be attentive and ready to act); "the kingdom of God is at hand" (God is about to speak and act); "repent" (be willing to change your mind and move with fresh direction); "believe in the gospel" (embrace the grace that has already embraced you).

Read books straight through, a self-contained section at a time, carefully, slowly, and meditatively. Stop where natural breaks occur at the end of stories or sequences of thought.

Beware the sense that you already know what a text is going to say. Read attentively, asking what God is teaching you through this text at this minute about your life or about your communities— family, church, work, neighborhood, nation. Trust the Holy Spirit to guide you to what you need.

Reading for Worship

The goal of reading the Bible is not learning new facts or getting merely private inspiration for living, but entering into deeper communion with God. Allow the Bible to teach you to pray by giving you the words to use in prayer. The psalms are especially apt for this, but any part of the Bible may be prayed. This practice, dating back more than fifteen hundred years, is called *lectio divina*, Latin for "sacred reading."

Read Scripture in relation to the Eucharist. The Bible both prepares for Jesus' real presence and helps us understand it. The same Jesus who healed the lepers, stilled the storm, and embraced the children is present to us in the Word and in the sacrament.

The Bible is a library of spiritual treasures waiting to be discovered. The Church intends that this treasury be "wide open to the Christian faithful" (*Dei Verbum* [*Dogmatic Constitution on Divine Revelation*], 22).

Resources

Brown, Raymond E., ss. *101 Questions and Answers on the Bible*. Mahwah, NJ: Paulist Press, 2003.

Casey, Michael. *Sacred Reading: The Ancient Art of Lectio Divina*. Liguori, MS: Liguori, 1997.

Frigge, Marielle, osb. *Beginning Biblical Studies*. Winona, MN: Anselm Academic, 2013.

Hahn, Scott. *Catholic Bible Dictionary*. New York: Doubleday, 2009.

Magrassi, Mariano. *Praying the Bible*. Collegeville, MN: Liturgical Press, 1998.

New Collegeville Bible Commentary Series. Collegeville, MN: Liturgical Press. (Short books on individual books of the Bible, various dates.)

Paprocki, Joe. *The Bible Blueprint, A Catholic's Guide to Understanding and Embracing God's Word*. Chicago: Loyola Press, 2009.

The Bible Documents: A Parish Resource. Chicago: Liturgy Training Publications, 2001.

The Catholic Study Bible, 3rd Edition. General editor, Donald Senior, cp. New York: Oxford, 2016.

Advent

Prayer before Reading the Word

Sustain us, O God,
on our Advent journey
as we go forth to welcome
the One who is to come.

Plant within our hearts
your living Word of promise,
and make haste to help us
as we seek to understand
what we went out to see in the Advent wilderness:
your patience nurturing your saving purpose
        to fulfillment,
your power in Jesus making all things new.

We ask this through our Lord Jesus Christ,
        your Son,
who lives and reigns with you
in the unity of the Holy Spirit,
one God, for ever and ever. Amen.

Prayer after Reading the Word

Joy and gladness, O God,
attend the advent of your reign in Jesus,
for whenever the Good News is proclaimed to
        the poor,
feeble limbs are made steady,
and fearful hearts grow strong.

Give us strength for witnessing,
that we may go and tell others what we see
        and hear.
Give us patience for waiting,
until the precious harvest of your Kingdom,
when the return of your Son
will make your saving work complete.

Grant this through our Lord Jesus Christ,
who was, who is, and who is to come,
your Son, who lives and reigns with you
in the unity of the Holy Spirit,
one God, for ever and ever. Amen.

Weekday Readings

November 30: *Romans 10:9–18; Matthew 4:18–22*

December 1: *Isaiah 11:1–10; Luke 10:21–24*

December 2: *Isaiah 25:6–10a; Matthew 15:29–37*

December 3: *Isaiah 26:1–6; Matthew 7:21, 24–27*

December 4: *Isaiah 29:17–24; Matthew 9:27–31*

December 5: *Isaiah 30:19–21, 23–26; Matthew 9:35—10:1, 5a, 6–8*

December 7: *Isaiah 35:1–10; Luke 5:17–26*

December 8: Solemnity of the Immaculate Conception of the Blessed Virgin Mary
Genesis 3:9–15, 20; Ephesians 1:3–6, 11–12; Luke 1:26–38

December 9: *Isaiah 40:25–31; Matthew 11:28–30*

December 10: *Isaiah 41:13–20; Matthew 11:11–15*

December 11: *Isaiah 48:17–19; Matthew 11:16–19*

December 12: Feast of Our Lady of Guadalupe
Zechariah 2:14–17; Luke 1:26–38

December 14: *Numbers 24:2–7, 15–17a; Matthew 21:23–27*

December 15: *Zephaniah 3:1–2, 9–13; Matthew 21:28–32*

December 16: *Isaiah 45:6c–8, 18, 21c–25; Luke 7:18b–23*

December 17: *Genesis 49:2, 8–10; Matthew 1:1–17*

December 18: *Jeremiah 23:5–8; Matthew 1:18–25*

December 19: *Judges 13:2–7, 24–25a; Luke 1:5–25*

December 21: *Song of Songs 2:8–14 or Zephaniah 3:14–18a; Luke 1:39–45*

December 22: *1 Samuel 1:24–28; Luke 1:46–56*

December 23: *Malachi 3:1–4, 23–24; Luke 1:57–66*

December 24: *Morning 2 Samuel 7:1–5, 8b–12, 14a, 16; Luke 1:67–79*

November 29, 2020 FIRST SUNDAY OF ADVENT

READING I
Isaiah 63:16b–17, 19b; 64:2–7

You, LORD, are our father,
  our redeemer you are named forever.
Why do you let us wander,
      O LORD, from your ways,
  and harden our hearts so that we fear
      you not?
Return for the sake of your servants,
  the tribes of your heritage.
Oh, that you would rend the
      heavens and come down,
  with the mountains quaking before you,
while you wrought awesome
      deeds we could not hope for,
  such as they had not heard of from
      of old.
No ear has ever heard, no eye ever
      seen, any God but you
  doing such deeds for those who wait
      for him.
Would that you might meet us doing right,
  that we were mindful of you in
      our ways!
Behold, you are angry, and we are sinful;
  all of us have become like unclean people,
  all our good deeds are like polluted rags;
we have all withered like leaves,
  and our guilt carries us away like
      the wind.
There is none who calls upon your name,
  who rouses himself to cling to you;
for you have hidden your face from us
  and have delivered us up to our guilt.
Yet, O LORD, you are our father;
  we are the clay and you the potter:
  we are all the work of your hands.

RESPONSORIAL PSALM
Psalm 80:2–3, 15–16, 18–19 (4)

R. Lord, make us turn to you; let us see your face
      and we shall be saved.

O shepherd of Israel, hearken,
  from your throne upon the cherubim,
      shine forth.

Rouse your power,
  and come to save us. R.

Once again, O LORD of hosts,
  look down from heaven, and see;
take care of this vine,
  and protect what your right hand has planted,
  the son of man whom you yourself
      made strong. R.

May your help be with the man of your right hand,
  with the son of man whom you yourself
      made strong.
Then we will no more withdraw from you;
  give us new life, and we will call upon
      your name. R.

READING II *1 Corinthians 1:3–9*

Brothers and sisters: Grace to you and peace from God our Father and the Lord Jesus Christ.

I give thanks to my God always on your account for the grace of God bestowed on you in Christ Jesus, that in him you were enriched in every way, with all discourse and all knowledge, as the testimony to Christ was confirmed among you, so that you are not lacking in any spiritual gift as you wait for the revelation of our Lord Jesus Christ. He will keep you firm to the end, irreproachable on the day of our Lord Jesus Christ. God is faithful, and by him you were called to fellowship with his Son, Jesus Christ our Lord.

GOSPEL *Mark 13:33–37*

Jesus said to his disciples: "Be watchful! Be alert! You do not know when the time will come. It is like a man traveling abroad. He leaves home and places his servants in charge, each with his own work, and orders the gatekeeper to be on the watch. Watch, therefore; you do not know when the lord of the house is coming, whether in the evening, or at midnight, or at cockcrow, or in the morning. May he not come suddenly and find you sleeping. What I say to you, I say to all: 'Watch!'"

Practice of Charity

"Would that you might meet us doing right," says Isaiah in the First Reading, followed by Mark's statement in the Gospel, "May he not come suddenly and find you sleeping." Our expectation of the coming of the Lord involves responsibility on our part. "Doing" is a very specific mandate. Pope Benedict XVI wrote, "Every authentic charitable action is thus a tangible manifestation of God's love for men and women and thereby becomes a proclamation of the Gospel." The readings call for discernment and watchfulness: we should set a watch on our hearts for our lack of charity, and we need to seek God incarnate in those we feed, clothe, and tend. ◆ Spend time in prayer to discern any lack of charity in your heart. ◆ Caritas International (https://www.caritas.org/) aims to end poverty, promote justice, and restore human dignity. Discover if there is a way you can be involved in their mission. ◆ Begin this Sunday to build a practice of deliberate charity founded on a mindfulness that is awakened to our role in restoring justice through our actions.

Download more questions and activities for families, Christian initiation groups, and other adult groups at http://www.ltp.org/ahw.

Scripture Insights

This First Sunday of Advent opens with a selection from the Book of Isaiah. More specifically, within these verses, we hear the plea of community members shortly after their return from exile. The rousing words of an earlier prophet who had proclaimed incredible words of hope must have seemed like false promises to the Jews whose homeland was far from what they had envisioned it would be. In a verse that is not part of the lectionary reading, God is asked: "Why have our enemies trampled your sanctuary?" (Isaiah 63:18).

This reading is a portion of a longer lament that shows pain, doubt, and expectation. The suffering community turns to God and pleads for God to respond, to make things right. While the implication is that God is responsible for the current state of affairs, this people who claim God as "our father" (twice in the text) and "our redeemer" firmly believe that God can change their situation.

An interesting element appears to link the First Reading with the Responsorial Psalm. The statement "you have hidden your face from us," near the end of the reading from Isaiah, is followed by the Psalm refrain "Lord, make us turn to you; let us see your face and we shall be saved."

The brief selection from Mark reminds us that we are indeed in the season of Advent. We are told to be watchful and alert while we await the coming of Christ. Although Mark's message was first addressed to Christians of the first century, we too are invited to actively await the kingdom of God.

◆ Today's laments from Isaiah and Psalm 80 can be seen as an invitation to reflect on the nature of our prayer. Can you bring all your concerns to God in prayer?

◆ Read carefully Paul's words of gratitude for the community in Corinth. Take time today to express to God your gratitude for the ways in which you have been blessed.

◆ How do you intend to enter into this season of waiting? Take some time to reflect on your hopes for this Advent.

December 6, 2020 SECOND SUNDAY OF ADVENT

READING I *Isaiah 40:1–5, 9–11*

Comfort, give comfort to my people,
	says your God.
Speak tenderly to Jerusalem, and proclaim
		to her
	that her service is at an end,
	her guilt is expiated;
indeed, she has received
		from the hand of the LORD
	double for all her sins.

	A voice cries out:
In the desert prepare the way of the LORD!
	Make straight in the wasteland
		a highway for our God!
Every valley shall be filled in,
	every mountain and hill shall be
		made low;
the rugged land shall be made a plain,
	the rough country, a broad valley.
Then the glory of the LORD shall be revealed,
	and all people shall see it together;
	for the mouth of the LORD has spoken.

Go up onto a high mountain,
	Zion, herald of glad tidings;
cry out at the top of your voice,
	Jerusalem, herald of good news!
Fear not to cry out
	and say to the cities of Judah:
	Here is your God!
Here comes with power
	the Lord GOD,
	who rules by his strong arm;
here is his reward with him,
	his recompense before him.
Like a shepherd he feeds his flock;
	in his arms he gathers the lambs,
carrying them in his bosom,
	and leading the ewes with care.

RESPONSORIAL PSALM
Psalm 85:9–10, 11–12, 13–14 (8)

R. Lord, let us see your kindness,
		and grant us your salvation.

I will hear what God proclaims;
	the LORD—for he proclaims peace to his people.

Near indeed is his salvation to those who
		fear him,
	glory dwelling in our land. R.

Kindness and truth shall meet;
	justice and peace shall kiss.
Truth shall spring out of the earth,
	and justice shall look down from heaven. R.

The LORD himself will give his benefits;
	our land shall yield its increase.
Justice shall walk before him,
	and prepare the way of his steps. R.

READING II *2 Peter 3:8–14*

Do not ignore this one fact, beloved, that with the Lord one day is like a thousand years and a thousand years like one day. The Lord does not delay his promise, as some regard "delay," but he is patient with you, not wishing that any should perish but that all should come to repentance. But the day of the Lord will come like a thief, and then the heavens will pass away with a mighty roar and the elements will be dissolved by fire, and the earth and everything done on it will be found out.

Since everything is to be dissolved in this way, what sort of persons ought you to be, conducting yourselves in holiness and devotion, waiting for and hastening the coming of the day of God, because of which the heavens will be dissolved in flames and the elements melted by fire. But according to his promise we await new heavens and a new earth in which righteousness dwells. Therefore, beloved, since you await these things, be eager to be found without spot or blemish before him, at peace.

GOSPEL *Mark 1:1–8*

The beginning of the gospel of Jesus Christ the Son of God.
	As it is written in Isaiah the prophet:

*Behold, I am sending my messenger ahead
		of you;
	he will prepare your way.
A voice of one crying out in the desert:
	"Prepare the way of the Lord,
	make straight his paths."*

John the Baptist appeared in the desert proclaiming a baptism of repentance for the forgiveness of sins. People of the whole Judean countryside and all the inhabitants of Jerusalem were going out to him and were being baptized by him in the Jordan River as they acknowledged their sins. John was clothed in camel's hair, with a leather belt around his waist. He fed on locusts and wild honey. And this is what he proclaimed: "One mightier than I is coming after me. I am not worthy to stoop and loosen the thongs of his sandals. I have baptized you with water; he will baptize you with the Holy Spirit."

Practice of Hope

Isaiah calls us to be comforted and promises that our service and our guilt are over—that we will see together the glory of the Lord. In the Second Reading, we are told of new heavens and a new earth. And in the Gospel, the fruition of these promises is defined when John the Baptist declares that soon, baptized with the Holy Spirit, we will be ushered into a new kind of being. Our hope in the fulfillment of these promises sustains us. Ask yourself how a truly hopeful person lives. ◆ Go for a walk in nature ("go up onto a high mountain"), even if only to a city park, and thank God for the gift of the natural world; let your hope make you joyful in your interactions with others. ◆ Reflect on a situation in which you have cause to feel comfort. Pray the Rosary, focusing on the Joyful Mysteries. ◆ Talk to your children, grandchildren, or a godchild about the day they were baptized, and if you remember your Baptism, or have heard stories about it, recount it for them.

Download more questions and activities for families, Christian initiation groups, and other adult groups at http://www.ltp.org/ahw.

Scripture Insights

What wonderful readings we hear on this Second Sunday of Advent! The text from Isaiah is often referred to as the opening of the "book of consolation," a work attributed to a prophet who ministered near the end of the exile in Babylon. The announcement of the return to Jerusalem under the tender care of a loving God must have seemed too good to be true for a community living under the rule of the Babylonians, the people who had devastated both the holy city and Temple and who were responsible for the circumstances of the exiles.

Today's reading from 2 Peter can be confusing since it addresses several related concerns. Perhaps our focus might best be directed to how we live each day while patiently awaiting the Lord's coming. Although we know not when the Lord will come, that coming has been promised, and God is faithful.

The opening lines of Mark's Gospel account state clearly that what is to follow is good news about the Son of God. While Mark attributes the next two sentences to the prophet Isaiah, the quotation is actually a conflation of material about guarding or preparing the way in the Books of Exodus, Malachi, and Isaiah. Although the author of Mark was quite familiar with the Hebrew Scriptures, his quotations are not always in perfect sync with the texts with which we are most familiar. Nevertheless, this reading introduces John the Baptist, who in turn prepares us for the arrival of Jesus in the next scene in Mark.

◆ Even if there had been a direct route, the distance from Babylon to Jerusalem would have been over five hundred miles. Reflect on Isaiah's depiction of this smooth journey home.

◆ Have you ever waited expectantly for a loved one's arrival? Imagine welcoming the coming of God's kingdom with that same anticipation.

◆ Is there something that you can do in your family, community, or workplace to actively bring forth God's kingdom of justice and peace?

December 13, 2020 THIRD SUNDAY OF ADVENT

READING I Isaiah 61:1–2a, 10–11

The spirit of the Lord GOD is upon me,
    because the LORD has anointed me;
he has sent me to bring glad tidings to the poor,
    to heal the brokenhearted,
to proclaim liberty to the captives
    and release to the prisoners,
to announce a year of favor from the LORD
    and a day of vindication by our God.

I rejoice heartily in the LORD,
    in my God is the joy of my soul;
for he has clothed me with a robe of salvation
    and wrapped me in a mantle of justice,
like a bridegroom adorned with a diadem,
    like a bride bedecked with her jewels.
As the earth brings forth its plants,
    and a garden makes its growth spring up,
so will the Lord GOD make justice and praise
    spring up before all the nations.

RESPONSORIAL PSALM Luke 1:46–48, 49–50, 53–54 (Isaiah 61:10b)

R. My soul rejoices in my God.

My soul proclaims the greatness of the LORD;
    my spirit rejoices in God my Savior,
for he has looked upon his lowly servant.
    From this day all generations will call
        me blessed. R.

The Almighty has done great things for me,
    and holy is his Name.
He has mercy on those who fear him
    in every generation. R.

He has filled the hungry with good things,
    and the rich he has sent away empty.
He has come to the help of his servant Israel
    for he has remembered his promise
        of mercy. R.

READING II 1 Thessalonians 5:16–24

Brothers and sisters: Rejoice always. Pray without ceasing. In all circumstances give thanks, for this is the will of God for you in Christ Jesus. Do not quench the Spirit. Do not despise prophetic utterances. Test everything; retain what is good. Refrain from every kind of evil.

May the God of peace make you perfectly holy and may you entirely, spirit, soul, and body, be preserved blameless for the coming of our Lord Jesus Christ. The one who calls you is faithful, and he will also accomplish it.

GOSPEL John 1:6–8, 19–28

A man named John was sent from God. He came for testimony, to testify to the light, so that all might believe through him. He was not the light, but came to testify to the light.

And this is the testimony of John. When the Jews from Jerusalem sent priests and Levites to him to ask him, "Who are you?" he admitted and did not deny it, but admitted, "I am not the Christ." So they asked him, "What are you then? Are you Elijah?" And he said, "I am not." "Are you the Prophet?" He answered, "No." So they said to him, "Who are you, so we can give an answer to those who sent us? What do you have to say for yourself?" He said:

"I am the voice of one crying out in the desert,
'make straight the way of the Lord,'

as Isaiah the prophet said." Some Pharisees were also sent. They asked him, "Why then do you baptize if you are not the Christ or Elijah or the Prophet?" John answered them, "I baptize with water; but there is one among you whom you do not recognize, the one who is coming after me, whose sandal strap I am not worthy to untie." This happened in Bethany across the Jordan, where John was baptizing.

Practice of Hope

Hope is a voice crying out, "The Lord is coming." As Christians, we are called to rejoice in that event, and to celebrate a long list of glad tidings: liberty, healing, release, justice, vindication. Hope is not, however, unbridled optimism but rather the virtue of securing one's happiness in the goodness of God despite affliction. Recall that hope and suffering are intertwined. Look for examples around you of those whose lives are not easy yet who maintain a hopeful spirit, and try to find a reason to hope in a circumstance that has caused you pain. ◆ Practice hope by submitting a challenge or trouble in your life to God. As you do, strengthen your hope by meditating on those things God has already done in your life. ◆ If Evening Prayer is scheduled at a nearby parish, attend and sing the Magnificat with your family of faith. ◆ Join with family and friends and sing or pray together today's Responsorial Psalm or Mary's great song of praise in Luke 1:46–55.

Download more questions and activities for families, Christian initiation groups, and other adult groups at http://www.ltp.org/ahw.

Scripture Insights

For the third consecutive week, our First Reading is from the Book of Isaiah. In today's selection we hear the words of one who is called by God to be an instrument of God's nurturing love to those most in need—the poor, the brokenhearted, and those imprisoned and held captive.

Our Responsorial Psalm today is one of the most well-known poems of the New Testament, Mary's Magnificat. The words are reminiscent of the song Hannah sings (1 Samuel 2:1–10) as she rejoices after having borne a son and offered him back to the Lord.

In Paul's letter to the Thessalonian community, we hear a series of rapid commands: *Rejoice. Pray. Do not quench the Spirit. Do not despise prophecy. Test everything.* Paul then offers a brief but beautiful prayer that reminds us that God is always faithful.

Today's Gospel from John hearkens back to last week's Gospel from Mark, where we were introduced to John the Baptist. Once again, we find ourselves at the beginning of a Gospel. Unlike Mark's straightforward telling of the Baptist's ministry, this Gospel presents the Baptist somewhat more mysteriously. He is one who came "to testify to the light." When questioned by the authorities about his identity, his responses are "I am not" and "no." Finally, John the Baptist identifies himself as the one who is preparing the way for one far greater than he. That one, although not named in this reading, is Jesus the Christ.

◆ Who are the people most in need of compassion to whom you are called to bring God's love?

◆ Reflect on some of the great things that God has done for you. Rejoice in how you have been blessed.

◆ How do you see yourself as a herald of Good News? Do you see this as a privilege or a burden?

READING I
2 Samuel 7:1–5, 8b–12, 14a, 16

When King David was settled in his palace, and the LORD had given him rest from his enemies on every side, he said to Nathan the prophet, "Here I am living in a house of cedar, while the ark of God dwells in a tent!" Nathan answered the king, "Go, do whatever you have in mind, for the LORD is with you." But that night the LORD spoke to Nathan and said: "Go, tell my servant David, 'Thus says the LORD: Should you build me a house to dwell in?

"'It was I who took you from the pasture and from the care of the flock to be commander of my people Israel. I have been with you wherever you went, and I have destroyed all your enemies before you. And I will make you famous like the great ones of the earth. I will fix a place for my people Israel; I will plant them so that they may dwell in their place without further disturbance. Neither shall the wicked continue to afflict them as they did of old, since the time I first appointed judges over my people Israel. I will give you rest from all your enemies. The LORD also reveals to you that he will establish a house for you. And when your time comes and you rest with your ancestors, I will raise up your heir after you, sprung from your loins, and I will make his kingdom firm. I will be a father to him, and he shall be a son to me. Your house and your kingdom shall endure forever before me; your throne shall stand firm forever.'"

RESPONSORIAL PSALM
Psalm 89:2–3, 4–5, 27, 29 (2a)

R. For ever I will sing the goodness of the Lord.

The promises of the LORD I will sing forever;
    through all generations my mouth shall
        proclaim your faithfulness.
For you have said, "My kindness is
        established forever";
    in heaven you have confirmed your
        faithfulness. R.

"I have made a covenant with my chosen one,
    I have sworn to David my servant:
forever will I confirm your posterity
    and establish your throne
        for all generations." R.

"He shall say of me, 'You are my father,
    my God, the Rock, my savior.'
Forever I will maintain my kindness toward him,
    and my covenant with him stands firm." R.

READING II *Romans 16:25–27*

Brothers and sisters: To him who can strengthen you, according to my gospel and the proclamation of Jesus Christ, according to the revelation of the mystery kept secret for long ages but now manifested through the prophetic writings and, according to the command of the eternal God, made known to all nations to bring about the obedience of faith, to the only wise God, through Jesus Christ be glory forever and ever. Amen.

GOSPEL *Luke 1:26–38*

The angel Gabriel was sent from God to a town of Galilee called Nazareth, to a virgin betrothed to a man named Joseph, of the house of David, and the virgin's name was Mary. And coming to her, he said, "Hail, full of grace! The Lord is with you." But she was greatly troubled at what was said and pondered what sort of greeting this might be. Then the angel said to her, "Do not be afraid, Mary, for you have found favor with God.

"Behold, you will conceive in your womb and bear a son, and you shall name him Jesus. He will be great and will be called Son of the Most High, and the Lord God will give him the throne of David his father, and he will rule over the house of Jacob forever, and of his kingdom there will be no end." But Mary said to the angel, "How can this be, since I have no relations with a man?" And the angel said to her in reply, "The Holy Spirit will come upon you, and the power of the Most High will overshadow you. Therefore the child to be born will be called holy, the Son of God." And behold, Elizabeth, your relative, has also conceived a son in her old age, and this is the sixth month for her who was called barren; for nothing will be impossible for God." Mary said, "Behold, I am the handmaid of the Lord. May it be done to me according to your word." Then the angel departed from her.

Practice of Faith

Throughout the ages, Mary's profound act of faith has provided artists with an endlessly fascinating subject, resulting in beautiful works of art depicting the Annunciation. In many of these, Mary's fear and confusion, her isolation and humility, are evident. Alone with a messenger of God, she needs convincing to accept that God has indeed chosen her to participate in his salvific act. In the end, her faith has its roots not in her strength but in God's. Faith does not do away with all fear but rather provides the possessor with an unwavering foundation. ◆ Look up paintings featuring the Annunciation. What do you see in them? How might Mary's situation reflect your relationship with God? How does it speak to the challenges presented to you as a person of faith in an increasingly secular time? ◆ Spend time in prayer and try to identify when your faith is strong and when it is weak. ◆ Talk to someone (a priest, a spiritual director, a close friend) about your life of faith. Do you see it as an ongoing journey or seem to be standing still?

Download more questions and activities for families, Christian initiation groups, and other adult groups at http://www.ltp.org/ahw.

Scripture Insights

The first of today's readings is one of the best-known texts from the historical books of the Old Testament. What has come to be known as "the Davidic promise" tells of David's desire to build a house for the Lord. While David's plan seems to get off to a good start, the prophet Nathan informs him that this plan will not go forward. Instead, God has something else in mind. God will establish a dynasty (the same word in Hebrew can be translated "house") for David. At its heart, this passage is about the faithfulness of God and God's Word. The Responsorial Psalm continues this theme and celebrates the faithfulness of God.

The three verses from Paul's Letter to the Romans remind us that human beings cannot understand the ways in which God works within human history. The mystery of God is revealed in the person of Jesus the Christ, the one whose mystery we ponder this season.

Luke is the only evangelist who recounts for us the annunciations of the births of both John the Baptist and Jesus. Today we focus on Mary's response to the announcement that she will give birth to a son and name him Jesus and that he will be recognized as "Son of the Most High." Further (and linking this text with today's First Reading), Mary is told that "the Lord God will give him the throne of David his father, and he will rule over the house of Jacob forever, and of his kingdom there will be no end."

These readings invite us to enter deeply into the mysterious ways of God. The story of David, a man favored by God, fills chapter upon chapter of the Old Testament, while Mary appears in only a few brief and scattered texts outside of this passage and the birth narrative of Matthew.

◆ Reflect on how you understand God's faithfulness to you and on your faithfulness to God.

◆ In what ways have you been invited to bring the mystery of God to light?

◆ How has God been made manifest to you and, through you, to those you encounter?

Christmas Time

Prayer before Reading the Word

Almighty God, Creator of all,
whose Word was present with you in
          the beginning
and whose wisdom was placed
at the service of your plan,
enlighten us to know the glorious hope
to which you have called us;
fill us with faith in Jesus and
with love toward all your people,
that we who have seen in Christ
the glory of your Word made flesh
may bear into the world you so love,
the Light no darkness can extinguish:
your Son, our Lord Jesus Christ,
who lives and reigns with you
in the unity of the Holy Spirit,
one God, for ever and ever. Amen.

Prayer after Reading the Word

Your Word, O God of ageless glory,
dwelling with you from before time,
has become flesh and lived among us,
and we have seen the glory of your Christ.

Place on our lips the word of salvation,
in our hearts a love that welcomes all,
and, in the depths of our being,
the light of faith and hope,
which the darkness can never overcome.
We ask this through our Lord Jesus Christ,
          your Son,
who lives and reigns with you
in the unity of the Holy Spirit,
one God, for ever and ever. Amen.

Weekday Readings

December 26: Feast of St. Stephen
  Acts 6:8–10; 7:54–59; Matthew 10:17–22

December 28: Feast of the Holy Innocents
  1 John 1:5—2:2; Matthew 2:13–18
December 29: Fifth Day within the Octave of the Lord
  1 John 2:3–11; Luke 2:22–35
December 30: Sixth Day within the Octave of the Lord
  1 John 2:12–17; Luke 2:36–40
December 31: Seventh Day within the Octave of the Lord
  1 John 2:18–21; John 1:1–18
January 1: Solemnity of Mary, Mother of God
  Numbers 6:22–27; Galatians 4:4–7; Luke 2:16–21
January 2: *1 John 2:22–28; John 1:19–28*

January 4: *1 John 3:22—4:6; Matthew 4:12–17, 23–25*
January 5: *1 John 4:7–10; Mark 6:34–44*
January 6: *1 John 4:11–18; Mark 6:45–52*
January 7: *1 John 4:19—5:4; Luke 4:14–22*
January 8: *1 John 5:5–13; Luke 5:12–16*
January 9: *1 John 5:14–21; John 3:22–30*

READING I *Isaiah 62:1–5*

For Zion's sake I will not be silent,
    for Jerusalem's sake I will not be quiet,
until her vindication shines forth like the dawn
    and her victory like a burning torch.

Nations shall behold your vindication,
    and all the kings your glory;
you shall be called by a new name
    pronounced by the mouth of the LORD.
You shall be a glorious crown in the hand
            of the LORD,
    a royal diadem held by your God.
No more shall people call you "Forsaken,"
    or your land "Desolate,"
but you shall be called "My Delight,"
    and your land "Espoused."
For the LORD delights in you
    and makes your land his spouse.
As a young man marries a virgin,
    your Builder shall marry you;
and as a bridegroom rejoices in his bride
    so shall your God rejoice in you.

RESPONSORIAL PSALM
Psalm 89:4–5, 16–17, 27, 29 (2a)

R. For ever I will sing the goodness of the LORD.

I have made a covenant with my chosen one,
    I have sworn to David my servant:
forever will I confirm your posterity
    and establish your throne for all
            generations. R.

Blessed the people who know the joyful shout;
    in the light of your countenance, O LORD,
            they walk.
At your name they rejoice all the day,
    and through your justice they are exalted. R.

He shall say of me, "You are my father,
    my God, the rock, my savior."
Forever I will maintain my kindness toward him,
    and my covenant with him stands firm. R.

READING II *Acts 13:16–17, 22–25*

When Paul reached Antioch in Pisidia and entered the synagogue, he stood up, motioned with his hand, and said, "Fellow Israelites and you others who are God-fearing, listen. The God of this people Israel chose our ancestors and exalted the people during their sojourn in the land of Egypt. With uplifted arm he led them out of it. Then he removed Saul and raised up David as king; of him he testified, 'I have found David, son of Jesse, a man after my own heart; he will carry out my every wish.' From this man's descendants God, according to his promise, has brought to Israel a savior, Jesus. John heralded his coming by proclaiming a baptism of repentance to all the people of Israel; and as John was completing his course, he would say, 'What do you suppose that I am? I am not he. Behold, one is coming after me; I am not worthy to unfasten the sandals of his feet.'"

GOSPEL *Matthew 1:18–25*

Longer: Matthew 1:1–25

This is how the birth of Jesus Christ came about. When his mother Mary was betrothed to Joseph, but before they lived together, she was found with child through the Holy Spirit. Joseph her husband, since he was a righteous man, yet unwilling to expose her to shame, decided to divorce her quietly. Such was his intention when, behold, the angel of the Lord appeared to him in a dream and said, "Joseph, son of David, do not be afraid to take Mary your wife into your home. For it is through the Holy Spirit that this child has been conceived in her. She will bear a son and you are to name him Jesus, because he will save his people from their sins." All this took place to fulfill what the Lord had said through the prophet:

Behold, the virgin shall conceive and bear a son,
    and they shall name him Emmanuel,

which means "God is with us." When Joseph awoke, he did as the angel of the Lord had commanded him and took his wife into his home. He had no relations with her until she bore a son, and he named him Jesus.

Practice of Faith

Poet Li-Young Lee ends the poem "Nativity" stating that a safe place in the heart needs to be made as God approaches. We have spent four weeks preparing for Emmanuel, God-with-us. Now that he is here, what does the Incarnation mean in your life? The Gospel reading takes care to place the birth of Jesus well within humanity's lineage: the human heart is the natural home for the Son of Man. ◆ Read the poem "Nativity" and Gerard Manley Hopkins's poem "God's Grandeur." Consider how you will make your heart safe for the approach of God. ◆ Contemplate the difference the presence of Christ brings to the world. How are you made different by the presence of God in your heart? ◆ Name one way your worldview is different because of your faith. What one thing could you do to manifest that difference?

Download more questions and activities for families, Christian initiation groups, and other adult groups at http://www.ltp.org/ahw.

Scripture Insights

Our First Reading returns to the latter part of the Book of Isaiah, with a selection attributed to the end of the exile or early postexilic period. The prophet's words announce that God is about to change Israel's fate. This people who have experienced devastation at the hands of the Babylonians and who must have felt "forsaken" by God are about to once again become God's "delight."

The Responsorial Psalm is almost identical to the verses proclaimed on the Fourth Sunday of Advent. In today's context, the Psalm seems to reaffirm that the hope-filled words of Isaiah are as trustworthy as God's everlasting covenant.

The reading from the Acts of the Apostles finds Paul addressing both Jews and Gentiles in the city of Antioch. Paul's words reinforce his belief that salvation history began when God chose Israel as God's own and guided them out of captivity in Egypt. Paul references two figures who have played prominent roles throughout Advent: King David, referred to as a man after God's own heart, and John the Baptist, who heralded Jesus' coming.

The Gospel readings for the Second, Third, and Fourth Sundays of Advent were from the opening chapters of Mark, John, and Luke, respectively. Today, on the Solemnity of the Nativity, the reading is from the first chapter of Matthew. This text recounts "how the birth of Jesus Christ came about," with considerable emphasis on Joseph, Mary's faithful spouse, whose voice is not heard in any Gospel text. Joseph, the quiet man, listened to the voice of God and became a powerful, though almost invisible, instrument in bringing about God's design.

◆ Read today's text from the prophet Isaiah. Imagine that God is calling you "My Delight." How would your life change if you truly believed that you were a delight to God?

◆ In Matthew's Gospel, God appears to Joseph in a dream. Reflect on the mysterious ways in which God has been revealed to you.

◆ How is Joseph a model of faith?

READING I *Genesis 15:1–6; 21:1–3*

Alternate: Sirach 3:2–6, 12–14

The word of the LORD came to Abram in a vision, saying:

"Fear not, Abram!
  I am your shield;
  I will make your reward very great."

But Abram said, "O Lord GOD, what good will your gifts be, if I keep on being childless and have as my heir the steward of my house, Eliezer?" Abram continued, "See, you have given me no offspring, and so one of my servants will be my heir." Then the word of the LORD came to him: "No, that one shall not be your heir; your own issue shall be your heir." The Lord took Abram outside and said, "Look up at the sky and count the stars, if you can. Just so," he added, "shall your descendants be." Abram put his faith in the LORD, who credited it to him as an act of righteousness.

The LORD took note of Sarah as he had said he would; he did for her as he had promised. Sarah became pregnant and bore Abraham a son in his old age, at the set time that God had stated. Abraham gave the name Isaac to this son of his whom Sarah bore him.

RESPONSORIAL PSALM
Psalm 105:1–2, 3–4, 6–7, 8–9 (7a, 8a)

Alternate: Psalm 128:1–2, 3, 4–5 (see 1)

R. The Lord remembers his covenant forever.

Give thanks to the LORD, invoke his name;
  make known among the nations his deeds.
Sing to him, sing his praise,
  proclaim all his wondrous deeds. R.

Glory in his holy name;
  rejoice, O hearts that seek the LORD!
Look to the LORD in his strength;
  constantly seek his face. R.

You descendants of Abraham, his servants,
  sons of Jacob, his chosen ones!
He, the LORD, is our God;
  throughout the earth his judgments
    prevail. R.

He remembers forever his covenant
  which he made binding for a
    thousand generations
which he entered into with Abraham
  and by his oath to Isaac. R.

READING II *Hebrews 11:8, 11–12, 17–19*

Alternate: Colossians 3:12–21 or 3:12–17

Brothers and sisters: By faith Abraham obeyed when he was called to go out to a place that he was to receive as an inheritance; he went out, not knowing where he was to go. By faith he received power to generate, even though he was past the normal age—and Sarah herself was sterile—for he thought that the one who had made the promise was trustworthy. So it was that there came forth from one man, himself as good as dead, descendants as numerous as the stars in the sky and as countless as the sands on the seashore.

By faith Abraham, when put to the test, offered up Isaac, and he who had received the promises was ready to offer his only son, of whom it was said, "Through Isaac descendants shall bear your name." He reasoned that God was able to raise even from the dead, and he received Isaac back as a symbol.

GOSPEL *Luke 2:22–40*

Shorter: Luke 2:22, 39–40

When the days were completed for their purification according to the law of Moses, they took him up to Jerusalem to present him to the Lord, just as it is written in the law of the Lord, *Every male that opens the womb shall be consecrated to the Lord,* and to offer the sacrifice of *a pair of turtledoves or two young pigeons,* in accordance with the dictate in the law of the Lord.

Now there was a man in Jerusalem whose name was Simeon. This man was righteous and devout, awaiting the consolation of Israel, and the Holy Spirit was upon him. It had been revealed to him by the Holy Spirit that he should not see death before he had seen the Christ of the Lord. He came in the Spirit into the temple; and when the parents brought in the child Jesus to perform the custom of the law in regard to him, he took him into his arms and blessed God, saying:

"Now, Master, you may let your servant go
　in peace, according to your word,
for my eyes have seen your salvation,
　which you prepared in sight of all the peoples,
a light for revelation to the Gentiles,
　and glory for your people Israel."

The child's father and mother were amazed at what was said about him; and Simeon blessed them and said to Mary his mother, "Behold, this child is destined for the fall and rise of many in Israel, and to be a sign that will be contradicted—and you yourself a sword will pierce—so that the thoughts of many hearts may be revealed." There was also a prophetess, Anna, the daughter of Phanuel, of the tribe of Asher. She was advanced in years, having lived seven years with her husband after her marriage, and then as a widow until she was eighty-four. She never left the temple, but worshiped night and day with fasting and prayer. And coming forward at that very time, she gave thanks to God and spoke about the child to all who were awaiting the redemption of Jerusalem.

When they had fulfilled all the prescriptions of the law of the Lord, they returned to Galilee, to their own town of Nazareth. The child grew and became strong, filled with wisdom; and the favor of God was upon him.

Practice of Faith

Through faith Abraham and Sarah conceived; because of his faith Simeon lived to see the Savior. The holiness of the Holy Family increased through acts of faith, as Mary and Joseph trusted God enough to say *yes* against overwhelming odds. Through similar acts of faith, families today are created and remain united to the Church; it is their faith in God's love for them that allows them to declare themselves holy, as Mary, Joseph, and Jesus were holy. ◆ Pray for a family you know that is going through a difficult time.

Download more questions and activities for families, Christian initiation groups, and other adult groups at http://www.ltp.org/ahw.

Scripture Insights

The readings from Genesis and the Gospel of Luke present us with scenes in the lives of two important families. The account from Genesis depicts Abram's frustration at not having fathered a child. When God consoles Abram with another promise of offspring, Abram responds by placing his faith in God. In turn, the text tells us that "the LORD took note of Sarah," and she gave birth to their long-awaited son.

The refrain from Psalm 105, "The Lord remembers his covenant forever," reinforces the message of the Genesis readings.

In the Letter to the Hebrews, the author summarizes the story of Abraham and identifies him as a person of faith. Upon hearing this summary of Abraham's life, the words of the Psalm refrain are readily brought back to mind. Although Abraham struggled with believing that God could make Sarah fruitful, Abraham "put his faith in the Lord," and for this reason, the praises of Abraham are extolled in the New Testament.

Luke tells us of the presentation of Jesus in the Temple. While Simeon and Anna are depicted as having long awaited the coming of this child, Mary and Joseph are described as being "amazed at what was said of him." Upon the family's return to Nazareth, the child Jesus "grew and became strong, filled with wisdom, and the favor of God was upon him." The following verses in Luke, vv. 41–52, tell the story of Jesus, at age twelve, in the Temple.

◆ The next time you have a clear view of the heavens, reflect on God's unfailing love.

◆ Read today's Responsorial Psalm. Give thanks for specific blessings you have received.

◆ Simeon's words in the Gospel are a part of the Church's Night Prayer. Reflect on why these words are appropriate for the end of the day.

READING I *Isaiah 60:1–6*

Rise up in splendor, Jerusalem!
　　Your light has come,
　　the glory of the Lord shines upon you.
See, darkness covers the earth,
　　and thick clouds cover the peoples;
but upon you the LORD shines,
　　and over you appears his glory.
Nations shall walk by your light,
　　and kings by your shining radiance.
Raise your eyes and look about;
　　they all gather and come to you:
your sons come from afar,
　　and your daughters in the arms of
　　　　their nurses.

Then you shall be radiant at what you see,
　　your heart shall throb and overflow,
for the riches of the sea shall be
　　　　emptied out before you,
　　the wealth of nations shall be brought to you.
Caravans of camels shall fill you,
　　dromedaries from Midian and Ephah;
all from Sheba shall come
　　bearing gold and frankincense,
　　and proclaiming the praises of the LORD.

RESPONSORIAL PSALM
Psalm 72:1–2, 7–8, 10–11, 12–13 (see 11)

R. Lord, every nation on earth will adore you.

O God, with your judgment endow the king,
　　and with your justice, the king's son;
he shall govern your people with justice
　　and your afflicted ones with judgment. R.

Justice shall flower in his days,
　　and profound peace, till the moon be no more.
May he rule from sea to sea,
　　and from the River to the ends of the earth. R.

The kings of Tarshish and the Isles shall offer gifts;
　　the kings of Arabia and Seba shall
　　　　bring tribute.
All kings shall pay him homage,
　　all nations shall serve him. R.

For he shall rescue the poor when he cries out,
　　and the afflicted when he has
　　　　no one to help him.
He shall have pity for the lowly and the poor;
　　the lives of the poor he shall save. R.

READING II *Ephesians 3:2–3a, 5–6*

Brothers and sisters: You have heard of the stewardship of God's grace that was given to me for your benefit, namely, that the mystery was made known to me by revelation. It was not made known to people in other generations as it has now been revealed to his holy apostles and prophets by the Spirit: that the Gentiles are coheirs, members of the same body, and copartners in the promise in Christ Jesus through the gospel.

GOSPEL *Matthew 2:1–12*

When Jesus was born in Bethlehem of Judea, in the days of King Herod, behold, magi from the east arrived in Jerusalem, saying, "Where is the newborn king of the Jews? We saw his star at its rising and have come to do him homage." When King Herod heard this, he was greatly troubled, and all Jerusalem with him. Assembling all the chief priests and the scribes of the people, he inquired of them where the Christ was to be born. They said to him, "In Bethlehem of Judea, for thus it has been written through the prophet:

　　And you, Bethlehem, land of Judah,
　　　　are by no means least among the rulers
　　　　　　of Judah;
　　since from you shall come a ruler,
　　　　who is to shepherd my people Israel."

Then Herod called the magi secretly and ascertained from them the time of the star's appearance. He sent them to Bethlehem and said, "Go and search diligently for the child. When you have found him, bring me word, that I too may go and do him homage." After their audience with the king they set out. And behold, the star that they had seen at its rising preceded them, until it came and stopped over the place where the child was. They were overjoyed at seeing the star, and on entering the house they saw the child with Mary his mother. They prostrated themselves and did him homage. Then they opened their treasures and offered him gifts of gold, frankincense, and myrrh. And having been warned in a dream not to return to Herod, they departed for their country by another way.

Practice of Hope

Humanity is compelled to seek the animating light that shines over all, to seek God above all things. Oneness with God is the purpose of our earthly life; we are seeking for what we believe, for what we desire: the kingdom of heaven. We persist in that belief despite hardship and danger. The reading from Isaiah shows that the virtue of hope is expressed in opposition to the troubles that naturally befall us. ("See, darkness covers the earth / . . . / but upon you the LORD shines.") For Christians, this is made manifest in the Beatitudes: Blessed are those—the poor, the meek, the suffering —whose hope is in the promise of the kingdom of heaven. ◆ Prayerfully study the Beatitudes (Matthew 5:1–12); what challenges you about this discourse? What gives you hope? ◆ Pray for those who are persecuted because of their Christian faith. ◆ Practice the virtue of hope this week by comforting someone who is suffering.

Download more questions and activities for families, Christian initiation groups, and other adult groups at http://www.ltp.org/ahw.

Scripture Insights

On this Feast of the Epiphany, on which we celebrate the manifestation of God among all peoples, we hear once again rousing words from the Book of Isaiah. Note that in our reading the text is addressed to Jerusalem, the holy city, not to either a prophet or the people. While the word *Jerusalem* does not appear in the Hebrew text, it would seem that the editors of the lectionary wanted to make clear to the listeners of this proclamation that the words are, indeed, addressed to the holy city. Commentators agree that this portion of Isaiah focuses on the role of Jerusalem, the soon-to-be-restored city, where God's glory will be made manifest.

The first two chapters of Matthew's Gospel account are commonly referred to as the infancy narrative, and this material is often divided into several sections. Today's verses are frequently identified as "the adoration of the Magi." Another element may be important to note. The word *Bethlehem*, the place of Jesus' birth, appears four times in these twelve verses. Might we consider this town, this earthly place, a specific location at a given time in human history, where Jesus, son of David and Son of God, is made manifest in human flesh? It is because of this mystery of the Incarnation that the author of the Letter to the Ephesians could write of the Spirit "that the Gentiles are coheirs, members of the same body, and copartners in the promise of Christ Jesus through the gospel."

◆ Reflect on the ways that God has been revealed to you.

◆ Today's Responsorial Psalm presents us with the depiction of an ideal king, a king who "rescues the poor when they cry out." What is your responsibility in helping to bring about such a world where justice and compassion reign?

◆ How has your image of Jesus coming into the world changed since your childhood? What does Christmas mean to you today?

READING I *Isaiah 55:1–11*

Alternate: Isaiah 42:1–4, 6–7

Thus says the LORD:
All you who are thirsty,
  come to the water!
You who have no money,
  come, receive grain and eat;
come, without paying and without cost,
  drink wine and milk!
Why spend your money for what is not bread,
  your wages for what fails to satisfy?
Heed me, and you shall eat well,
  you shall delight in rich fare.
Come to me heedfully,
  listen, that you may have life.
I will renew with you the everlasting covenant,
  the benefits assured to David.
As I made him a witness to the peoples,
  a leader and commander of nations,
so shall you summon a nation you knew not,
  and nations that knew you not shall run
        to you,
because of the LORD, your God,
  the Holy One of Israel, who has glorified you.

Seek the LORD while he may be found,
  call him while he is near.
Let the scoundrel forsake his way,
  and the wicked man his thoughts;
let him turn to the LORD for mercy;
  to our God, who is generous in forgiving.
For my thoughts are not your thoughts,
  nor are your ways my ways, says the LORD.
As high as the heavens are above the earth
  so high are my ways above your ways
  and my thoughts above your thoughts.

For just as from the heavens
  the rain and snow come down
and do not return there
  till they have watered the earth,
  making it fertile and fruitful,
giving seed to the one who sows
  and bread to the one who eats,
so shall my word be
  that goes forth from my mouth;
my word shall not return to me void,
  but shall do my will,
  achieving the end for which I sent it.

RESPONSORIAL PSALM
Isaiah 12:2–3, 4bcd, 5–6 (3)

R. You will draw water joyfully from the springs
      of salvation.

God indeed is my savior;
  I am confident and unafraid.
My strength and my courage is the LORD,
  and he has been my savior.
With joy you will draw water
  at the fountain of salvation. R.

Give thanks to the LORD, acclaim his name;
  among the nations make known his deeds,
  proclaim how exalted is his name. R.

Sing praise to the LORD for his glorious
      achievement;
  let this be known throughout all the earth.
Shout with exultation, O city of Zion,
  for great in your midst
  is the Holy One of Israel! R.

READING II *1 John 5:1–9*

Alternate: Acts 10:34–38

Beloved: Everyone who believes that Jesus is the
Christ is begotten by God, and everyone who loves
the Father loves also the one begotten by him. In
this way we know that we love the children of God
when we love God and obey his commandments.
For the love of God is this, that we keep his commandments. And his commandments are not
burdensome, for whoever is begotten by God conquers the world. And the victory that conquers the
world is our faith. Who indeed is the victor over
the world but the one who believes that Jesus is the
Son of God?

  This is the one who came through water and
blood, Jesus Christ, not by water alone, but by
water and blood. The Spirit is the one who testifies,
and the Spirit is truth. So there are three that testify, the Spirit, the water and the blood, and the

three are of one accord. If we accept human testimony, the testimony of God is surely greater. Now the testimony of God is this, that he has testified on behalf of his Son.

GOSPEL *Mark 1:7–11*

This is what John the Baptist proclaimed: "One mightier than I is coming after me. I am not worthy to stoop and loosen the thongs of his sandals. I have baptized you with water; he will baptize you with the Holy Spirit."

It happened in those days that Jesus came from Nazareth of Galilee and was baptized in the Jordan by John. On coming up out of the water he saw the heavens being torn open and the Spirit, like a dove, descending upon him. And a voice came from the heavens, "You are my beloved Son; with you I am well pleased."

Practice of Hope

Today's Gospel describes the baptism of Jesus in startling detail: "On coming up out of the water he saw the heavens being torn open, and the Spirit, like a dove, descending on him." We are with Jesus as he is pulled gasping from the stream, blinking water out of his eyes to see the promise of heaven and, shaken, to hear the voice that claims him as God's beloved. Like Isaiah ("Come to the water! / Come, without paying and without cost"), the author of this Gospel offers an explicit invitation as he allows us to experience this moment with Jesus. Shaken by the experience, we are claimed by God. ◆ Meditate on how the psalm describes the moment that hope is given to us through Baptism as a time of profound joy. You will draw water joyfully from the springs of salvation. For Christians, the immediate fruit of hope is joy. ◆ Today, find reasons for hope, and allow that hope to give you joy. ◆ Reflect on and connect moments of joy in your life to your Christian hope for eternal life with God.

Download more questions and activities for families, Christian initiation groups, and other adult groups at http://www.ltp.org/ahw.

Scripture Insights

This selection from Isaiah 55 is sandwiched between chapters that have the common theme of "covenant." In today's reading, all who are thirsty are invited to come and be nourished, to come and be satisfied by God, who invites us again and again into a covenant relationship.

The Responsorial Psalm (taken from a much earlier chapter in the Book of Isaiah) picks up the theme of nourishing water in its refrain, "You will draw water joyfully from the springs of salvation." As a gathered community of faith, we pray these words and celebrate God's faithfulness.

Our Gospel reading for this feast is from the first chapter of Mark. Mark, who unlike Matthew and Luke, does not provide a story of the Nativity, opens his Gospel with what he identifies as a quotation from Isaiah (in actuality, it is a combination of words from two prophetic books, Malachi and Isaiah). In a few short verses, the first six of which we do not hear today, the Gospel writer tells us that the Good News has begun. John the Baptist is introduced and he immediately begins his ministry of preparing the way for Jesus. As Jesus comes up from the water, we hearers of this Gospel, along with Jesus, are told quite clearly that Jesus is the Son of God.

◆ God invites each of us to draw near and to be nourished. In a few moments of quiet prayer, express your longing to be nourished.

◆ With today's psalm, reflect on the words "God is indeed my savior; / I am confident and unafraid."

◆ Take some time today to hear God saying to you: "You are my beloved daughter/son; with you I am well pleased."

Ordinary Time, Winter

Prayer before Reading the Word

Not to the wise and powerful of this world,
O God of all blessedness,
but to those who are poor in spirit
do you reveal in Jesus
the righteousness of your Kingdom.

Gathered here,
like the disciples on the mountain,
we long to listen as Jesus, the teacher, speaks.
By the power of his word
refashion our lives
in the pattern of the Beatitudes.

We ask this through our Lord Jesus Christ,
       your Son,
who lives and reigns with you
in the unity of the Holy Spirit,
one God, for ever and ever. Amen.

Prayer after Reading the Word

God of all the nations,
we proclaim your wisdom and your power
in the mystery of Christ's Cross.
We have heard Christ's call
and it compels us to follow.

Let the truth of the Gospel
break the yoke of our selfishness.
Let the Cross draw us and all people
to the joy of salvation.

We ask this through our Lord Jesus Christ,
       your Son,
who lives and reigns with you
in the unity of the Holy Spirit,
one God, for ever and ever. Amen.

Weekday Readings

January 11: *Hebrews 1:1–6; Mark 1:14–20*
January 12: *Hebrews 2:5–12; Mark 1:21–28*
January 13: *Hebrews 2:14–18; Mark 1:29–39*
January 14: *Hebrews 3:7–14; Mark 1:40–45*
January 15: *Hebrews 4:1–5, 11; Mark 2:1–12*
January 16: *Hebrews 4:12–16; Mark 2:13–17*

January 18: *Hebrews 5:1–10; Mark 2:18–22*
January 19: *Hebrews 6:10–20; Mark 2:23–28*
January 20: *Hebrews 7:1–3, 15–17; Mark 3:1–6*
January 21: *Hebrews 7:25—8:6; Mark 3:7–12*
January 22: Day of Prayer for the
  Legal Protection of Unborn Children
  Hebrews 8:6–13; Mark 3:13–19
January 23: *Hebrews 9:2–3, 11–14; Mark 3:20–21*

January 25: Feast of the Conversion
  of St. Paul the Apostle
  Acts 22:3–16 or Acts 9:1–22; Mark 16:15–18
January 26: *2 Timothy 1:1–8 or Titus 1:1–5; Mark 3:31–35*
January 27: *Hebrews 10:11–18; Mark 4:1–20*
January 28: *Hebrews 10:19–25; Mark 4:21–25*
January 29: *Hebrews 10:32–39; Mark 4:26–34*
January 30: *Hebrews 11:1–2, 8–19; Mark 4:35–41*

February 1: *Hebrews 11:32–40; Mark 5:1–20*
February 2: Feast of the Presentation of the Lord
  Malachi 3:1–4; Hebrews 2:14–18; Luke 2:22–40
February 3: *Hebrews 12:4–7, 11–15; Mark 6:1–6*
February 4: *Hebrews 12:18–19, 21–24; Mark 6:7–13*
February 5: *Hebrews 13:1–8; Mark 6:14–29*
February 6: *Hebrews 13:15–17, 20–21; Mark 6:30–34*

February 8: *Genesis 1:1–19; Mark 6:53–56*
February 9: *Genesis 1:20—2:4a; Mark 7:1–13*
February 10: *Genesis 2:4b–9, 15–17; Mark 7:14–23*
February 11: *Genesis 2:18–25; Mark 7:24–30*
February 12: *Genesis 3:1–8; Mark 7:31–37*
February 13: *Genesis 3:9–24; Mark 8:1–10*

February 15: *Genesis 4:1–15, 25; Mark 8:11–13*
February 16: *Genesis 6:5–8; 7:1–5, 10; Mark 8:14–21*

READING I *1 Samuel 3:3b–10, 19*

Samuel was sleeping in the temple of the LORD where the ark of God was. The LORD called to Samuel, who answered, "Here I am." Samuel ran to Eli and said, "Here I am. You called me." "I did not call you," Eli said. "Go back to sleep." So he went back to sleep. Again the LORD called Samuel, who rose and went to Eli. "Here I am," he said. "You called me." But Eli answered, "I did not call you, my son. Go back to sleep."

At that time Samuel was not familiar with the LORD, because the LORD had not revealed anything to him as yet. The LORD called Samuel again, for the third time. Getting up and going to Eli, he said, "Here I am. You called me." Then Eli understood that the LORD was calling the youth. So he said to Samuel, "Go to sleep, and if you are called, reply, 'Speak, LORD, for your servant is listening.'" When Samuel went to sleep in his place, the LORD came and revealed his presence, calling out as before, "Samuel, Samuel!" Samuel answered, "Speak, for your servant is listening."

Samuel grew up, and the LORD was with him, not permitting any word of his to be without effect.

RESPONSORIAL PSALM
Psalm 40:2, 4, 7–8, 8–9, 10 (8a, 9a)

R. Here am I, Lord; I come to do your will.

I have waited, waited for the LORD,
    and he stooped toward me and heard my cry.
And he put a new song into my mouth,
    a hymn to our God. R.

Sacrifice or offering you wished not,
    but ears open to obedience you gave me.
Holocausts or sin-offerings you sought not;
    then said I, "Behold I come." R.

"In the written scroll it is prescribed for me,
to do your will, O my God, is my delight,
    and your law is within my heart!" R.

I announced your justice in the vast assembly;
    I did not restrain my lips, as you,
        O LORD, know. R.

READING II
1 Corinthians 6:13c–15a, 17–20

Brothers and sisters: The body is not for immorality, but for the Lord, and the Lord is for the body; God raised the Lord and will also raise us by his power.

Do you not know that your bodies are members of Christ? But whoever is joined to the Lord becomes one Spirit with him. Avoid immorality. Every other sin a person commits is outside the body, but the immoral person sins against his own body. Do you not know that your body is a temple of the Holy Spirit within you, whom you have from God, and that you are not your own? For you have been purchased at a price. Therefore glorify God in your body.

GOSPEL *John 1:35–42*

John was standing with two of his disciples, and as he watched Jesus walk by, he said, "Behold, the Lamb of God." The two disciples heard what he said and followed Jesus. Jesus turned and saw them following him and said to them, "What are you looking for?" They said to him, "Rabbi"—which translated means Teacher—, "where are you staying?" He said to them, "Come, and you will see." So they went and saw where Jesus was staying, and they stayed with him that day. It was about four in the afternoon. Andrew, the brother of Simon Peter, was one of the two who heard John and followed Jesus. He first found his own brother Simon and told him, "We have found the Messiah"—which is translated Christ. Then he brought him to Jesus. Jesus looked at him and said, "You are Simon the son of John; you will be called Cephas"—which is translated Peter.

Practice of Faith

Samuel and John have very different responses when God appears in their daily life. Samuel is confused and slow to respond, while John is strikingly certain and bold, but both are dependent on a quality of openness and an initial willingness to see and hear God. Two models of faith—one that has to be nurtured and grown; one that is authoritative and in full force—lead to a life of following God. Faith is a habit of initial openness followed by responsiveness, often patiently cultivated by a trusted parent, role model, or mentor. ◆ Review your week and ask where you saw and heard God. What did you do in that moment? ◆ Eli and John both played roles in helping others see God. Do you have a spiritual director, even an informal one? ◆ Consider attending or leading a faith formation class, Bible study, or religious education program in your parish.

Download more questions and activities for families, Christian initiation groups, and other adult groups at http://www.ltp.org/ahw.

Scripture Insights

The genre of today's First Reading is that of a "call narrative." While many call narratives are in Scripture, the call of Samuel is unique. Other such narratives depict an individual hearing the voice of God and understanding who it is that is speaking (consider, for example, Abraham, Isaiah, and Jeremiah). Samuel does not grasp whose voice is calling him. The priest Eli, however, understands this call and instructs Samuel in how to respond, should he hear that voice again. Verses that are cut from today's text are especially interesting since within them we learn that by responding faithfully to God's call, Samuel has difficult words that he must deliver to his mentor, Eli.

In the Gospel selection from John, we are presented with a remarkable story. Like the First Reading for today, it can be described as a call narrative. The scene opens with John the Baptist standing with two of his disciples when Jesus walks by. When John refers to Jesus as the "Lamb of God," John's disciples immediately leave him to follow Jesus. It is as if John has fulfilled his responsibility to these two men. He has helped them to recognize Jesus. Andrew, one of John's disciples who left John and followed Jesus, in turn, "found his own brother Simon [Peter]" and "brought him to Jesus."

Seemingly evident in today's selections from First Samuel and the Gospel of John is that people of faith are called to assist one another in recognizing the mystery and presence of God among them. Clearly, the priest Eli, John the Baptist, and Andrew were instruments of God.

◆ Consider the significance of someone who has helped you recognize the voice of God in your life. Give thanks to God for the gift of this individual.

◆ Reflect on how remarkable it is to be alive and how your body has allowed you to know some of God's many blessings.

◆ How are you a disciple of Jesus and how do you help others to recognize the living God?

READING I *Jonah 3:1–5, 10*

The word of the LORD came to Jonah, saying: "Set out for the great city of Nineveh, and announce to it the message that I will tell you." So Jonah made ready and went to Nineveh, according to the LORD's bidding. Now Nineveh was an enormously large city; it took three days to go through it. Jonah began his journey through the city, and had gone but a single day's walk announcing, "Forty days more and Nineveh shall be destroyed," when the people of Nineveh believed God; they proclaimed a fast and all of them, great and small, put on sackcloth.

When God saw by their actions how they turned from their evil way, he repented of the evil that he had threatened to do to them; he did not carry it out.

RESPONSORIAL PSALM
Psalm 25:4–5, 6–7, 8–9 (4a)

R. Teach me your ways, O Lord.

Your ways, O LORD, make known to me;
    teach me your paths,
guide me in your truth and teach me,
    for you are God my savior. R.

Remember that your compassion, O LORD,
    and your love are from of old.
In your kindness remember me,
    because of your goodness, O LORD. R.

Good and upright is the LORD;
    thus he shows sinners the way.
He guides the humble to justice
    and teaches the humble his way. R.

READING II *1 Corinthians 7:29–31*

I tell you, brothers and sisters, the time is running out. From now on, let those having wives act as not having them, those weeping as not weeping, those rejoicing as not rejoicing, those buying as not owning, those using the world as not using it fully. For the world in its present form is passing away.

GOSPEL *Mark 1:14–20*

After John had been arrested, Jesus came to Galilee proclaiming the gospel of God: "This is the time of fulfillment. The kingdom of God is at hand. Repent, and believe in the gospel."

As he passed by the Sea of Galilee, he saw Simon and his brother Andrew casting their nets into the sea; they were fishermen. Jesus said to them, "Come after me, and I will make you fishers of men." Then they abandoned their nets and followed him. He walked along a little farther and saw James, the son of Zebedee, and his brother John. They too were in a boat mending their nets. Then he called them. So they left their father Zebedee in the boat along with the hired men and followed him.

Practice of Charity

When we make the decision to become a disciple of Christ, we not only decide to take on an utterly changed way of being but also agree to leave behind anything that might present an obstacle to our new mission. Indifference (to injustice, to suffering), selfishness, a stubborn pursuit of unworthy aims—none of these can be part of our new path. The Christian life is a continual process of discernment and formation. ◆ Today, discern the path you are traveling. What must you leave behind to continue on your baptismal journey? ◆ What concrete things can you do to show that you love God above all? ◆ At the "Issues and Actions" page on the US bishops' website (http://usccb.org/issues-and-action/index.cfm), find practical ways to become involved in charitable actions in the world, your country, or your region.

Download more questions and activities for families, Christian initiation groups, and other adult groups at http://www.ltp.org/ahw.

Scripture Insights

Today's First Reading from the Book of Jonah can easily give us the wrong impression of this prophet. Why? This selection provides the picture of a prophet who hears the Word of God and immediately responds to what the Lord commands. It is important for us to know that in the first three verses of the book, we hear God giving Jonah a more detailed command to preach against Nineveh. How does Jonah respond? He completely ignores this command and flees in the opposite direction! The material between Jonah's first and second command from the Lord is familiar to many. While on a ship headed away from Nineveh, the prophet is thrown overboard during a storm, is swallowed by a large fish, and then prays to God, after which he is spewed onto dry land. Then, only then, do we hear today's reading that portrays Jonah as the obedient prophet. Interestingly, the Psalm refrain "Teach me your ways, O Lord," would certainly have been an appropriate prayer for this prophet.

Our short passage from Paul's First Letter to the Corinthians and the opening lines from Mark's Gospel account remind us that God's kingdom is near. The Gospel continues with material not unlike what we heard from the Book of Jonah. Both of these excerpts can be referred to as "call narratives," texts in which an individual or individuals are called by God and given a particular command. You may notice that Mark's call of Simon and Andrew (as well as James and John) is somewhat different from how John presented the call of these two men in last Sunday's Gospel.

◆ Knowing that Jonah was not immediately obedient to God's command, consider how much you are like this prophet.

◆ How might you incorporate into your prayer life the psalm refrain "Teach me your ways, O Lord"?

◆ Consider times in your life when God has extended an invitation to you. How did you feel about that invitation? How did you respond to that call?

READING I *Deuteronomy 18:15–20*

Moses spoke to all the people, saying: "A prophet like me will the LORD, your God, raise up for you from among your own kin; to him you shall listen. This is exactly what you requested of the LORD, your God, at Horeb on the day of the assembly, when you said, 'Let us not again hear the voice of the LORD, our God, nor see this great fire any more, lest we die.' And the LORD said to me, 'This was well said. I will raise up for them a prophet like you from among their kin, and will put my words into his mouth; he shall tell them all that I command him. Whoever will not listen to my words which he speaks in my name, I myself will make him answer for it. But if a prophet presumes to speak in my name an oracle that I have not commanded him to speak, or speaks in the name of other gods, he shall die.'"

RESPONSORIAL PSALM
Psalm 95:1–2, 6–7, 7–9 (8)

R. If today you hear his voice, harden not
        your hearts.

Come, let us sing joyfully to the LORD;
    let us acclaim the rock of our salvation.
Let us come into his presence with thanksgiving;
    let us joyfully sing psalms to him. R.

Come, let us bow down in worship;
    let us kneel before the LORD who made us.
For he is our God,
    and we are the people he shepherds,
        the flock he guides. R.

Oh, that today you would hear his voice:
    "Harden not your hearts as at Meribah,
    as in the day of Massah in the desert,
where your fathers tempted me;
    they tested me though they had seen
        my works." R.

READING II *1 Corinthians 7:32–35*

Brothers and sisters: I should like you to be free of anxieties. An unmarried man is anxious about the things of the Lord, how he may please the Lord. But a married man is anxious about the things of the world, how he may please his wife, and he is divided. An unmarried woman or a virgin is anxious about the things of the Lord, so that she may be holy in both body and spirit. A married woman, on the other hand, is anxious about the things of the world, how she may please her husband. I am telling you this for your own benefit, not to impose a restraint upon you, but for the sake of propriety and adherence to the Lord without distraction.

GOSPEL *Mark 1:21–28*

Then they came to Capernaum, and on the sabbath Jesus entered the synagogue and taught. The people were astonished at his teaching, for he taught them as one having authority and not as the scribes. In their synagogue was a man with an unclean spirit; he cried out, "What have you to do with us, Jesus of Nazareth? Have you come to destroy us? I know who you are—the Holy One of God!" Jesus rebuked him and said, "Quiet! Come out of him!" The unclean spirit convulsed him and with a loud cry came out of him. All were amazed and asked one another, "What is this? A new teaching with authority. He commands even the unclean spirits and they obey him." His fame spread everywhere throughout the whole region of Galilee.

Practice of Faith

In the history of salvation, God has spoken to his people through a variety of messengers, revealing himself fully in Jesus, the Word Incarnate. Even after Jesus returned to the Father, God continues to speak to us. The Church, Scripture, the traditions, and the practices of Christian communities through the ages—we trust that these authentically convey God's message. Our attentiveness to these and our response through our prayer life and spiritual practices deepen our faith. In the long history of the Church, different spiritualties have flourished as ways of reflecting on and responding to God's message. ◆ See if a community near you offers Taizé prayer or if a group in your parish regularly prays the Rosary. ◆ Look into the intensely reflective Carmelite way of praying, St. Francis' passionate vision of Creation, or any other of the Church's prayer traditions. ◆ Pray for authentic guidance through the Holy Spirit.

Download more questions and activities for families, Christian initiation groups, and other adult groups at http://www.ltp.org/ahw.

Scripture Insights

The First Reading from the Book of Deuteronomy introduces us to the role and the responsibilities of a prophet. The commonly held opinion that prophets can predict the future is a naïve understanding of the biblical prophet. The best way to perceive the prophets of the Bible may be as spokespersons, or messengers, of God. Exactly how God's "Word" came to each prophet is a complicated matter. Nevertheless, Scripture identifies a considerable number of both women and men who served God as messengers of the divine Word.

The key figure in the Book of Deuteronomy is Moses, whom tradition identifies as the prophet par excellence. This is because Moses is identified as having communed with God face to face. Today's text makes clear that the prophet is responsible for communicating God's Word, not the prophet's word, to the people. The text also speaks of a prophet to come (and there were many) who would also speak God's Word as commanded.

In First Corinthians, we find Paul speaking about whether it is better to be married or single. It is important to grasp Paul's reason for recommending the single life over the married life. Paul was under the impression that the Lord would soon return to this earth. With that consideration, Paul thought that marriage, with its responsibilities to spouse and family, was a distraction from focusing on the impending return of the Lord Jesus.

Mark's Gospel passage for today emphasizes the astonishing authority of Jesus' teaching. It was while teaching in the synagogue that a man with an unclean spirit presented himself to Jesus. With the simple words "Quiet! Come out of him!" the spirit left the man. The primary focus of this reading is not the exorcism but rather the awesome manifestation of Jesus' power.

◆ How is God's Word made manifest today?

◆ What does it mean to be a messenger of God today?

◆ Reflect on a time that you were transformed by the power of God's Word.

READING I *Job 7:1–4, 6–7*

Job spoke, saying:
    Is not man's life on earth a drudgery?
        Are not his days those of hirelings?
    He is a slave who longs for the shade,
        a hireling who waits for his wages.
    So I have been assigned months of misery,
        and troubled nights have been allotted to me.
    If in bed I say, "When shall I arise?"
        then the night drags on;
        I am filled with restlessness until the dawn.
    My days are swifter than a weaver's shuttle;
        they come to an end without hope.
    Remember that my life is like the wind;
        I shall not see happiness again.

RESPONSORIAL PSALM
Psalm 147:1–2, 3–4, 5–6 (see 3a)

R. Praise the Lord, who heals the brokenhearted.
    or: Alleluia.

Praise the LORD, for he is good;
    sing praise to our God, for he is gracious;
    it is fitting to praise him.
The LORD rebuilds Jerusalem;
    the dispersed of Israel he gathers. R.

He heals the brokenhearted
    and binds up their wounds.
He tells the number of the stars;
    he calls each by name. R.

Great is our Lord and mighty in power;
    to his wisdom there is no limit.
The LORD sustains the lowly;
    the wicked he casts to the ground. R.

READING II
1 Corinthians 9:16–19, 22–23

Brothers and sisters: If I preach the gospel, this is no reason for me to boast, for an obligation has been imposed on me, and woe to me if I do not preach it! If I do so willingly, I have a recompense, but if unwillingly, then I have been entrusted with a stewardship. What then is my recompense? That, when I preach, I offer the gospel free of charge so as not to make full use of my right in the gospel.

Although I am free in regard to all, I have made myself a slave to all so as to win over as many as possible. To the weak I became weak, to win over the weak. I have become all things to all, to save at least some. All this I do for the sake of the gospel, so that I too may have a share in it.

GOSPEL *Mark 1:29–39*

On leaving the synagogue Jesus entered the house of Simon and Andrew with James and John. Simon's mother-in-law lay sick with a fever. They immediately told him about her. He approached, grasped her hand, and helped her up. Then the fever left her and she waited on them.

When it was evening, after sunset, they brought to him all who were ill or possessed by demons. The whole town was gathered at the door. He cured many who were sick with various diseases, and he drove out many demons, not permitting them to speak because they knew him.

Rising very early before dawn, he left and went off to a deserted place, where he prayed. Simon and those who were with him pursued him and on finding him said, "Everyone is looking for you." He told them, "Let us go on to the nearby villages that I may preach there also. For this purpose have I come." So he went into their synagogues, preaching and driving out demons throughout the whole of Galilee.

Practice of Faith

What is sometimes called the prosperity gospel teaches that faithfulness to God leads to happiness and worldly success. The story of Job, a faithful man who endures great suffering, directly contradicts this belief. What does a life of faith confer, if not worldly success? It may be that such a life provides restoration, healing, and a share in the Good News, which compels service to others. We who are entrusted with the Gospel must share it as far as we are able. This is not a denial of happiness; rather, the *Catechism of the Catholic Church* describes an "aspiration to happiness that God has placed in the heart of every person" that is realized via a "transformative evangelization." ◆ In light of today's readings, consider Pope Francis' words from *The Joy of the Gospel:* "The Gospel, radiant with the glory of Christ's cross, constantly invites us to rejoice." ◆ Research Catholic missionary societies (http://www.usccb.org/about/evangelization-and-catechesis/world-missions/world-mission-organizations.cfm) and consider how you can help. ◆ In what way does your daily way of living evangelize those who know you?

Download more questions and activities for families, Christian initiation groups, and other adult groups at http://www.ltp.org/ahw.

Scripture Insights

Today's Scripture readings might be understood as invitations to reflect on the mystery of suffering. In the First Reading, Job, the blameless and upright man who was rich in family, land, and animals until his life was turned upside down, reflects on the human condition. He, who had recognized that he had once been the recipient of God's many blessings, now sees life with different eyes. Interestingly, today's verses begin with rather generic remarks about the human state and move to lines that speak specifically of Job's experience of misery and darkness. The Psalm refrain proclaims, "Praise the Lord, who heals the brokenhearted." If seen as a direct response to Job, the refrain would indicate that Job's condition is not permanent.

For the third consecutive week, the Gospel is from the first chapter of Mark. The verses for today's selection immediately follow last week's reading, in which Jesus performed his first miracle. With no time wasted and no verses excluded, Jesus moves from the synagogue to Simon's house, accompanied by Simon, Andrew, and James (two weeks ago, these men were "called" in the Gospel reading).

Mark's Gospel moves quickly. Immediately after entering the house, Jesus is told that Simon's mother-in-law was ill. Jesus took her hand and "helped her up." Later that evening, Jesus cured "many who were sick . . . and he drove out many demons." Before dawn, Jesus and his companions left the house, and the text tells us that Jesus prayed. It would seem, however, that this prayer was brief, since "everyone" was looking for him. Jesus' response is one of incredible kindness. He is ready to move on to wherever he can preach and heal.

◆ Have you ever found yourself feeling like Job? If so, express your pain to God, either quietly in your heart or in a journal.

◆ If you have experienced the darkness expressed by Job, take time to reflect on today's Psalm. Use the words "the Lord heals the brokenhearted" as a mantra.

◆ Reflect on the readiness of Jesus to heal those in need of healing. Ask that he might heal your wounds.

READING I *Leviticus 13:1–2, 44–46*

The LORD said to Moses and Aaron, "If someone has on his skin a scab or pustule or blotch which appears to be the sore of leprosy, he shall be brought to Aaron, the priest, or to one of the priests among his descendants. If the man is leprous and unclean, the priest shall declare him unclean by reason of the sore on his head.

"The one who bears the sore of leprosy shall keep his garments rent and his head bare, and shall muffle his beard; he shall cry out, 'Unclean, unclean!' As long as the sore is on him he shall declare himself unclean, since he is in fact unclean. He shall dwell apart, making his abode outside the camp."

RESPONSORIAL PSALM
Psalm 32:1–2, 5, 11 (7)

R. I turn to you, Lord, in time of trouble,
    and you fill me with the joy of salvation.

Blessed is he whose fault is taken away,
    whose sin is covered.
Blessed the man to whom the LORD imputes
        not guilt,
    in whose spirit there is no guile. R.

Then I acknowledged my sin to you,
    my guilt I covered not.
I said, "I confess my faults to the LORD,"
    and you took away the guilt of my sin. R.

Be glad in the LORD and rejoice, you just;
    exult, all you upright of heart. R.

READING II *1 Corinthians 10:31—11:1*

Brothers and sisters, whether you eat or drink, or whatever you do, do everything for the glory of God. Avoid giving offense, whether to the Jews or Greeks or the church of God, just as I try to please everyone in every way, not seeking my own benefit but that of the many, that they may be saved. Be imitators of me, as I am of Christ.

GOSPEL *Mark 1:40–45*

A leper came to Jesus and kneeling down begged him and said, "If you wish, you can make me clean." Moved with pity, he stretched out his hand, touched him, and said to him, "I do will it. Be made clean." The leprosy left him immediately, and he was made clean. Then, warning him sternly, he dismissed him at once.

He said to him, "See that you tell no one anything, but go, show yourself to the priest and offer for your cleansing what Moses prescribed; that will be proof for them."

The man went away and began to publicize the whole matter. He spread the report abroad so that it was impossible for Jesus to enter a town openly. He remained outside in deserted places, and people kept coming to him from everywhere.

Practice of Charity

Illness can be isolating. Sometimes the sick person is unable to go about as before; sometimes, because of ignorance or fear, society shuns the individual. Either way, both the sick person and the community suffer. Society benefits from contemplating and responding to the trust of its most vulnerable, yet so often, confronted with misery, we look away or deliberately harden our response. We are called, like Jesus, to be moved with pity, and in that moment, to do what we can to reduce the suffering and isolation of the people society forgets. ◆ On this Valentine's Day, allow yourself to be moved to provide comfort to someone who is in need. Bring valentine cards to a nursing home. ◆ Donate blood if you are able. ◆ Offer to provide a respite to a caregiver of a chronically ill person.

Download more questions and activities for families, Christian initiation groups, and other adult groups at http://www.ltp.org/ahw.

Scripture Insights

Today's readings from the Book of Leviticus and the Gospel of Mark give attention to a disease identified as leprosy. A bit of background can be quite helpful in understanding these texts.

First, what the Scriptures refer to as leprosy (*tzaraat* in the Old Testament and *lepra* in the New Testament) should not be understood as synonymous with the illness of this name today. The word *leprosy* seems to have been a generic term used to refer to a variety of skin conditions, one of which might have been leprosy (Hansen's disease). Second, specific laws were designated for the purpose of restricting the spread of communicable illnesses, with skin diseases being among them. While these laws may sound harsh to us today, they are best understood as safeguarding the well-being of the community. Third, in addition to making a person unclean, which resulted in isolation from the community, leprosy was often associated with sin.

In our passage from Mark, we hear that a leper approached Jesus and said: "If you wish, you can make me clean." Jesus wasted no time in responding. He touched the man! This was unheard of! He touched a leper! Jesus then said to the leper, "I do will it. Be made clean." And immediately the leprosy left the man. Jesus then instructs the man to follow the prescriptions of the Law. Interestingly, within the next thirty-four verses of Mark, in five episodes, some consider Jesus as one who does not uphold the Law but violates it.

Today's Psalm refrain could easily be understood as the prayer of the leper whom Jesus cleansed. "I turn to you, Lord, in time of trouble, and you fill me with the joy of salvation."

◆ Can you identify laws or common practices that exclude people on the basis of appearances?

◆ Imagine yourself as the leper in today's Gospel. How do you feel when you experience the touch of Jesus?

◆ Read today's Responsorial Psalm. Can you identify with the psalmist who has experienced the saving action of a tender and loving God?

Lent

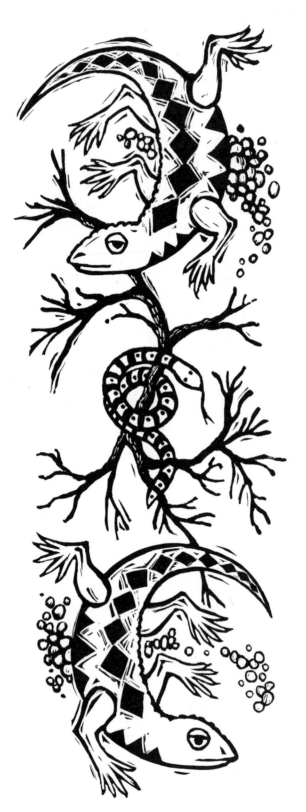

Prayer before Reading the Word

To Abraham and Sarah you called out,
O God of mystery,
inviting them to journey to a land of promise.
To us also you call out,
inviting us to pass through Lent to Easter's glory.
Open our ears, therefore, to listen to Jesus,
the Beloved Son in whom you are well pleased,
so that, embracing the mystery of the Cross,
we may come to the holy mountain,
       to immortal life,
and a share in Christ's transfigured glory.
We ask this through our Lord Jesus Christ,
       your Son,
who lives and reigns with you
in the unity of the Holy Spirit,
one God, for ever and ever. Amen.

Prayer after Reading the Word

O God, the living fountain of new life,
to the human race, parched with thirst,
you offer the living water of grace
that springs up from the rock,
our Savior Jesus Christ.
Grant your people the gift of the Spirit,
that we may learn to profess our faith
with courage and conviction
and announce with joy
the wonders of your saving love.
We ask this through our Lord Jesus Christ,
       your Son,
who lives and reigns with you
in the unity of the Holy Spirit,
one God, for ever and ever. Amen.

Weekday Readings

February 17: Ash Wednesday
   Joel 2:12–18; 2 Corinthians 5:20—6:2;
   Matthew 6:1–6, 16–18
February 18: *Deuteronomy 30:15–20; Luke 9:22–25*
February 19: *Isaiah 58:1–9a; Matthew 9:14–15*
February 20: *Isaiah 58:9b–14; Luke 5:27–32*

February 22: Feast of the Chair of St. Peter the Apostle
   1 Peter 5:1–4; Matthew 16:13–19
February 23: *Isaiah 55:10–11; Matthew 6:7–15*
February 24: *Jonah 3:1–10; Luke 11:29–32*
February 25: *Esther C:12, 14–16, 23–25; Matthew 7:7–12*
February 26: *Ezekiel 18:21–28; Matthews 5:20–26*
February 27: *Deuteronomy 26:16–19; Matthew 5:43–48*

March 1: *Daniel 9:4b–10; Luke 6:36–38*
March 2: *Isaiah 1:10, 16–20; Matthew 23:1–12*
March 3: *Jeremiah 18:18–20; Matthew 20:17–28;*
March 4: *Jeremiah 17:5–10; Luke 16:19–31*
March 5: *Genesis 37:3–4, 12–13a, 17b–28a;*
   Matthew 21:33–43, 45–46
March 6: *Micah 7:14–15, 18–20; Luke 15:1–3, 11–32*

March 8: *2 Kings 5:1–15b; Luke 4:24–30*
March 9: *Daniel 3:25, 34–43; Matthew 18:21–35*
March 10: *Deuteronomy 4:1, 5–9; Matthew 5:17–19*
March 11: *Jeremiah 7:23–28; Luke 11:14–23*
March 12: *Hosea 14:2–10; Mark 12:28–34*
March 13: *Hosea 6:1–6; Luke 18:9–14*

March 15: *Isaiah 65:17–21; John 4:43–54*
March 16: *Ezekiel 47:1–9, 12; John 5:1–16*
March 17: *Isaiah 49:8–15; John 5:17–30*
March18: *Exodus 32:7–14; John 5:31–47*
March 19: Solemnity of St. Joseph,
   Spouse of the Blessed Virgin Mary
   2 Samuel 7:4–5a, 12–14a, 16; Romans 4:13, 16–18, 22;
   Matthew 1:16, 18–21, 24a or Luke 2:41–51a
March 20: *Jeremiah 11:18–20; John 7:40–53*

March 22: *Daniel 13:1–9, 15–17, 19–30, 33–62*
   or 13:41c–62; John 8:1–11
March 23: *Numbers 21:4–9; John 8:21–30*
March 24: *Daniel 3:14–20, 91–92, 95; John 8:31–42*
March 25: Solemnity of the Annunciation of the Lord
   Isaiah 7:10–14; 8:10; Hebrews 10:4–10; Luke 1:26–38
March 26: *Jeremiah 20:10–13; John 10:31–42*
March 27: *Ezekiel 37:21–28; John 11:45–56*

March 29: *Isaiah 42:1–7; John 12:1–11*
March 30: *Isaiah 49:1–6; John 13:21–33, 36–38*
March 31: *Isaiah 50:4–9a; Matthew 26:14–25*

READING I *Genesis 9:8–15*

God said to Noah and to his sons with him: "See, I am now establishing my covenant with you and your descendants after you and with every living creature that was with you: all the birds, and the various tame and wild animals that were with you and came out of the ark. I will establish my covenant with you, that never again shall all bodily creatures be destroyed by the waters of a flood; there shall not be another flood to devastate the earth." God added: "This is the sign that I am giving for all ages to come, of the covenant between me and you and every living creature with you: I set my bow in the clouds to serve as a sign of the covenant between me and the earth. When I bring clouds over the earth, and the bow appears in the clouds, I will recall the covenant I have made between me and you and all living beings, so that the waters shall never again become a flood to destroy all mortal beings."

RESPONSORIAL PSALM
Psalm 25:4–5, 6–7, 8–9 (see 10)

R. Your ways, O Lord, are love and truth to
those who keep your covenant.

Your ways, O LORD, make known to me;
teach me your paths.
Guide me in your truth and teach me,
for you are God my savior. R.

Remember that your compassion, O LORD,
and your love are from of old.
In your kindness remember me,
because of your goodness, O LORD. R.

Good and upright is the LORD,
thus he shows sinners the way.
He guides the humble to justice,
and he teaches the humble his way. R.

READING II *1 Peter 3:18–22*

Beloved: Christ suffered for sins once, the righteous for the sake of the unrighteous, that he might lead you to God. Put to death in the flesh, he was brought to life in the Spirit. In it he also went to preach to the spirits in prison, who had once been disobedient while God patiently waited in the days of Noah during the building of the ark, in which a few persons, eight in all, were saved through water. This prefigured baptism, which saves you now. It is not a removal of dirt from the body but an appeal to God for a clear conscience, through the resurrection of Jesus Christ, who has gone into heaven and is at the right hand of God, with angels, authorities, and powers subject to him.

GOSPEL *Mark 1:12–15*

The Spirit drove Jesus out into the desert, and he remained in the desert for forty days, tempted by Satan. He was among wild beasts, and the angels ministered to him.

After John had been arrested, Jesus came to Galilee proclaiming the gospel of God: "This is the time of fulfillment. The kingdom of God is at hand. Repent, and believe in the gospel."

Practice of Hope

Quite likely, Jesus' followers felt both dismay and expectation with his words: "This is the time of fulfillment. The kingdom of God is at hand." We too are embarking on a desert time; and if there are places of discord in our lives, this passage may give us unease. Jesus has told us how to prepare: "Repent, and believe in the gospel." ◆ This First Sunday of Lent, examine any anxiety you may have, and prayerfully attempt to identify the source. ◆ What can you do to demonstrate your trust in God and your hope in his promise? Does your life reflect God's care for "all living beings"? ◆ More than a billion people in the world lack access to clean water. Reflecting on the Genesis story and your Baptism, consider limiting your use of water and giving to ministries that provide clean water for those who do not have access to it: http://www.filtersfast.com/articles/Water-Charities-A-Comprehensive-List.php.

Download more questions and activities for families, Christian initiation groups, and other adult groups at http://www.ltp.org/ahw.

Scripture Insights

On this First Sunday of Lent, a time when most of us are inclined to reflect more deeply on how we live as Christians, we are reminded of God's everlasting love. Our First Reading from Genesis follows the well-known story of the great flood. While the text states that God addresses Noah and his sons, it is important to note that the covenant God makes goes well beyond this remnant of humankind and their future descendants. This covenant is with all that God had created. The "bow," which we associate with the rainbow, is said to have had its origins in the mythology of the Ancient Near East. Since it might have been a reference to a warrior's bow, we might easily imagine this bow as representing God's decision to hang up this weapon of destruction while promising anew to be in relationship with all of creation.

The Psalm refrain picks up the already-mentioned theme with the words "Your ways, O Lord, are love and truth to those who keep your covenant." The Psalm's verses continue to remind us of God's compassion and goodness.

Words from the First Letter of Peter take us back to the First Reading by referencing the days of Noah. The author then indirectly connects the floodwaters to the life-giving waters of Baptism and proceeds to refer to the Resurrection of Jesus.

Four verses compose the Gospel reading. Verses 12 and 13 speak very briefly of Jesus' temptation in the desert, while verses 14 and 15 find Jesus beginning his public ministry of proclaiming the Good News that God's kingdom is near.

◆ Mindful that the Genesis reading speaks of God's love for all creation, reflect on your disposition toward Earth. This Lent, consider making choices that reverence all life on our planet.

◆ Reread today's Psalm. Which lines from this prayer would you like to carry with you throughout these forty days?

◆ What is the invitation you hear in today's Gospel?

READING I
Genesis 22:1–2, 9a, 10–13, 15–18

God put Abraham to the test. He called to him, "Abraham!" "Here I am!" he replied. Then God said: "Take your son Isaac, your only one, whom you love, and go to the land of Moriah. There you shall offer him up as a holocaust on a height that I will point out to you."

When they came to the place of which God had told him, Abraham built an altar there and arranged the wood on it. Then he reached out and took the knife to slaughter his son. But the LORD's messenger called to him from heaven, "Abraham, Abraham!" "Here I am!" he answered. "Do not lay your hand on the boy," said the messenger. "Do not do the least thing to him. I know now how devoted you are to God, since you did not withhold from me your own beloved son." As Abraham looked about, he spied a ram caught by its horns in the thicket. So he went and took the ram and offered it up as a holocaust in place of his son.

Again the LORD's messenger called to Abraham from heaven and said: "I swear by myself, declares the LORD, that because you acted as you did in not withholding from me your beloved son, I will bless you abundantly and make your descendants as countless as the stars of the sky and the sands of the seashore; your descendants shall take possession of the gates of their enemies, and in your descendants all the nations of the earth shall find blessing—all this because you obeyed my command."

RESPONSORIAL PSALM
Psalm 116:10, 15, 16–17, 18–19 (9)

R. I will walk before the Lord,
    in the land of the living.

I believed, even when I said,
  "I am greatly afflicted."
Precious in the eyes of the LORD
  is the death of his faithful ones. R.

O LORD, I am your servant;
  I am your servant, the son of your handmaid;
  you have loosed my bonds.
To you will I offer sacrifice of thanksgiving,
  and I will call upon the name of the LORD. R.

My vows to the LORD I will pay
  in the presence of all his people,
in the courts of the house of the LORD,
  in your midst, O Jerusalem. R.

READING II *Romans 8:31b–34*

Brothers and sisters: If God is for us, who can be against us? He who did not spare his own Son but handed him over for us all, how will he not also give us everything else along with him?

Who will bring a charge against God's chosen ones? It is God who acquits us, who will condemn? Christ Jesus it is who died—or, rather, was raised—who also is at the right hand of God, who indeed intercedes for us.

GOSPEL *Mark 9:2–10*

Jesus took Peter, James, and John and led them up a high mountain apart by themselves. And he was transfigured before them, and his clothes became dazzling white, such as no fuller on earth could bleach them. Then Elijah appeared to them along with Moses, and they were conversing with Jesus. Then Peter said to Jesus in reply, "Rabbi, it is good that we are here! Let us make three tents: one for you, one for Moses, and one for Elijah." He hardly knew what to say, they were so terrified. Then a cloud came, casting a shadow over them; from the cloud came a voice, "This is my beloved Son. Listen to him." Suddenly, looking around, they no longer saw anyone but Jesus alone with them.

As they were coming down from the mountain, he charged them not to relate what they had seen to anyone, except when the Son of Man had risen from the dead. So they kept the matter to themselves, questioning what rising from the dead meant.

Practice of Faith

It can be difficult to reconcile the story of God bidding Abraham to take the life of his only son with a belief in a loving God. The reconciliation comes in the person of Jesus. The account can be read as a challenge to our complacency. By allowing difficult questions into our lives and accepting them with faith, we become like the first disciples. In the Gospel reading, the question "What does it mean to rise from the dead?" challenges Peter, James, and John. The passage does not provide a ready solution, but it tells us where to begin the search for an answer: "This is my beloved Son. Listen to him." ◆ Sometimes faith is practiced in acts of courage. Consider where you may be letting fear overcome faith. ◆ Reflect on whether you are courageous enough to live with unanswered questions. ◆ With a friend or spiritual adviser, discuss a question of faith that troubles you; if you cannot reconcile it, be deliberate about accepting that question with an open heart.

Download more questions and activities for families, Christian initiation groups, and other adult groups at http://www.ltp.org/ahw.

Scripture Insights

For some Christians, today's reading from Genesis is understood as presenting a model of faithfulness; for others, this text is a source of deep consternation. Chapter 22 of Genesis, sometimes referred to as "the trial" or "the test" of Abraham, has produced multiple interpretations within both Judaism and Christianity. While these verses indeed present Abraham as one who trusted in God, we might also keep in mind that child sacrifice was not unheard of in the ancient world. Might this test be one in which Abraham came to understand something that the later Hebrew Scriptures forbid? In an age when we are aware that countless innocent children have been victimized for the pleasure of abusive adults, it is essential to know that child sacrifice is condemned in the Bible.

Turning to Paul's Letter to the Romans, we hear only a portion of a larger literary unit consisting of verses 31–39. The fuller text contains a series of five rhetorical questions, of which the first four would elicit a response of "No one!" with the final response, "Absolutely not!" *If God is for us, who can be against us? Who will bring a charge against God's chosen ones? Who will condemn? What will separate us from the love of Christ? Will anguish, or distress, or persecution, or famine, or nakedness, or peril, or the sword?* The purpose of this text is to help its hearers comprehend the unsurpassable love of God. Nothing can separate us from God's love made manifest in Jesus.

Our Gospel for today is Mark's version of the Transfiguration. In this pericope, we find Peter, James, and John experiencing a mysterious revelation of Jesus' identity. While these companions do not fully comprehend this experience, their eyes are beginning to open.

◆ When you have entered into serious discernment over a difficult issue, have you wondered if you have discerned properly?

◆ Do some decisions require intense prayer and reflection?

◆ When you read today's text from Genesis, can you imagine what Abraham might have experienced? What about Sarah's suffering?

READING I *Exodus 20:1–17*

Shorter: Exodus 20:1–3, 7–8, 12–17

In those days, God delivered all these commandments: "I, the LORD, am your God, who brought you out of the land of Egypt, that place of slavery. You shall not have other gods besides me. You shall not carve idols for yourselves in the shape of anything in the sky above or on the earth below or in the waters beneath the earth; you shall not bow down before them or worship them. For I, the LORD, your God, am a jealous God, inflicting punishment for their fathers' wickedness on the children of those who hate me, down to the third and fourth generation; but bestowing mercy down to the thousandth generation on the children of those who love me and keep my commandments.

"You shall not take the name of the LORD, your God, in vain. For the LORD will not leave unpunished the one who takes his name in vain.

"Remember to keep holy the sabbath day. Six days you may labor and do all your work, but the seventh day is the sabbath of the LORD, your God. No work may be done then either by you, or your son or daughter, or your male or female slave, or your beast, or by the alien who lives with you. In six days the LORD made the heavens and the earth, the sea and all that is in them; but on the seventh day he rested. That is why the LORD has blessed the sabbath day and made it holy.

"Honor your father and your mother, that you may have a long life in the land which the LORD, your God, is giving you. You shall not kill. You shall not commit adultery. You shall not steal. You shall not bear false witness against your neighbor. You shall not covet your neighbor's house. You shall not covet your neighbor's wife, nor his male or female slave, nor his ox or ass, nor anything else that belongs to him."

RESPONSORIAL PSALM
Psalm 19:8, 9, 10, 11 (John 6:68c)

R. Lord, you have the words of everlasting life.

The law of the LORD is perfect,
    refreshing the soul;
the decree of the LORD is trustworthy,
    giving wisdom to the simple. R.

The precepts of the LORD are right,
    rejoicing the heart;
the command of the LORD is clear,
    enlightening the eye. R.

The fear of the LORD is pure,
    enduring forever;
the ordinances of the LORD are true,
    all of them just. R.

They are more precious than gold,
    than a heap of purest gold;
sweeter also than syrup
    or honey from the comb. R.

READING II *1 Corinthians 1:22–25*

Brothers and sisters: Jews demand signs and Greeks look for wisdom, but we proclaim Christ crucified, a stumbling block to Jews and foolishness to Gentiles, but to those who are called, Jews and Greeks alike, Christ the power of God and the wisdom of God. For the foolishness of God is wiser than human wisdom, and the weakness of God is stronger than human strength.

GOSPEL *John 2:13–25*

Since the Passover of the Jews was near, Jesus went up to Jerusalem. He found in the temple area those who sold oxen, sheep, and doves, as well as the money changers seated there. He made a whip out of cords and drove them all out of the temple area, with the sheep and oxen, and spilled the coins of the money changers and overturned their tables, and to those who sold doves he said, "Take these out of here, and stop making my Father's house a marketplace." His disciples recalled the words of Scripture, *Zeal for your house will consume me.* At this the Jews answered and said to him, "What sign can you show us for doing this?" Jesus answered and said to them, "Destroy this temple and in three days I will raise it up." The Jews said, "This temple has been under construction for forty-six years, and you will raise it up in three days?" But he was speaking about the temple of his body. Therefore, when he was raised from the dead, his disciples remembered that he had said this, and they came to believe the Scripture and the word Jesus had spoken.

While he was in Jerusalem for the feast of Passover, many began to believe in his name when they saw the signs he was doing. But Jesus would not trust himself to them because he knew them all, and did not need anyone to testify about human nature. He himself understood it well.

Practice of Charity

Today's is a disturbing Gospel, a depiction of the wrath of Jesus taking form as a deliberate act of violence—he makes a whip, driving out the male-factors, spilling and overturning their money tables. Our culture needs the message implicit in this Gospel. As Christians, it is our responsibility to reject destructive values and take on those that Christ exemplified. This can begin by resisting the urge to commodify everything and exploit what should be sacred: the natural world, religious belief, and most especially other people. An estimated 600,000 to 800,000 children, women, and men are trafficked annually across international borders into every kind of degradation and slavery, humans created in the likeness of God reduced to their monetary value. ◆ Discover what can be done to stop human trafficking at www.freetheslaves.net /our-model-for-freedom/slavery-today/. ◆ Volunteer to clean your parish church in preparation for Easter, remembering that the building is the sacred house for God's holy people. ◆ Reflect on how you treat people who perform services, such as the wait staff at restaurants and sales clerks at stores.

Download more questions and activities for families, Christian initiation groups, and other adult groups at http://www.ltp.org/ahw.

Scripture Insights

Even people with little familiarity with Judeo-Christian beliefs are well acquainted with the reading from Exodus of the giving of the Ten Commandments. While these commands may be quite familiar to us, it is essential to recognize that they were delivered within the context of God entering into a covenant relationship with Israel. To be God's treasured possession, Israel must follow the behaviors specified in the words of the Commandments, also called the Decalogue. To be in close relationship with God requires that Israel assume responsibilities toward its neighbor.

Psalm 19 is a song of praise for God's *torah*, or "instruction." Far different from the North American mentality that views torah as "law" in a restrictive sense, today's Psalm expresses quite clearly how Israel understood God's instruction as a guide for living well. Thus, the psalmist can speak of God's torah as being sweeter than "honey from the comb."

Within the first two chapters of John's Gospel, readers learn Jesus' identity, see him perform his first sign at the wedding celebration in Cana, and hear him confront the religious authorities in the Temple in Jerusalem. The most obvious focus in today's reading is Jesus' cleansing of the Temple, followed by reference to his impending death and Resurrection. Looking carefully at the passage, though, we see that the last verses turn attention to the people who had begun "to believe in his name when they saw the signs he was doing. But Jesus would not trust himself to them because he knew them all." The reading is clear that a reciprocal relationship between Jesus and true believers exits. It is implied that some people were beginning to follow Jesus because they were interested in seeing great works, not because they trusted in him.

◆ How has your understanding of the Commandments changed over the years?

◆ Pray the words of today's Psalm reflectively. How do you perceive the instruction that God presents to you?

◆ It is important to recognize that Jesus is fully human as well as fully divine. Reread this Gospel text and reflect on what it says about Jesus.

READING I *Exodus 17:3–7*

In those days, in their thirst for water, the people grumbled against Moses, saying, "Why did you ever make us leave Egypt? Was it just to have us die here of thirst with our children and our livestock?" So Moses cried out to the LORD, "What shall I do with this people? A little more and they will stone me!" The LORD answered Moses, "Go over there in front of the people, along with some of the elders of Israel, holding in your hand, as you go, the staff with which you struck the river. I will be standing there in front of you on the rock in Horeb. Strike the rock, and the water will flow from it for the people to drink." This Moses did, in the presence of the elders of Israel. The place was called Massah and Meribah, because the Israelites quarreled there and tested the LORD, saying, "Is the LORD in our midst or not?"

RESPONSORIAL PSALM
Psalm 95:1–2, 6–7, 8–9 (8)

R. If today you hear his voice, harden not
      your hearts.

Come, let us sing joyfully to the LORD;
  let us acclaim the Rock of our salvation.
Let us come into his presence with thanksgiving;
  let us joyfully sing psalms to him. R.

Come, let us bow down in worship;
  let us kneel before the LORD who made us.
For he is our God,
    and we are the people he shepherds, the flock
      he guides. R.

Oh, that today you would hear his voice:
  "Harden not your hearts as at Meribah,
  as in the day of Massah in the desert.
Where your fathers tempted me;
    they tested me though they had seen
      my works." R.

READING II *Romans 5:1–2, 5–8*

Brothers and sisters: Since we have been justified by faith, we have peace with God through our Lord Jesus Christ, through whom we have gained access by faith to this grace in which we stand, and we boast in hope of the glory of God.

And hope does not disappoint, because the love of God has been poured out into our hearts through the Holy Spirit who has been given to us. For Christ, while we were still helpless, died at the appointed time for the ungodly. Indeed, only with difficulty does one die for a just person, though perhaps for a good person one might even find courage to die. But God proves his love for us in that while we were still sinners Christ died for us.

GOSPEL
John 4:5–15, 19b–26, 39a, 40–42
Longer: John 4:5–42

Jesus came to a town of Samaria called Sychar, near the plot of land that Jacob had given to his son Joseph. Jacob's well was there. Jesus, tired from his journey, sat down there at the well. It was about noon.

A woman of Samaria came to draw water. Jesus said to her, "Give me a drink." His disciples had gone into the town to buy food. The Samaritan woman said to him, "How can you, a Jew, ask me, a Samaritan woman, for a drink?"—For Jews use nothing in common with Samaritans.— Jesus answered and said to her, "If you knew the gift of God and who is saying to you, 'Give me a drink,' you would have asked him and he would have given you living water." The woman said to him, "Sir, you do not even have a bucket and the cistern is deep; where then can you get this living water? Are you greater than our father Jacob, who gave us this cistern and drank from it himself with his children and his flocks?" Jesus answered and said to her, "Everyone who drinks this water will be thirsty again; but whoever drinks the water I shall give will never thirst; the water I shall give will become in him a spring of water welling up to eternal life." The woman said to him, "Sir, give me this water, so that I may not be thirsty or have to keep coming here to draw water.

"I can see that you are a prophet. Our ancestors worshiped on this mountain; but you people say that the place to worship is in Jerusalem." Jesus said to her, "Believe me, woman, the hour is coming when you will worship the Father neither on this mountain nor in Jerusalem. You people worship what you do not understand; we worship what we understand, because salvation is from the Jews. But the hour is coming, and is now here, when true worshipers will worship the Father in Spirit and truth; and indeed the Father seeks such people to worship him. God is Spirit, and those who worship him must worship in Spirit and truth." The woman said to him, "I know that the Messiah is coming, the one called the Christ; when he comes, he will tell us everything." Jesus said to her, "I am he, the one who is speaking with you."

Many of the Samaritans of that town began to believe in him. When the Samaritans came to him, they invited him to stay with them; and he stayed there two days. Many more began to believe in him because of his word, and they said to the woman, "We no longer believe because of your word; for we have heard for ourselves, and we know that this is truly the savior of the world."

Practice of Hope

When we refuse to believe in the unlimited mercy of God, we are like the Samaritan woman. Our refusal may stem from an unwillingness to associate ourselves intimately with something so foreign in its total acceptance and goodness. Jesus brings hope with his words "whoever drinks the water I shall give will never thirst; the water I shall give will become in him a spring of water welling up to eternal life." Become in him: this can occur only when the love of God meets acceptance in the human heart. ◆ Today, ask: What sins am I holding on to as being unforgivable? ◆ Find one positive action you can accomplish this week that gives you hope. ◆ The Second Vatican Council's *Pastoral Constitution on the Church in the Modern World* (*Gaudium et spes*) begins by stating that the joys and hopes, the griefs and anxieties of others are the joys and hopes, the griefs and anxieties of the followers of Christ. What does this mean to you?

Download more questions and activities for families, Christian initiation groups, and other adult groups at http://www.ltp.org/ahw.

Scripture Insights

In today's First Reading from Exodus, we hear Israel *grumbling* (this Hebrew word can also be translated "quarreling") with Moses. The people are thirsty, and they blame Moses for their circumstances. Only one chapter earlier in Exodus the people "grumbled" to Moses and wished that they had died in Egypt! In response to that first grumbling, God provided the people with manna and quail. Now, God provides them with water. The place names, Massah and Meribah, referred to in this reading, are associated with the words *test* and *quarrel*. They appear again, in today's Psalm, with the instruction "Harden not your hearts as at Meribah, as in the day of Massah in the desert, where your fathers tempted me; they tested me though they had seen my works."

Turning to Romans, we hear of our salvation. Paul emphasizes that we have come to know God through the self-gift of Jesus and the outpouring of the Holy Spirit. The main point of this passage is God's tremendous love for us.

Having journeyed from Jerusalem, Jesus rests at Jacob's well. Jesus, a Jewish man, initiates a conversation with a woman of Samaria. In addition to the fact that such an encounter between an unknown man and woman would have been deemed inappropriate, that the woman was a Samaritan made this even more astonishing. The Samaritans did not recognize the Temple in Jerusalem as the true place of worship, so sharp tensions existed between Samaritans and Jews. Crossing cultural and religious norms, Jesus demonstrates that his mission is to all who would accept him as the Christ.

◆ Reread the text from Exodus.

◆ Have you ever questioned whether God was near?

◆ If you were to have a conversation with Jesus, what do you imagine he would ask you?

READING I
2 Chronicles 36:14–16, 19–23

In those days, all the princes of Judah, the priests, and the people added infidelity to infidelity, practicing all the abominations of the nations and polluting the LORD's temple which he had consecrated in Jerusalem.

Early and often did the LORD, the God of their fathers, send his messengers to them, for he had compassion on his people and his dwelling place. But they mocked the messengers of God, despised his warnings, and scoffed at his prophets, until the anger of the LORD against his people was so inflamed that there was no remedy. Their enemies burnt the house of God, tore down the walls of Jerusalem, set all its palaces afire, and destroyed all its precious objects. Those who escaped the sword were carried captive to Babylon, where they became servants of the king of the Chaldeans and his sons until the kingdom of the Persians came to power. All this was to fulfill the word of the LORD spoken by Jeremiah: "Until the land has retrieved its lost sabbaths, during all the time it lies waste it shall have rest while seventy years are fulfilled."

In the first year of Cyrus, king of Persia, in order to fulfill the word of the LORD spoken by Jeremiah, the LORD inspired King Cyrus of Persia to issue this proclamation throughout his kingdom, both by word of mouth and in writing: "Thus says Cyrus, king of Persia: All the kingdoms of the earth the LORD, the God of heaven, has given to me, and he has also charged me to build him a house in Jerusalem, which is in Judah. Whoever, therefore, among you belongs to any part of his people, let him go up, and may his God be with him!"

RESPONSORIAL PSALM
Psalm 137:1–2, 3, 4–5, 6 (6ab)

R. Let my tongue be silenced, if I ever forget you!

By the streams of Babylon
　　we sat and wept
　　when we remembered Zion.
On the aspens of that land
　　we hung up our harps. R.

For there our captors asked of us
　　the lyrics of our songs,
and our despoilers urged us to be joyous:
　　"Sing for us the songs of Zion!" R.

How could we sing a song of the LORD
　　in a foreign land?
If I forget you, Jerusalem,
　　may my right hand be forgotten! R.

May my tongue cleave to my palate
　　if I remember you not,
if I place not Jerusalem
　　ahead of my joy. R.

READING II Ephesians 2:4–10

Brothers and sisters: God, who is rich in mercy, because of the great love he had for us, even when we were dead in our transgressions, brought us to life with Christ—by grace you have been saved—, raised us up with him, and seated us with him in the heavens in Christ Jesus, that in the ages to come he might show the immeasurable riches of his grace in his kindness to us in Christ Jesus. For by grace you have been saved through faith, and this is not from you; it is the gift of God; it is not from works, so no one may boast. For we are his handiwork, created in Christ Jesus for the good works that God has prepared in advance, that we should live in them.

GOSPEL John 3:14–21

Jesus said to Nicodemus: "Just as Moses lifted up the serpent in the desert, so must the Son of Man be lifted up, so that everyone who believes in him may have eternal life."

For God so loved the world that he gave his only Son, so that everyone who believes in him might not perish but might have eternal life. For God did not send his Son into the world to condemn the world, but that the world might be saved through him. Whoever believes in him will not be condemned, but whoever does not believe has already been condemned, because he has not believed in the name of the only Son of God. And this is the verdict, that the light came into the world, but people preferred darkness to light, because their works were evil. For everyone who does wicked things hates the light and does not come toward the light, so that his works might not be exposed. But whoever lives the truth comes to the light, so that his works may be clearly seen as done in God.

Practice of Faith

"For God so loved the world that he gave his only Son." This succinct summary of the mission of Jesus is among the best-known verses in Scripture. Less beloved, and certainly less inspiring, is the verse that comes later: "And this is the verdict, that the light came into the world, but people preferred darkness to light, because their works were evil." This is a matter-of-fact expression of a dispiriting reality: the light of Christ shines into our darkest places and shows us what we would prefer to keep hidden, even from ourselves. ◆ Reflect on where you are giving preference to darkness instead of light. ◆ Read "The Sun This March," Wallace Stevens' poetic description of personal darkness and conversion, recalling that Jesus is sometimes called "Rabbi." ◆ If there are young children in your life, help them to plant pea, nasturtium, or sunflower seeds, explaining to them that seeds, once sprouted, need to be carefully nurtured and turned each day in the light in order to grow properly, and that our souls likewise need to be carefully tended and constantly reoriented to God.

Download more questions and activities for families, Christian initiation groups, and other adult groups at http://www.ltp.org/ahw.

Scripture Insights

Three things are presented in the First Reading. The conclusion of the Second Book of Chronicles contains a condensed account of the fall of Jerusalem, Israel's exile in Babylon, and the possibility of Israel's return to Judah. The Persian defeat of the Babylonians under King Cyrus brought an end to the exile and ushered in the period often referred to as "the restoration."

Psalm 137 provides insight into the exilic experience that was glossed over in the First Reading. As the psalmist tells us, the Judeans were taunted by the Babylonians, who asked the exiles to sing songs from their homeland. The exiles refused to sing for their captors and instead held fast to their fond memories of Jerusalem as expressed in today's refrain: "Let my tongue be silenced, if I ever forget you!" This Psalm is a lament, a song of longing for the world that the exiles had known prior to their defeat by the Babylonians.

Today's New Testament readings broaden our understanding of what it means to believe in Jesus, the Christ. Ephesians reminds us that God's mercy and grace are freely given to all who believe in Jesus and that our faith is a gift of God. While we know from the very first chapter of Genesis that we are made in the image and likeness of God, in Ephesians we hear that, in addition to being God's "handiwork," we are created "in Christ Jesus" for good works. Meanwhile, the Gospel reminds us that the life we have in Jesus is eternal. If eternal life is desired, we must choose to walk in the light of God.

◆ Have you ever been ridiculed or persecuted for your faith? Reflect on the significance of holding fast, even during periods of difficulty.

◆ Ephesians states that we are God's "handiwork." Ask God to help you know that you are a masterpiece of God.

◆ Reflect on the images of light and darkness that appear so often in the Scriptures. What does it mean for you to choose to walk in the light?

READING I *1 Samuel 16:1b, 6–7, 10–13a*

The LORD said to Samuel: "Fill your horn with oil, and be on your way. I am sending you to Jesse of Bethlehem, for I have chosen my king from among his sons."

As Jesse and his sons came to the sacrifice, Samuel looked at Eliab and thought, "Surely the LORD's anointed is here before him." But the LORD said to Samuel: "Do not judge from his appearance or from his lofty stature, because I have rejected him. Not as man sees does God see, because man sees the appearance but the LORD looks into the heart." In the same way Jesse presented seven sons before Samuel, but Samuel said to Jesse, "The LORD has not chosen any one of these." Then Samuel asked Jesse, "Are these all the sons you have?" Jesse replied, "There is still the youngest, who is tending the sheep." Samuel said to Jesse, "Send for him; we will not begin the sacrificial banquet until he arrives here." Jesse sent and had the young man brought to them. He was ruddy, a youth handsome to behold and making a splendid appearance. The LORD said, "There—anoint him, for this is the one!" Then Samuel, with the horn of oil in hand, anointed David in the presence of his brothers; and from that day on, the spirit of the LORD rushed upon David.

RESPONSORIAL PSALM
Psalm 23:1–3a, 3b–4, 5, 6 (1)

R. The Lord is my shepherd;
> there is nothing I shall want.

The LORD is my shepherd; I shall not want.
> In verdant pastures he gives me repose;
beside restful waters he leads me;
> he refreshes my soul. R.

He guides me in right paths
> for his name's sake.
Even though I walk in the dark valley
> I fear no evil; for you are at my side
with your rod and your staff
> that give me courage. R.

You spread the table before me
> in the sight of my foes;
you anoint my head with oil;
> my cup overflows. R.

Only goodness and kindness follow me
> all the days of my life;
and I shall dwell in the house of the LORD
> for years to come. R.

READING II *Ephesians 5:8–14*

Brothers and sisters: You were once darkness, but now you are light in the Lord. Live as children of light, for light produces every kind of goodness and righteousness and truth. Try to learn what is pleasing to the Lord. Take no part in the fruitless works of darkness; rather expose them, for it is shameful even to mention the things done by them in secret; but everything exposed by the light becomes visible, for everything that becomes visible is light. Therefore, it says:
> "Awake, O sleeper,
> and arise from the dead,
> and Christ will give you light."

GOSPEL *John 9:1, 6–9, 13–17, 34–38*

Longer: John 9:1–41

As Jesus passed by he saw a man blind from birth. He spat on the ground and made clay with the saliva, and smeared the clay on his eyes, and said to him, "Go wash in the Pool of Siloam"—which means Sent—. So he went and washed, and came back able to see.

His neighbors and those who had seen him earlier as a beggar said, "Isn't this the one who used to sit and beg?" Some said, "It is," but others said, "No, he just looks like him." He said, "I am."

They brought the one who was once blind to the Pharisees. Now Jesus had made clay and opened his eyes on a sabbath. So then the Pharisees also asked him how he was able to see. He said to them, "He put clay on my eyes, and I washed, and now I can see." So some of the Pharisees said, "This man is not from God, because he does not keep the sabbath." But others said, "How can a sinful man do such signs?" And there was a division among them. So they said to the blind man again, "What do you have to say about him, since he opened your eyes?" He said, "He is a prophet."

They answered and said to him, "You were born totally in sin, and are you trying to teach us?" Then they threw him out.

When Jesus heard that they had thrown him out, he found him and said, "Do you believe in the Son of Man?" He answered and said, "Who is he, sir, that I may believe in him?" Jesus said to him, "You have seen him, and the one speaking with you is he." He said, "I do believe, Lord," and he worshiped him.

Practice of Hope

For Jews in the time of Jesus, the light that dispelled the world's darkness was the Law, given to them by Moses from God. For Christians, that light is Jesus. Both positions are evident in the Pharisees' approach to the blind man and in his response to them and to the miracle itself. The Pharisees focus their questions on the law that Jesus broke, completely ignoring the main event. No matter what the Pharisees say, the man whose sight has been restored is adamant: "Now I can see." This unwavering stance leads to his acceptance of Jesus as the Son of Man. ◆ At Mass, focus on an openness to Jesus Christ in the Word, in the community, and in the Eucharist. How does your experience of the liturgy change when you approach it this way? ◆ Would you be afraid if someone in your life could suddenly "see" you? Why? How can you change that? ◆ Practice honesty by entering difficult conversations with an open mind rather than defensively.

Download more questions and activities for families, Christian initiation groups, and other adult groups at http://www.ltp.org/ahw.

Scripture Insights

Our reading from the First Book of Samuel introduces us to David, the future king of Israel. His story will dominate the remainder of First and Second Samuel. In these verses, we find Samuel fulfilling the Lord's instructions to visit Jesse and to anoint God's chosen one from among Jesse's sons. As in several other texts from the Old Testament, God's choice does not follow human standards, in which the eldest son is most often the recipient of special blessings over the youngest (consider the stories of Esau and Jacob and Reuben and Joseph, where the youngest received God's favor). When Samuel fulfills the Lord's command and anoints David, the Lord's spirit rushes upon him. As king of Israel, David will have the responsibility of shepherding, caring for God's people.

It is not surprising, then, that the lectionary uses Psalm 23, one of the most well-known and loved texts of the psalter, as today's Responsorial Psalm. While continuing the theme of the shepherd, the poem clearly identifies the Lord as Israel's true and tender shepherd.

In the Gospel of John, Jesus cures a man who had been blind since birth. Today's abbreviated version of a lengthier account is itself an intricate story involving a dispute among the Pharisees and observers of Jesus' cure, a declaration by the cured man that Jesus is a prophet, and another encounter with Jesus in which the man declares his belief that Jesus is the Son of Man and then worships him. When read in its entirety, chapter 9 is recognized as the story of an individual's developing faith in Jesus.

◆ Reread the passage from First Samuel. Ponder the lines that reveal that God does not see as we see, by appearance; rather, God looks into the heart. What does God see within your heart?

◆ Today's reading from Ephesians invites us to reflect on what it means to be "children of light." When you walk in the light of Christ, how are you different?

◆ How are you like the blind man?

READING I *Jeremiah 31:31–34*

The days are coming, says the LORD, when I will make a new covenant with the house of Israel and the house of Judah. It will not be like the covenant I made with their fathers the day I took them by the hand to lead them forth from the land of Egypt; for they broke my covenant, and I had to show myself their master, says the LORD. But this is the covenant that I will make with the house of Israel after those days, says the LORD. I will place my law within them and write it upon their hearts; I will be their God, and they shall be my people. No longer will they have need to teach their friends and relatives how to know the LORD. All, from least to greatest, shall know me, says the LORD, for I will forgive their evildoing and remember their sin no more.

RESPONSORIAL PSALM
Psalm 51:3–4, 12–13, 14–15 (12a)

R. Create a clean heart in me, O God.

Have mercy on me, O God, in your goodness;
    in the greatness of your compassion wipe out
        my offense.
Thoroughly wash me from my guilt
    and of my sin cleanse me. R.

A clean heart create for me, O God,
    and a steadfast spirit renew within me.
Cast me not out from your presence,
    and your Holy Spirit take not from me. R.

Give me back the joy of your salvation,
    and a willing spirit sustain in me.
I will teach transgressors your ways,
    and sinners shall return to you. R.

READING II *Hebrews 5:7–9*

In the days when Christ Jesus was in the flesh, he offered prayers and supplications with loud cries and tears to the one who was able to save him from death, and he was heard because of his reverence. Son though he was, he learned obedience from what he suffered; and when he was made perfect, he became the source of eternal salvation for all who obey him.

GOSPEL *John 12:20–33*

Some Greeks who had come to worship at the Passover Feast came to Philip, who was from Bethsaida in Galilee, and asked him, "Sir, we would like to see Jesus." Philip went and told Andrew; then Andrew and Philip went and told Jesus. Jesus answered them, "The hour has come for the Son of Man to be glorified. Amen, amen, I say to you, unless a grain of wheat falls to the ground and dies, it remains just a grain of wheat; but if it dies, it produces much fruit. Whoever loves his life loses it, and whoever hates his life in this world will preserve it for eternal life. Whoever serves me must follow me, and where I am, there also will my servant be. The Father will honor whoever serves me.

"I am troubled now. Yet what should I say? 'Father, save me from this hour'? But it was for this purpose that I came to this hour. Father, glorify your name." Then a voice came from heaven, "I have glorified it and will glorify it again." The crowd there heard it and said it was thunder; but others said, "An angel has spoken to him." Jesus answered and said, "This voice did not come for my sake but for yours. Now is the time of judgment on this world; now the ruler of this world will be driven out. And when I am lifted up from the earth, I will draw everyone to myself." He said this indicating the kind of death he would die.

Practice of Faith

The Gospel reading this Sunday is St. John's final depiction of the cycle of seeking, witness, and mission that is at the heart of Christianity. Some Greeks who are seeking Jesus approach his disciples first. Andrew and Philip then go to Jesus on behalf of the seekers. Jesus responds by petitioning the Father, perhaps because, in his troubled state, he feels unequal to this moment. But when God speaks to the crowd, some do not hear the voice truly. Only those with faith hear it for what it is.

◆ This week, think of the people in your life who brought you to Christ or who prayed to him on your behalf. Pray to Christ for someone who needs your prayers. Find one small way to be a witness to someone who is looking for Jesus. ◆ Help someone who seems to be struggling through a difficult time in their life. ◆ Read the story of your patron saint or the saint whose Christian example you admire. How did that saint bring others to Christ?

Download more questions and activities for families, Christian initiation groups, and other adult groups at http://www.ltp.org/ahw.

Scripture Insights

Today's passage from Jeremiah tells of a covenant unlike what Israel has known. Whereas the Sinai covenant identified multiple stipulations that Israel was required to uphold, in this covenant Israel is passive. God would place this new covenant within the heart of the people. Israel would receive this covenant freely. While similar images exist in a variety of texts in the Old Testament (for example, Ezekiel 11:19–20; 36:26; and Isaiah 42:9), nowhere else do we hear of a new covenant until we turn to the New Testament.

Psalm 51, often associated with King David, though not necessarily composed by him, is one of the better-known psalms of the psalter and certainly one of the best known of the seven penitential psalms. The refrain "Create a clean heart in me, O God," is a plea for newness. The heart, in Hebrew anthropology, was the most vital of all organs. It also was understood to be that place where discernment took place and where decisions were made.

As the liturgical year draws closer to the celebration of the Triduum, the New Testament readings bring our attention to the death of Jesus. In the Letter to the Hebrews, Jesus' humanity is detailed. He was a being who prayed, cried, learned, and suffered. In the Gospel, Jesus states, "The hour has come for the Son of Man to be glorified," indicating that the time of his suffering, death, and Resurrection is at hand.

◆ Reread the text from Jeremiah and today's Responsorial Psalm. Ask God to touch your heart as you move closer to the celebration of the Lord's Resurrection.

◆ Catholics regularly pray the words of the Apostles' Creed, "he suffered . . . died and was buried." Have you consciously reflected on Jesus as one who prayed, cried, and learned, much as we do?

◆ The Gospel presents us with the image of the "grain of wheat," which bears much fruit when it dies. How does Jesus' death do this?

READING I *Ezekiel 37:12–14*

Thus says the Lord GOD: O my people, I will open your graves and have you rise from them, and bring you back to the land of Israel. Then you shall know that I am the LORD, when I open your graves and have you rise from them, O my people! I will put my spirit in you that you may live, and I will settle you upon your land; thus you shall know that I am the LORD. I have promised, and I will do it, says the LORD.

RESPONSORIAL PSALM
Psalm 130:1–2, 3–4, 5–6, 7–8 (7)

R. With the Lord there is mercy and fullness
of redemption.

Out of the depths I cry to you, O LORD;
LORD, hear my voice!
Let your ears be attentive
to my voice in supplication. R.

If you, O LORD, mark iniquities,
LORD, who can stand?
But with you is forgiveness,
that you may be revered. R.

I trust in the LORD;
my soul trusts in his word.
More than sentinels wait for the dawn,
let Israel wait for the LORD. R.

For with the LORD is kindness
and with him is plenteous redemption;
and he will redeem Israel
from all their iniquities. R.

READING II *Romans 8:8–11*

Brothers and sisters: Those who are in the flesh cannot please God. But you are not in the flesh; on the contrary, you are in the spirit, if only the Spirit of God dwells in you. Whoever does not have the Spirit of Christ does not belong to him. But if Christ is in you, although the body is dead because of sin, the spirit is alive because of righteousness. If the Spirit of the One who raised Jesus from the dead dwells in you, the One who raised Christ from the dead will give life to your mortal bodies also, through his Spirit dwelling in you.

GOSPEL *John 11:3–7, 17, 20–27, 33b–45*
Longer: John 11:1–45

The sisters of Lazarus sent word to Jesus, saying, "Master, the one you love is ill." When Jesus heard this he said, "This illness is not to end in death, but is for the glory of God, that the Son of God may be glorified through it." Now Jesus loved Martha and her sister and Lazarus. So when he heard that he was ill, he remained for two days in the place where he was. Then after this he said to his disciples, "Let us go back to Judea."

When Jesus arrived, he found that Lazarus had already been in the tomb for four days. When Martha heard that Jesus was coming, she went to meet him; but Mary sat at home. Martha said to Jesus, "Lord, if you had been here, my brother would not have died. But even now I know that whatever you ask of God, God will give you." Jesus said to her, "Your brother will rise." Martha said, "I know he will rise, in the resurrection on the last day." Jesus told her, "I am the resurrection and the life; whoever believes in me, even if he dies, will live, and everyone who lives and believes in me will never die. Do you believe this?" She said to him, "Yes, Lord. I have come to believe that you are the Christ, the Son of God, the one who is coming into the world."

He became perturbed and deeply troubled, and said, "Where have you laid him?" They said to him, "Sir, come and see." And Jesus wept. So the Jews said, "See how he loved him." But some of them said, "Could not the one who opened the eyes of the blind man have done something so that this man would not have died?"

So Jesus, perturbed again, came to the tomb. It was a cave, and a stone lay across it. Jesus said, "Take away the stone." Martha, the dead man's sister, said to him, "Lord, by now there will be a stench; he has been dead for four days." Jesus said to her, "Did I not tell you that if you believe you will see the glory of God?" So they took away the stone. And Jesus raised his eyes and said, "Father,

I thank you for hearing me. I know that you always hear me; but because of the crowd here I have said this, that they may believe that you sent me." And when he had said this, he cried out in a loud voice, "Lazarus, come out!" The dead man came out, tied hand and foot with burial bands, and his face was wrapped in a cloth. So Jesus said to them, "Untie him and let him go."

Now many of the Jews who had come to Mary and seen what he had done began to believe in him.

Practice of Charity

Again, another disturbing passage, more uncomfortable images: Jesus weeping at the entrance to a tomb, the betrayal-tinged accusation of a friend, the stench of a decaying body. These images provide many contrasts. A physical death is contrasted with the miracle of resurrection; an event we can relate to is contrasted with one that is past our understanding. The images also contrast the relationship between Jesus and his friends, who are full of human grief, anger, and love, with the love of God that is more encompassing. ◆ This week pray for the dying and for those who care for them or grieve for them. If you have loved ones buried nearby, visit their graves and pray in gratitude that they have entered eternal life with God. ◆ If you can, volunteer at a local hospital. ◆ Love God by loving the people in front of you and by tending to their needs; by so doing, you affirm the Resurrection.

Download more questions and activities for families, Christian initiation groups, and other adult groups at http://www.ltp.org/ahw.

Scripture Insights

Today's short reading from Ezekiel is the conclusion of one of the best-known oracles in this prophetic book. The fuller text, commonly referred to as "the dry bones," is an oracle of salvation that speaks of a time in the near future, when exiled Israel will be brought back to life and return to Judah. The metaphor of bodily resurrection is most appropriate at this time in the liturgical year.

The Responsorial Psalm for today is another of the seven penitential psalms. The refrain for this lament, "With the Lord there is mercy and fullness of redemption," stems from the personal experience of the psalmist.

In Paul's Letter to the Romans, he contrasts two ways of living, "in the flesh" and "in the Spirit." For Paul, life in the flesh refers to human life with all its weaknesses, whereas life in the Spirit refers to life that is focused on God and God's ways. Paul reminds us that, indeed, the Spirit of God dwells within us.

In the Gospel account of Lazarus being raised from the dead, Jesus waits several days before going to his ill friend. When Jesus appears, he tells Martha that her brother will rise, allowing her to profess her belief in the resurrection on the last day. When Jesus states that he is the resurrection and the life, Martha again professes her belief in Jesus. Martha's faith in Jesus does not require that he perform miraculous deeds, whereas many of the people who had come to be with Martha and Mary believed in Jesus only after they had seen the great deeds he had performed.

◆ As you reread today's Responsorial Psalm, ponder the refrain and reflect on the ways that God has shown mercy to you.

◆ Have you experienced the Spirit of God dwelling in you? Ask God to help you live in the Spirit.

◆ The Gospel states, "Jesus loved Martha and her sister and Lazarus." Have you thought of Jesus as a man who had friendships?

Gospel at procession with palms: Mark 11:1–10 or John 12:12–16

READING I *Isaiah 50:4–7*

The Lord GOD has given me
    a well-trained tongue,
that I might know how to speak to the weary
    a word that will rouse them.
Morning after morning
    he opens my ear that I may hear;
and I have not rebelled,
    have not turned back.
I gave my back to those who beat me,
    my cheeks to those who plucked my beard;
my face I did not shield
    from buffets and spitting.

The Lord GOD is my help,
    therefore I am not disgraced;
I have set my face like flint,
    knowing that I shall not be put to shame.

RESPONSORIAL PSALM *Psalm 22:8–9, 17–18, 19–20, 23–24 (2a)*

R. My God, my God, why have you
    abandoned me?

All who see me scoff at me;
    they mock me with parted lips,
        they wag their heads:
"He relied on the LORD; let him deliver him,
    let him rescue him, if he loves him." R.

Indeed, many dogs surround me,
    a pack of evildoers closes in upon me;
they have pierced my hands and my feet;
    I can count all my bones. R.

They divide my garments among them,
    and for my vesture they cast lots.
But you, O LORD, be not far from me;
    O my help, hasten to aid me. R.

I will proclaim your name to my brethren;
    in the midst of the assembly I will praise you:
"You who fear the LORD, praise him;
    all you descendants of Jacob,
        give glory to him;
    revere him, all you descendants of Israel!" R.

READING II *Philippians 2:6–11*

Christ Jesus, though he was in the form of God,
   did not regard equality with God
   something to be grasped.
Rather, he emptied himself,
   taking the form of a slave,
   coming in human likeness;
   and found human in appearance,
   he humbled himself,
   becoming obedient to the point of death,
   even death on a cross.
Because of this, God greatly exalted him
   and bestowed on him the name
   which is above every name,
   that at the name of Jesus
   every knee should bend,
   of those in heaven and on earth and under
      the earth,
   and every tongue confess that
   Jesus Christ is Lord,
   to the glory of God the Father.

GOSPEL *Mark 14:1—15:47*

Shorter: Mark 15:1–39

The Passover and the Feast of Unleavened Bread were to take place in two days' time. So the chief priests and the scribes were seeking a way to arrest him by treachery and put him to death. They said, "Not during the festival, for fear that there may be a riot among the people."

When he was in Bethany reclining at table in the house of Simon the leper, a woman came with an alabaster jar of perfumed oil, costly genuine spikenard. She broke the alabaster jar and poured it on his head. There were some who were indignant. "Why has there been this waste of perfumed oil? It could have been sold for more than three hundred days' wages and the money given to the poor." They were infuriated with her. Jesus said, "Let her alone. Why do you make trouble for her? She has done a good thing for me. The poor you will always have with you, and whenever you wish you can do good to them, but you will not always have me. She has done what she could. She has anticipated anointing my body for burial. Amen, I say to you, wherever the gospel is proclaimed to the whole world, what she has done will be told in memory of her."

Then Judas Iscariot, one of the Twelve, went off to the chief priests to hand him over to them. When they heard him they were pleased and promised to pay him money. Then he looked for an opportunity to hand him over.

On the first day of the Feast of Unleavened Bread, when they sacrificed the Passover lamb, his disciples said to him, "Where do you want us to go and prepare for you to eat the Passover?" He sent two of his disciples and said to them, "Go into the city and a man will meet you, carrying a jar of water. Follow him. Wherever he enters, say to the master of the house, 'The Teacher says, "Where is my guest room where I may eat the Passover with my disciples?"' Then he will show you a large upper room furnished and ready. Make the preparations for us there." The disciples then went off, entered the city, and found it just as he had told them; and they prepared the Passover.

When it was evening, he came with the Twelve. And as they reclined at table and were eating, Jesus said, "Amen, I say to you, one of you will betray me, one who is eating with me." They began to be distressed and to say to him, one by one, "Surely it is not I?" He said to them, "One of the Twelve, the one who dips with me into the dish. For the Son of Man indeed goes, as it is written of him, but woe to that man by whom the Son of Man is betrayed. It would be better for that man if he had never been born."

While they were eating, he took bread, said the blessing, broke it, and gave it to them, and said, "Take it; this is my body." Then he took a cup, gave thanks, and gave it to them, and they all drank from it. He said to them, "This is my blood of the covenant, which will be shed for many. Amen, I say to you, I shall not drink again the fruit of the vine until the day when I drink it new in the kingdom of God." Then, after singing a hymn, they went out to the Mount of Olives.

Then Jesus said to them, "All of you will have your faith shaken, for it is written:

> I will strike the shepherd,
>   and the sheep will be dispersed.

But after I have been raised up, I shall go before you to Galilee." Peter said to him, "Even though all should have their faith shaken, mine will not be." Then Jesus said to him, "Amen, I say to you, this very night before the cock crows twice you will deny me three times." But he vehemently replied, "Even though I should have to die with you, I will not deny you." And they all spoke similarly.

Then they came to a place named Gethsemane, and he said to his disciples, "Sit here while I pray." He took with him Peter, James, and John, and began to be troubled and distressed. Then he said to them, "My soul is sorrowful even to death. Remain here and keep watch." He advanced a little and fell to the ground and prayed that if it were possible the hour might pass by him; he said, "Abba, Father, all things are possible to you. Take this cup away from me, but not what I will but what you will." When he returned he found them asleep. He said to Peter, "Simon, are you asleep? Could you not keep watch for one hour? Watch and pray that you may not undergo the test. The spirit is willing but the flesh is weak." Withdrawing again, he prayed, saying the same thing. Then he returned once more and found them asleep, for they could not keep their eyes open and did not know what to answer him. He returned a third time and said to them, "Are you still sleeping and taking your rest? It is enough. The hour has come. Behold, the Son of Man is to be handed over to sinners. Get up, let us go. See, my betrayer is at hand."

Then, while he was still speaking, Judas, one of the Twelve, arrived, accompanied by a crowd with swords and clubs who had come from the chief priests, the scribes, and the elders. His betrayer had arranged a signal with them, saying, "The man I shall kiss is the one; arrest him and lead him away securely." He came and immediately went over to him and said, "Rabbi." And he kissed him. At this they laid hands on him and arrested him. One of the bystanders drew his sword, struck the high priest's servant, and cut off his ear. Jesus said to them in reply, "Have you come out as against a robber, with swords and clubs, to seize me? Day after day I was with you teaching in the temple area, yet you did not arrest me; but that the Scriptures may be fulfilled." And they all left him and fled. Now a young man followed him wearing nothing but a linen cloth about his body. They seized him, but he left the cloth behind and ran off naked.

They led Jesus away to the high priest, and all the chief priests and the elders and the scribes came together. Peter followed him at a distance into the high priest's courtyard and was seated with the guards, warming himself at the fire. The chief priests and the entire Sanhedrin kept trying to obtain testimony against Jesus in order to put him to death, but they found none. Many gave false witness against him, but their testimony did not agree. Some took the stand and testified falsely against him, alleging, "We heard him say, 'I will destroy this temple made with hands and within three days I will build another not made with hands.'" Even so their testimony did not agree. The high priest rose before the assembly and questioned Jesus, saying, "Have you no answer? What are these men testifying against you?" But he was silent and answered nothing. Again the high priest asked him and said to him, "Are you the Christ, the son of the Blessed One?" Then Jesus answered, "I am;

> and 'you will see the Son of Man
>> seated at the right hand of the Power
>> and coming with the clouds of heaven.'"

At that the high priest tore his garments and said, "What further need have we of witnesses? You have heard the blasphemy. What do you think?" They all condemned him as deserving to die. Some began to spit on him. They blindfolded him and struck him and said to him, "Prophesy!" And the guards greeted him with blows.

While Peter was below in the courtyard, one of the high priest's maids came along. Seeing Peter warming himself, she looked intently at him and said, "You too were with the Nazarene, Jesus." But he denied it saying, "I neither know nor understand what you are talking about." So he went out into the outer court. Then the cock crowed. The maid saw him and began again to say to the bystanders, "This man is one of them." Once again he denied it. A little later the bystanders said to Peter once more, "Surely you are one of them; for you too are a Galilean." He began to curse and to swear, "I do not know this man about whom you are talking." And immediately a cock crowed a second time. Then Peter remembered the word that Jesus had said to him, "Before the cock crows twice you will deny me three times." He broke down and wept.

As soon as morning came, the chief priests with the elders and the scribes, that is, the whole Sanhedrin held a council. They bound Jesus, led him away, and handed him over to Pilate. Pilate questioned him, "Are you the king of the Jews?" He said to him in reply, "You say so." The chief priests accused him of many things. Again Pilate questioned him, "Have you no answer? See how many things they accuse you of." Jesus gave him no further answer, so that Pilate was amazed.

Now on the occasion of the feast he used to release to them one prisoner whom they requested. A man called Barabbas was then in prison along with the rebels who had committed murder in a rebellion. The crowd came forward and began to ask him to do for them as he was accustomed. Pilate answered, "Do you want me to release to you the king of the Jews?" For he knew that it was out of envy that the chief priests had handed him over. But the chief priests stirred up the crowd to have him release Barabbas for them instead. Pilate again said to them in reply, "Then what do you want me to do with the man you call the king of the Jews?" They shouted again, "Crucify him." Pilate said to them, "Why? What evil has he done?" They only shouted the louder, "Crucify him." So Pilate, wishing to satisfy the crowd, released Barabbas to them and, after he had Jesus scourged, handed him over to be crucified.

The soldiers led him away inside the palace, that is, the praetorium, and assembled the whole cohort. They clothed him in purple and, weaving a crown of thorns, placed it on him. They began to salute him with, "Hail, King of the Jews!" and kept striking his head with a reed and spitting upon him. They knelt before him in homage. And when they had mocked him, they stripped him of the purple cloak, dressed him in his own clothes, and led him out to crucify him.

They pressed into service a passer-by, Simon, a Cyrenian, who was coming in from the country, the father of Alexander and Rufus, to carry his cross.

They brought him to the place of Golgotha—which is translated Place of the Skull—. They gave him wine drugged with myrrh, but he did not take it. Then they crucified him and divided his garments by casting lots for them to see what each should take. It was nine o'clock in the morning when they crucified him. The inscription of the charge against him read, "The King of the Jews." With him they crucified two revolutionaries, one on his right and one on his left. Those passing by reviled him, shaking their heads and saying, "Aha! You who would destroy the temple and rebuild it in three days, save yourself by coming down from the cross." Likewise the chief priests, with the scribes, mocked him among themselves and said, "He saved others; he cannot save himself. Let the Christ, the King of Israel, come down now from the cross that we may see and believe." Those who were crucified with him also kept abusing him.

At noon darkness came over the whole land until three in the afternoon. And at three o'clock Jesus cried out in a loud voice, *"Eloi, Eloi, lema sabachthani?"* which is translated, "My God, my

God, why have you forsaken me?" Some of the bystanders who heard it said, "Look, he is calling Elijah." One of them ran, soaked a sponge with wine, put it on a reed and gave it to him to drink saying, "Wait, let us see if Elijah comes to take him down." Jesus gave a loud cry and breathed his last.

[Here all kneel and pray for a short time.]

The veil of the sanctuary was torn in two from top to bottom. When the centurion who stood facing him saw how he breathed his last he said, "Truly this man was the Son of God!" There were also women looking on from a distance. Among them were Mary Magdalene, Mary the mother of the younger James and of Joses, and Salome. These women had followed him when he was in Galilee and ministered to him. There were also many other women who had come up with him to Jerusalem.

When it was already evening, since it was the day of preparation, the day before the sabbath, Joseph of Arimathea, a distinguished member of the council, who was himself awaiting the kingdom of God, came and courageously went to Pilate and asked for the body of Jesus. Pilate was amazed that he was already dead. He summoned the centurion and asked him if Jesus had already died. And when he learned of it from the centurion, he gave the body to Joseph. Having bought a linen cloth, he took him down, wrapped him in the linen cloth, and laid him in a tomb that had been hewn out of the rock. Then he rolled a stone against the entrance to the tomb. Mary Magdalene and Mary the mother of Joses watched where he was laid.

Practice of Charity

Holy Week begins with the long story of the arrest, torture, and death of Jesus. Before Jesus suffers, a woman anoints him with costly oil. Though some of his followers were "infuriated" with the woman for being wasteful, Jesus defends her loving action, saying, "She has done what she could." He knows that he will soon die as a criminal, in which case his body cannot receive the traditional burial anointing. He sees beyond their limited view. ◆ Do you do what you can to bless and tend those around you? Charity is often blocked for practical reasons that have no bearing on what is required of followers of Christ. ◆ Ask yourself if you have failed in charity because of a perspective focused on practicalities. ◆ Reflect on whether you are generous or judgmental in how you view the actions of others. Spend some quiet time today in prayerful preparation for Holy Week.

Download more questions and activities for families, Christian initiation groups, and other adult groups at http://www.ltp.org/ahw.

Scripture Insights

Today begins the first day of Holy Week. Palm Sunday commemorates the entry of Jesus into Jerusalem, where he is proclaimed king.

Our First Reading from the book of Isaiah is one of four poems that are called "the Servant Songs." Another of these poems will be heard on Good Friday. While these texts are believed to have originated during the exile, the Church sees these words as speaking to the identity of Jesus, the one who has given himself for the life of others.

The Psalm refrain, "My God, my God, why have you abandoned me?" will be heard in today's Gospel reading from Mark. Since this line also appears in the Gospel of Matthew, Psalm 22 is perhaps one of the best known of the lament psalms.

Today's text from Philippians is often referred to as the "Christ hymn." Paul uses this poem of uncertain origin to speak of the humiliation and the exaltation of Jesus. Similarities between this text and the reading from Isaiah are self-evident.

Since Mark's Passion account is lengthy, involving multiple scenarios, it can be difficult to follow the details of the Gospel. The text opens with the religious authorities plotting to arrest Jesus and put him to death and is followed by a meal in Bethany where Jesus was anointed, preparation for the Passover meal and the meal itself, Jesus' foretelling of Peter's denial, Jesus' prayer in the garden, Judas' denial, Jesus' arrest and trial, and, finally, his death and burial.

◆ Reread the selections from Isaiah and Philippians. How do these readings depict Jesus?

◆ Carefully pray today's Responsorial Psalm. Have you ever considered that Jesus might have felt completely abandoned by his Father? Notice how the final verses reflect a renewed confidence in God.

◆ With which character in the Gospel do you most identify? The religious authorities? The woman who anointed Jesus? Peter? James? John? Judas Iscariot? Jesus?

Holy Thursday brings to an end the forty days of Lent, which make up the season of anticipation of the great Three Days. Composed of prayer, almsgiving, fasting, and the preparation of the catechumens for Baptism, the season of Lent is now brought to a close, and the Three Days begin as we approach the liturgy of Holy Thursday evening. As those to be initiated into the Church have prepared themselves for their entrance into the fullness of life, so have we been awakening in our hearts, minds, and bodies our own entrances into the life of Christ, experienced in the life of the Church.

The Sacred Paschal Triduum (Latin for "three days") is the center, the core, of the entire year for Christians. These Three Days mark the mystery around which our entire lives are played out. Adults in the community are invited to plan ahead so that the whole time from Thursday night until Easter Sunday is free of social engagements, free of entertainment, and free of meals except for the most basic nourishment. We measure these days—indeed, our very salvation in the life of God—in step with the catechumens themselves; we are revitalized as we support them along the way and participate in their initiation rites.

We are asked to fast on Good Friday and to continue fasting, if possible, all through Holy Saturday as strictly as we can so that we come to the Easter Vigil hungry and full of excitement, parched and longing to feel the sacred water of the font on our skin. We pare down distractions on Good Friday and Holy Saturday so that we may be free for prayer and anticipation, for reflection, preparation, and silence. The Church is getting ready for the great night of the Easter Vigil.

As one who has been initiated into the Church, as one whose life has been wedded to this community gathered at the table, you should anticipate the Triduum with concentration and vigor. With you, the whole Church knows that our presence for the liturgies of the Triduum is not just an invitation. Everyone is needed. We pull out all the stops for these days. As humans, wedded to humanity by the joys and travails of life and grafted onto the body of the Church by the sanctifying waters of Baptism, we lead the new members into new life in this community of faith.

To this end, the Three Days are seen not as three distinct liturgies, but as one movement. These days have been connected liturgically from the early days of the Christian Church. As members of this community, we should be personally committed to preparing for and attending the Triduum and its culmination in the Easter Vigil of Holy Saturday.

The Church proclaims the direction of the Triduum with the opening antiphon of Holy Thursday, which comes from Paul's Letter to the Galatians (6:14). With this verse the Church sets a spiritual environment into which we as committed Christians enter the Triduum:

> *We should glory in the Cross*
> *of our Lord Jesus Christ,*
> *in whom is our salvation, life and resurrection,*
> *through whom we are saved and delivered.*

HOLY THURSDAY

On Thursday evening we enter into this Triduum together. Whether presider, lector, preacher, greeter, altar server, minister of the Eucharist, decorator, or person in the remote corner in the last pew of the church, we begin, as always, by hearkening to the Word of God. These are the Scriptures for the liturgy of Holy Thursday:

Exodus 12:1–8, 11–14
Ancient instructions for the meal of the Passover.

1 Corinthians 11:23–26
Eat the bread and drink the cup until the return of the Lord.

John 13:1–15
Jesus washes the feet of the disciples.

Then the priest, like Jesus, does something strange: he washes feet. Jesus gave us this image of what the Church is supposed to look like, feel like, act like. Our position—whether as observer, washer or washed, servant or served—may be difficult. Yet we learn from the discomfort, from the awkwardness.

Then we celebrate the Eucharist. Because it is connected to the other liturgies of the Triduum on Good Friday and Holy Saturday night, the evening liturgy of Holy Thursday has no ending. Whether we stay to pray awhile or leave, we are now in the quiet, peace, and glory of the Triduum.

Good Friday

We gather quietly in community on Friday and again listen to the Word of God:

Isaiah 52:13—53:12
The servant of the Lord was crushed for our sins.

Hebrews 4:14–16; 5:7–9
The Son of God learned obedience through his suffering.

John 18:1—19:42
The passion of Jesus Christ.

After the homily, we pray at length for all the world's needs: for the Church; for the pope, the clergy and all the baptized; for those preparing for initiation; for the unity of Christians; for Jews; for non-Christians; for atheists; for all in public office; and for those in special need.

Then there is another once-a-year event: the holy cross is held up in our midst, and we come forward one by one to do reverence with a kiss, bow, or genuflection. This communal reverence of an instrument of torture recalls the painful price, in the past and today, of salvation, the way in which our redemption is wrought, the scourging and humiliation of Jesus Christ that bring direction and life back to a humanity that is lost and dead. During the adoration of the cross, we sing not only of the sorrow, but of the glory of the cross by which we have been saved.

Again, we bring to mind the words of Paul (Galatians 6:14), on which last night's entrance antiphon is loosely based: "May I never boast except in the cross of our Lord Jesus Christ, through which the world has been crucified to me, and I to the world."

We continue in fasting and prayer and vigil, in rest and quiet, through Saturday. This Saturday for us is God's rest at the end of creation. It is Christ's repose in the tomb. It is Christ's visit with the dead.

Easter Vigil

Hungry now, pared down to basics, lightheaded from vigilance and full of excitement, we, the already baptized, gather in darkness and light a new fire. From this blaze we light a great candle that will make this night bright for us and will burn throughout Easter Time.

We hearken again to the Word of God with some of the most powerful narratives and proclamations of our tradition:

Genesis 1:1—2:2
The creation of the world.

Genesis 22:1–18
The sacrifice of Isaac.

Exodus 14:15—15:1
The crossing of the Red Sea.

Isaiah 54:5–14
You will not be afraid.

Isaiah 55:1–11
Come, come to the water.

Baruch 3:9–15, 32—4:4
Walk by the light of wisdom.

Ezekiel 36:16–17a, 18–28
The Lord says: I will sprinkle water.

Romans 6:3–11
United with him in death.

Year A: Matthew 28:1–10, Year B: Mark 16:1–7, Year C: Luke 24:1–12
Jesus has been raised.

After the readings, we call on our saints to stand with us as we go to the font and the priest celebrant blesses the waters. The chosen of all times and all places attend to what is about to take place. The elect renounce evil, profess the faith of the Church, and are baptized and anointed.

All of us renew our Baptism. These are the moments when death and life meet, when we reject evil and make our promises to God. All of this is in the communion of the Church. So together we go to the table and celebrate the Easter Eucharist.

Easter Time

Prayer before Reading the Word

God of all creation,
whose mighty power raised Jesus from the dead,
be present to this community of disciples
whom you have called to the hope
of a glorious inheritance among the saints.
As we hear the word that brings salvation,
make our hearts burn within us,
that we may recognize Christ crucified and risen,
who opens our hearts to
        understand the Scriptures,
who is made known to us in the breaking of
        the bread,
and who lives and reigns with you
in the unity of the Holy Spirit,
one God, for ever and ever. Amen.

Prayer after Reading the Word

O God of Easter glory,
gather your baptized people
around the teaching of the Apostles,
devoted to the life we share in the Church,
devoted to the breaking of the bread.
Make us so embrace the name of Christ,
that we glorify you in the world
and bear witness to your Word
made known to us by Jesus,
our Passover and our peace,
who lives and reigns with you
in the unity of the Holy Spirit,
one God, for ever and ever. Amen.

Weekday Readings

April 5: Monday within the Octave of Easter
Acts 2:14, 22–33; Matthew 28:8–15
April 6: Tuesday within the Octave of Easter
Acts 2:36–41; John 20:11–18
April 7: Wednesday within the Octave of Easter
Acts 3:1–10; Luke 24:13–35
April 8: Thursday within the Octave of Easter
Acts 3:11–26; Luke 24:35–48
April 9: Friday within the Octave of Easter
Acts 4:1–12; John 21:1–14
April 10: Saturday within the Octave of Easter
Acts 4:13–21; Mark 16:9–15

April 12: *Acts 4:23–31; John 3:1–8*
April 13: *Acts 4:32–37; John 3:7b–15*
April 14: *Acts 5:17–26; John 3:16–21*
April 15: *Acts 5:27–33; John 3:31–36*
April 16: *Acts 5:34–42; John 6:1–15*
April 17: *Acts 6:1–7; John 6:16–21*

April 19: *Acts 6:8–15; John 6:22–29*
April 20: *Acts 7:51—8:1a; John 6:30–35*
April 21: *Acts 8:1b–8; John 6:35–40*
April 22: *Acts 8:26–40; John 6:44–51*
April 23: *Acts 9:1–20; John 6:52–59*
April 24: *Acts 9:31–42; John 6:60–69*

April 26: *Acts 11:1–18; John 10:1–10*
April 27: *Acts 11:19–26; John 10:22–30*
April 28: *Acts 12:24—13:5a; John 12:44–50*
April 29: *Acts 13:13–25; John 13:16–20*
April 30: *Acts 13:26–33; John 14:1–6*
May 1: *Acts 13:44–52; John 14:7–14*

May 3: Feast of Sts. Philip and James, Apostles
1 Corinthians 15:1–8; John 14:6–14
May 4: *Acts 14:19–28; John 14:27–31a*
May 5: *Acts 15:1–6; John 15:1–8*
May 6: *Acts 15:7–21; John 15:9–11*
May 7: *Acts 15:22–31; John 15:12–17*
May 8: *Acts 16:1–10; John 15:18–21*

May 10: *Acts 16:11–15; John 15:26—16:4a*
May 11: *Acts 16:22–34; John 16:5–11*
May 12: *Acts 17:15, 22—18:1; John 16:12–15*
May 13: Solemnity of the Ascension of the Lord
    [Ecclesiastical provinces of Boston, Hartford, New York, Newark, Omaha, and Philadelphia]
    Acts 1:1–11; Ephesians 1:17–23; Mark 16:15–20
(If the Ascension of the Lord is celebrated
    on the following Sunday:)
    May 13: Acts 18:1–8; John 16:16–20
May 14: Feast of St. Matthias
    Acts 1:15–17, 20–26; John 15:9–17
May 15: *Acts 18:23–28; John 16:23b–28*

May 17: *Acts 19:1–8; John 16:29–33*
May 18: *Acts 20:17–27; John 17:1–11a*
May 19: *Acts 20:28–38; John 17:11b–19*
May 20: *Acts 22:30; 23:6–11; John 17:20–26*
May 21: *Acts 25:13b–21; John 21:15–19*
May 22: *Acts 28:16–20, 30–31; John 21:20–25*

READING I *Acts 10:34a, 37–43*

Peter proceeded to speak and said: "You know what has happened all over Judea, beginning in Galilee after the baptism that John preached, how God anointed Jesus of Nazareth with the Holy Spirit and power. He went about doing good and healing all those oppressed by the devil, for God was with him. We are witnesses of all that he did both in the country of the Jews and in Jerusalem. They put him to death by hanging him on a tree. This man God raised on the third day and granted that he be visible, not to all the people, but to us, the witnesses chosen by God in advance, who ate and drank with him after he rose from the dead. He commissioned us to preach to the people and testify that he is the one appointed by God as judge of the living and the dead. To him all the prophets bear witness, that everyone who believes in him will receive forgiveness of sins through his name."

RESPONSORIAL PSALM
Psalm 118:1–2, 16–17, 22–23 (24)

R. This is the day the Lord has made;
    let us rejoice and be glad.

or: Alleluia.

Give thanks to the LORD, for he is good,
    for his mercy endures forever.
Let the house of Israel say,
    "His mercy endures forever." R.

"The right hand of the LORD
        has struck with power;
    the right hand of the LORD is exalted.
I shall not die, but live,
    and declare the works of the LORD." R.

The stone which the builders rejected
    has become the cornerstone.
By the LORD has this been done;
    it is wonderful in our eyes. R.

READING II *Colossians 3:1–4*

Alternate: 1 Corinthians 5:6b–8

Brothers and sisters: If then you were raised with Christ, seek what is above, where Christ is seated at the right hand of God. Think of what is above, not of what is on earth. For you have died, and your life is hidden with Christ in God. When Christ your life appears, then you too will appear with him in glory.

GOSPEL *John 20:1–9*

Alternates: Mark 16:1–7; or at an afternoon or evening Mass: Luke 24:13–35

On the first day of the week, Mary of Magdala came to the tomb early in the morning, while it was still dark, and saw the stone removed from the tomb. So she ran and went to Simon Peter and to the other disciple whom Jesus loved, and told them, "They have taken the Lord from the tomb, and we don't know where they put him." So Peter and the other disciple went out and came to the tomb. They both ran, but the other disciple ran faster than Peter and arrived at the tomb first; he bent down and saw the burial cloths there, but did not go in. When Simon Peter arrived after him, he went into the tomb and saw the burial cloths there, and the cloth that had covered his head, not with the burial cloths but rolled up in a separate place. Then the other disciple also went in, the one who had arrived at the tomb first, and he saw and believed. For they did not yet understand the Scripture that he had to rise from the dead.

Practice of Faith

The beginning of the reading from Acts notes that Peter is speaking to people familiar with the life of Jesus ("You know what has happened all over Judea"). Peter tells the gathered community what the events of Jesus' life mean: Jesus is "the one appointed by God," through whom all who believe will receive forgiveness of sins. Paul persists with Peter's message in the Letter to the Colossians: "Think of what is above. . . . When Christ your life appears, then you too will appear with him in glory." Those with faith have a different view than those focused on earthly matters: what is seen means more than what may be perceived. Even Mary Magdalene at first does not understand what she sees. ◆ Reflect on what it means to see with eyes of faith. ◆ If your parish provides a Mass in another language, attend that Mass to experience Eucharistic unity through a means other than language. ◆ You know the story of Jesus, but do you know what it means? Consider what you must do to appear with Christ in glory.

Download more questions and activities for families, Christian initiation groups, and other adult groups at http://www.ltp.org/ahw.

Scripture Insights

Jesus has been raised from the dead. Alleluia! Alleluia!

From today through the Solemnity of Pentecost, the First Reading each Sunday will be from the Acts of the Apostles. These readings are not in sequential order, so while today's text is from chapter 10 of Acts, next Sunday's reading is from chapter 4. None of the readings during the next six weeks are from the latter chapters of the book, chapters 11–28. It can be helpful to bear this in mind since we understand Acts to be the story of the early followers of Jesus, after his Resurrection. These texts, then, will focus only on the beginnings of the early Church community. Today's reading opens with the words "Peter proceeded to speak and said." In Greek, these words are recognized as a particular literary form that lets the readers and the listeners know that what follows is inspired speech, similar to the Hebrew form in prophetic literature that begins "Thus says the Lord." The message that Peter proclaims is about God's great deeds in Jesus.

The four verses from Colossians in the Second Reading are part of a larger unit that began in the previous chapter and whose focus was more negative in tone than what we find here. These few lines encourage the community to turn their attention to Christ, with whom they are already united.

The Gospel reading is from select verses of a longer and powerful story that provide us with a brief and dramatic scene at the empty tomb. While verse 10, not included in today's reading, states that the disciples returned home, verse 11 tells us that Mary remained outside the tomb and wept. A beautiful encounter between Mary and the Risen Lord takes place within the next few verses.

◆ How does the Resurrection impact the way that you live?

◆ From your Bible, read the longer account of the Resurrection, John 20:1–18 or 1–29. Imagine yourself weeping and searching for Jesus.

◆ If you heard Christ call your name, how do you imagine you would respond to him?

READING I *Acts 4:32–35*

The community of believers was of one heart and mind, and no one claimed that any of his possessions was his own, but they had everything in common. With great power the apostles bore witness to the resurrection of the Lord Jesus, and great favor was accorded them all. There was no needy person among them, for those who owned property or houses would sell them, bring the proceeds of the sale, and put them at the feet of the apostles, and they were distributed to each according to need.

RESPONSORIAL PSALM
Psalm 118:2–4, 13–15, 22–24 (1)

R. Give thanks to the Lord, for he is good; his
      love is everlasting.
  or: Alleluia.

Let the house of Israel say,
    "His mercy endures forever."
Let the house of Aaron say,
    "His mercy endures forever."
Let those who fear the LORD say,
    "His mercy endures forever." R.

I was hard pressed and was falling,
    but the LORD helped me.
My strength and my courage is the LORD,
    and he has been my savior.
The joyful shout of victory
    in the tents of the just. R.

The stone which the builders rejected
    has become the cornerstone.
By the LORD has this been done;
    it is wonderful in our eyes.
This is the day the LORD has made;
    let us be glad and rejoice in it. R.

READING II *1 John 5:1–6*

Beloved: Everyone who believes that Jesus is the Christ is begotten by God, and everyone who loves the Father loves also the one begotten by him. In this way we know that we love the children of God when we love God and obey his commandments. For the love of God is this, that we keep his commandments. And his commandments are not burdensome, for whoever is begotten by God conquers the world. And the victory that conquers the world is our faith. Who indeed is the victor over the world but the one who believes that Jesus is the Son of God?

This is the one who came through water and blood, Jesus Christ, not by water alone, but by water and blood. The Spirit is the one that testifies, and the Spirit is truth.

GOSPEL *John 20:19–31*

On the evening of that first day of the week, when the doors were locked, where the disciples were, for fear of the Jews, Jesus came and stood in their midst and said to them, "Peace be with you." When he had said this, he showed them his hands and his side. The disciples rejoiced when they saw the Lord. Jesus said to them again, "Peace be with you. As the Father has sent me, so I send you." And when he had said this, he breathed on them and said to them, "Receive the Holy Spirit. Whose sins you forgive are forgiven them, and whose sins you retain are retained."

Thomas, called Didymus, one of the Twelve, was not with them when Jesus came. So the other disciples said to him, "We have seen the Lord." But he said to them, "Unless I see the mark of the nails in his hands and put my finger into the nailmarks and put my hand into his side, I will not believe."

Now a week later his disciples were again inside and Thomas was with them. Jesus came, although the doors were locked, and stood in their midst and said, "Peace be with you." Then he said to Thomas, "Put your finger here and see my hands, and bring your hand and put it into my side, and do not be unbelieving, but believe." Thomas answered and said to him, "My Lord and my God!" Jesus said to him, "Have you come to believe because you have seen me? Blessed are those who have not seen and have believed."

Now Jesus did many other signs in the presence of his disciples that are not written in this book. But these are written that you may come to believe that Jesus is the Christ, the Son of God, and that through this belief you may have life in his name.

Practice of Faith

The joy inherent in the First Reading is the joy of a people united in faith. ("The community of believers was of one heart and mind," and "there was no needy person among them.") In contrast, Thomas represents an individual who, due to his lack of faith, remains isolated within his community. It takes an experience of the Risen Lord to change his unbelief, and then he honors Jesus as "my Lord and my God." All Christians after Thomas' time must rely on the testimony and lives of those who came before them, who have handed on their experience of the Risen Lord. ◆ Be aware that you belong to a people united in faith. Pray for another parish in your city or region. If you can, plan to visit the cathedral in your diocese. ◆ Put some good of yours—a talent, a service, money, or material goods—at the disposal of your community. ◆ Consider the many titles given to Jesus throughout the ages and what they mean. Reflect on the times that you have been surprised into recognizing Christ.

Download more questions and activities for families, Christian initiation groups, and other adult groups at http://www.ltp.org/ahw.

Scripture Insights

On this Second Sunday of Easter, the Liturgy of the Word begins with a most beautiful and idealistic text from Acts. Of special significance is the description that the Jerusalem community "was of one heart and mind," with "everything in common." How many of us struggle daily to live for the common good!

Appropriately, today's Responsorial Psalm is one of thanksgiving, with emphasis placed on God's everlasting love. While this love is celebrated throughout the liturgical year, it is uniquely emphasized during the Easter season, when we remember the Paschal Mystery most intensely.

The reading from the First Letter of John, like our Responsorial Psalm, invites us to reflect on the incomprehensible love of God. God's commandments are not intended to be a burden for us; rather, they have been given to us as guides for living faith-filled lives.

While locked behind closed doors, Jesus appears to the disciples and offers them peace. Upon recognizing Jesus, the disciples rejoice. Jesus extends peace to them a second time, then bestows the Holy Spirit on them. In yet another encounter behind locked doors, Jesus appears again. This time, after extending peace to the disciples, Jesus invites Thomas to touch him and to believe in him. This scene concludes with reference to other signs that Jesus performed so that we might have life in Jesus' name.

◆ Reread the short passage from the Acts of the Apostles. What would it require for a community to be "of one heart and mind"? What would such a lifestyle require of you? Do you believe that such a way of life is possible?

◆ Consider writing a short psalm of thanksgiving using the refrain "Give thanks to the Lord, for he is good; his love is everlasting." Compose several verses in which you identify specific people and acts of God for which you are grateful.

◆ Had you been locked behind closed doors and heard the voice of Jesus extending you his peace, how do you imagine that you would respond?

READING I *Acts 3:13–15, 17–19*

Peter said to the people: "The God of Abraham, the God of Isaac, and the God of Jacob, the God of our fathers, has glorified his servant Jesus, whom you handed over and denied in Pilate's presence when he had decided to release him. You denied the Holy and Righteous One and asked that a murderer be released to you. The author of life you put to death, but God raised him from the dead; of this we are witnesses. Now I know, brothers, that you acted out of ignorance, just as your leaders did; but God has thus brought to fulfillment what he had announced beforehand through the mouth of all the prophets, that his Christ would suffer. Repent, therefore, and be converted, that your sins may be wiped away."

RESPONSORIAL PSALM
Psalm 4:2, 4, 7–8, 9 (7a)

R. Lord, let your face shine on us.
  or: Alleluia.

When I call, answer me, O my just God,
    you who relieve me when I am in distress;
    have pity on me, and hear my prayer! R.

Know that the LORD does wonders for his
        faithful one;
    the LORD will hear me when I call
        upon him. R.

O LORD, let the light of your countenance shine
        upon us!
    You put gladness into my heart. R.

As soon as I lie down, I fall peacefully asleep,
    for you alone, O LORD,
    bring security to my dwelling. R.

READING II *1 John 2:1–5a*

My children, I am writing this to you so that you may not commit sin. But if anyone does sin, we have an Advocate with the Father, Jesus Christ the righteous one. He is expiation for our sins, and not for our sins only but for those of the whole world. The way we may be sure that we know him is to keep his commandments. Those who say, "I know him," but do not keep his commandments are liars, and the truth is not in them. But whoever keeps his word, the love of God is truly perfected in him.

GOSPEL *Luke 24:35–48*

The two disciples recounted what had taken place on the way, and how Jesus was made known to them in the breaking of bread.

While they were still speaking about this, he stood in their midst and said to them, "Peace be with you." But they were startled and terrified and thought that they were seeing a ghost. Then he said to them, "Why are you troubled? And why do questions arise in your hearts? Look at my hands and my feet, that it is I myself. Touch me and see, because a ghost does not have flesh and bones as you can see I have." And as he said this, he showed them his hands and his feet. While they were still incredulous for joy and were amazed, he asked them, "Have you anything here to eat?" They gave him a piece of baked fish; he took it and ate it in front of them.

He said to them, "These are my words that I spoke to you while I was still with you, that everything written about me in the law of Moses and in the prophets and psalms must be fulfilled." Then he opened their minds to understand the Scriptures. And he said to them, "Thus it is written that the Christ would suffer and rise from the dead on the third day and that repentance, for the forgiveness of sins, would be preached in his name to all the nations, beginning from Jerusalem. You are witnesses of these things."

Practice of Hope

Jesus opens the two disciples' minds and presses them to understand the true import of the Scriptures now fulfilled, telling them, "You are witnesses of these things." His message is urgent, as his time on earth is coming to a close. He wants them to know that the hope of salvation depends on their witness and asks them to carry his message of hope to the nations. ◆ Many families in America have no dwelling, no security, and very little hope. Give these families hope. Find a local Habitat for Humanity or similar charity where you can volunteer. ◆ Enroll in a Bible study course so you can understand more fully how Jesus is the culmination of God's relationship with humanity, as described in Scripture. ◆ Consider how you can tell someone of your reason for hope.

Download more questions and activities for families, Christian initiation groups, and other adult groups at http://www.ltp.org/ahw.

Scripture Insights

Today's First Reading from Acts is an excerpt of a lengthier text that tells of a healing that Peter and John had performed. A lame man had requested alms from the Apostles, but instead of receiving monetary assistance from them, he was cured of his impairment. Peter's words that we hear today are addressed to the crowd that had gathered to see the lame man walking and praising God. Peter seeks to make the point that the marvelous act that had just been performed was a direct result of the Apostles' having spoken "in the name of Jesus Christ of Nazareth." Peter reminds the crowd that, although they had put Jesus to death, they have the opportunity to repent of their sin and become one with Christ.

The Gospel reading from Luke follows the story of the two disciples on the road to Emmaus. Upon returning to Jerusalem, these disciples learn that Jesus had also appeared to Simon. As the two recounted their experience of Jesus to the others, the Risen Lord appears among them and offers them peace. After encouraging the disciples to "touch" him, and after they have seen him eat, the disciples appear to have remained puzzled. Jesus speaks to them again, and then "he opened their minds to understand the Scriptures." Whereas Jesus had opened the eyes of the two disciples on the road, Jesus now opens the minds of the gathered disciples. The verse that follows this account has not been included in the reading. That verse, however, helps us understand what occurs next. Jesus instructs the disciples to remain in the city (Jerusalem) until they are clothed and receive the power from on high. That power is the Holy Spirit.

◆ Reread today's Second Reading. Ponder what it means for you to keep God's Word.

◆ Reflect on the experience of Jesus' disciples. When you question the strength of your faith, consider how difficult it was for the people who knew the earthly Jesus to recognize him among them.

◆ Where in your life is repentance needed?

April 25, 2021 FOURTH SUNDAY OF EASTER

READING I *Acts 4:8–12*

Peter, filled with the Holy Spirit, said: "Leaders of the people and elders: If we are being examined today about a good deed done to a cripple, namely, by what means he was saved, then all of you and all the people of Israel should know that it was in the name of Jesus Christ the Nazorean whom you crucified, whom God raised from the dead; in his name this man stands before you healed. He is *the stone rejected by you, the builders, which has become the cornerstone.* There is no salvation through anyone else, nor is there any other name under heaven given to the human race by which we are to be saved."

RESPONSORIAL PSALM *Psalm 118:1, 8–9, 21–23, 26, 28, 29 (22)*

R. The stone rejected by the builders has become
the cornerstone.
or: Alleluia.

Give thanks to the LORD, for he is good,
for his mercy endures forever.
It is better to take refuge in the LORD
than to trust in man.
It is better to take refuge in the LORD
than to trust in princes. R.

I will give thanks to you, for you have
answered me
and have been my savior.
The stone which the builders rejected
has become the cornerstone.
By the LORD has this been done;
it is wonderful in our eyes. R.

Blessed is he who comes in the name of the LORD;
we bless you from the house of the LORD.
I will give thanks to you,
for you have answered me
and have been my savior.
Give thanks to the LORD, for he is good;
for his kindness endures forever. R.

READING II *1 John 3:1–2*

Beloved: See what love the Father has bestowed on us that we may be called the children of God. Yet so we are. The reason the world does not know us is that it did not know him. Beloved, we are God's children now; what we shall be has not yet been revealed. We do know that when it is revealed we shall be like him, for we shall see him as he is.

GOSPEL *John 10:11–18*

Jesus said: "I am the good shepherd. A good shepherd lays down his life for the sheep. A hired man, who is not a shepherd and whose sheep are not his own, sees a wolf coming and leaves the sheep and runs away, and the wolf catches and scatters them. This is because he works for pay and has no concern for the sheep. I am the good shepherd, and I know mine and mine know me, just as the Father knows me and I know the Father; and I will lay down my life for the sheep. I have other sheep that do not belong to this fold. These also I must lead, and they will hear my voice, and there will be one flock, one shepherd. This is why the Father loves me, because I lay down my life in order to take it up again. No one takes it from me, but I lay it down on my own. I have power to lay it down, and power to take it up again. This command I have received from my Father."

Practice of Charity

Jesus is the Good Shepherd, not only because he offered himself for his sheep, but because he knows his sheep intimately, having lived with them from birth to death. In an address to priests, Pope Francis has said, "This is what I am asking you— be shepherds with the smell of sheep." That is, he asks them to go out and take part in the lives of those they lead. This is the task of all the baptized. Like the "priest who seldom goes out himself," the Christian who fails to minister in some way to the rest of the flock fails in charity. A person who takes an overly academic approach to faith misses the heart of the Gospel message. ◆ On the Vatican website (www.vatican.va), read Pope Francis' address to the world's priests at the Chrism Mass on Holy Thursday. Reflect on how his message applies to you. ◆ Perform one loving act that you have been avoiding out of a feeling of discomfort or distaste. ◆ Reach out to someone outside your "fold"; yours might be the voice they need to hear.

Download more questions and activities for families, Christian initiation groups, and other adult groups at http://www.ltp.org/ahw.

Scripture Insights

Today's First Reading from Acts is a continuation of events that we heard last Sunday. After curing a lame man, Peter and John are questioned by the Temple authorities. When asked, "by what power or by what name have you done this?" Peter boldly responds that it was in the name of Jesus that the man was cured and that it is in this name only that all people will be saved.

The Gospel for today is a portion of the longer and very familiar discourse on the Good Shepherd. Most people reading this passage have had no experience with tending sheep, but it is important to keep in mind that this discourse is about relationship. The Jewish community would have been familiar with the images of the shepherd and the hired hand. The hired hand to whom Jesus refers is an individual (or individuals) who had no relationship with the sheep he is paid to tend. The shepherd, on the other hand, is the one who knows and tends to the sheep with tender care. When Jesus says, "I am the good shepherd," he not only is identifying himself as the one with whom he and his sheep have a mutual relationship, but also saying that he and the Father have a mutual relationship. While using the familiar shepherd imagery of the Old Testament, Jesus expands the image of shepherd to include "other sheep that do not belong to this fold." Jesus will lay down his life for many, not for an elite few.

◆ Consider the significance of knowing someone's name. Of what importance is this in the First Reading? in your daily life?

◆ In today's Gospel, Jesus says that there are other sheep that he will lead and who will hear his voice. Reflect on what the voice of a loved one stirs within you.

◆ What might Jesus mean when he states that he must also lead sheep who are not of this fold but that "they will hear my voice, and there will be one flock, one shepherd"?

READING I *Acts 9:26–31*

When Saul arrived in Jerusalem he tried to join the disciples, but they were all afraid of him, not believing that he was a disciple. Then Barnabas took charge of him and brought him to the apostles, and he reported to them how he had seen the Lord, and that he had spoken to him, and how in Damascus he had spoken out boldly in the name of Jesus. He moved about freely with them in Jerusalem, and spoke out boldly in the name of the Lord. He also spoke and debated with the Hellenists, but they tried to kill him. And when the brothers learned of this, they took him down to Caesarea and sent him on his way to Tarsus.

The church throughout all Judea, Galilee, and Samaria was at peace. It was being built up and walked in the fear of the Lord, and with the consolation of the Holy Spirit it grew in numbers.

RESPONSORIAL PSALM
Psalm 22:26–27, 28, 30, 31–32 (26a)

R. I will praise you, Lord, in the assembly of
      your people.
  or: Alleluia.

I will fulfill my vows before those who fear
    the LORD.
  The lowly shall eat their fill;
they who seek the LORD shall praise him:
  "May your hearts live forever!" R.

All the ends of the earth
  shall remember and turn to the LORD;
all the families of the nations
  shall bow down before him. R.

To him alone shall bow down
  all who sleep in the earth;
before him shall bend
  all who go down into the dust. R.

And to him my soul shall live;
  my descendants shall serve him.
Let the coming generation be told of the LORD
  that they may proclaim to a people yet
      to be born
  the justice he has shown. R.

READING II *1 John 3:18–24*

Children, let us love not in word or speech but in deed and truth.

Now this is how we shall know that we belong to the truth and reassure our hearts before him in whatever our hearts condemn, for God is greater than our hearts and knows everything. Beloved, if our hearts do not condemn us, we have confidence in God and receive from him whatever we ask, because we keep his commandments and do what pleases him. And his commandment is this: we should believe in the name of his Son, Jesus Christ, and love one another just as he commanded us. Those who keep his commandments remain in him, and he in them, and the way we know that he remains in us is from the Spirit he gave us.

GOSPEL *John 15:1–8*

Jesus said to his disciples: "I am the true vine, and my Father is the vine grower. He takes away every branch in me that does not bear fruit, and every one that does he prunes so that it bears more fruit. You are already pruned because of the word that I spoke to you. Remain in me, as I remain in you. Just as a branch cannot bear fruit on its own unless it remains on the vine, so neither can you unless you remain in me. I am the vine, you are the branches. Whoever remains in me and I in him will bear much fruit, because without me you can do nothing. Anyone who does not remain in me will be thrown out like a branch and wither; people will gather them and throw them into a fire and they will be burned. If you remain in me and my words remain in you, ask for whatever you want and it will be done for you. By this is my Father glorified, that you bear much fruit and become my disciples."

Practice of Charity

During the Easter season, the readings describe the Church as it takes root and grows and discovers its nature and mission. Paul struggles with his past and his task; John explains that Christians follow Christ and love one another "in deed and truth," an active love. But it is in the Gospel that the one essential condition is so vividly expressed: the Christian life must be lived in Christ, dependent on him as a branch is dependent on the vine. Since Christ is so intimately united to humanity, it is only in unity with each other that Christians bear fruit. ◆ Today, pray for farmworkers and their families, so many of whom are migrants in tenuous situations. ◆ Pray also for missionaries, many of whom, like Paul, have suffered—even died—carrying Christ's message across the globe. ◆ Look up Catholic missionary societies and consider how you can assist in their work.

Download more questions and activities for families, Christian initiation groups, and other adult groups at http://www.ltp.org/ahw.

Scripture Insights

Today's First Reading appears near the end of chapter 9 of Acts. The opening verses of this chapter recount Saul's request for letters of approval from Temple officials. These letters would acknowledge Saul's authority once he reached Damascus, where he intended to persecute followers of Jesus. In verse 3 of this chapter, the first of three accounts of Saul's conversion begins. (Two other recordings of this experience are found in Acts 22:3–16 and 26:4–23.) Thus, it is no wonder that in today's pericope, beginning in verse 26, we hear that the disciples were reticent to believe that Saul had become a follower of Jesus. In a few words, the text details how Barnabas intervened and how the Apostles accepted Saul as one who had seen the Lord. Immediately, Saul began to proclaim that Jesus is Lord.

The reading from the First Letter of John reminds us that love expresses itself most perfectly in action. While words are important, the lived expression of our words speaks a truth more strongly. Belief in Jesus is identified by our actions, our love for one another.

The Gospel of John presents us with the metaphor of the vine and the branches. Jesus identifies himself as the true vine and speaks of his relationship to the Father. Earlier texts that referred to Israel as the vine, primarily prophetic texts, quite obviously did not speak of the Father. Here, Jesus identifies his Father as the vine grower, or vine dresser, the one who carefully tends to the vine so that it will bear fruit.

◆ Given the reputation that Saul/Paul had as a persecutor of those who followed Jesus, how likely would you have been to believe that he had experienced a conversion?

◆ Have you experienced a conversion, even a small one, that resulted in a life-changing practice?

◆ How do you see yourself as part of the true vine?

READING I
Acts 10:25–26, 34–35, 44–48

When Peter entered, Cornelius met him and, falling at his feet, paid him homage. Peter, however, raised him up, saying, "Get up. I myself am also a human being."

Then Peter proceeded to speak and said, "In truth, I see that God shows no partiality. Rather, in every nation whoever fears him and acts uprightly is acceptable to him."

While Peter was still speaking these things, the Holy Spirit fell upon all who were listening to the word. The circumcised believers who had accompanied Peter were astounded that the gift of the Holy Spirit should have been poured out on the Gentiles also, for they could hear them speaking in tongues and glorifying God. Then Peter responded, "Can anyone withhold the water for baptizing these people, who have received the Holy Spirit even as we have?" He ordered them to be baptized in the name of Jesus Christ.

RESPONSORIAL PSALM
Psalm 98:1, 2–3, 3–4 (see 2b)

R. The Lord has revealed to the nations his
       saving power.
   or: Alleluia.

Sing to the LORD a new song,
   for he has done wondrous deeds;
His right hand has won victory for him,
   his holy arm. R.

The LORD has made his salvation known:
   in the sight of the nations he has revealed
       his justice.
He has remembered his kindness and
       his faithfulness
   toward the house of Israel. R.

All the ends of the earth have seen
   the salvation by our God.
Sing joyfully to the LORD, all you lands;
   break into song; sing praise. R.

READING II *1 John 4:7–10*

Beloved, let us love one another, because love is of God; everyone who loves is begotten by God and knows God. Whoever is without love does not know God, for God is love. In this way the love of God was revealed to us: God sent his only Son into the world so that we might have life through him. In this is love: not that we have loved God, but that he loved us and sent his Son as expiation for our sins.

GOSPEL *John 15:9–17*

Jesus said to his disciples: "As the Father loves me, so I also love you. Remain in my love. If you keep my commandments, you will remain in my love, just as I have kept my Father's commandments and remain in his love.

"I have told you this so that my joy may be in you and your joy might be complete. This is my commandment: love one another as I love you. No one has greater love than this, to lay down one's life for one's friends. You are my friends if you do what I command you. I no longer call you slaves, because a slave does not know what his master is doing. I have called you friends, because I have told you everything I have heard from my Father. It was not you who chose me, but I who chose you and appointed you to go and bear fruit that will remain, so that whatever you ask the Father in my name he may give you. This I command you: love one another."

Practice of Charity

In today's Gospel, Jesus is intimate and urgent, repeating himself and using words such as "command." How many times does he ask his followers to love him and each other, to remain united? "Remain in my love, keep my commandments," "love one another as I love you," "this I command you: love one another." He is begging those who follow him to accept what he has offered, no less than his life, by becoming and staying a unified body of love and faith. ◆ Read John 17:21, and reflect further on Jesus' overriding desire for us. Are you living out that desire? ◆ In what way do you foster unity in your faith community? Where do you perhaps encourage division? ◆ Open your heart to one devotional practice that you find uncomfortable, and pray that way once this week.

Download more questions and activities for families, Christian initiation groups, and other adult groups at http://www.ltp.org/ahw.

Scripture Insights

In today's First Reading from Acts, we are introduced to the Gentile Cornelius. In the verses immediately preceding today's selection, Cornelius has a vision in which he is instructed to meet Peter. Meanwhile, Peter has a vision that confounds him and that he will later understand as a sign that Gentiles who proclaim Jesus as Lord should be welcomed into this new community. Upon his first meeting with Peter, Cornelius falls before Peter's feet. While a conversation between the two ensues, a large crowd gathers. For the first time, Peter begins to teach "that God shows no partiality" between Jew and Gentile. The Holy Spirit descended upon the believers, and the Baptism of Cornelius and his household followed.

Our Responsorial Psalm is identified as a psalm of God's kingship. Psalms of this type proclaim that God is king over history, all the earth, and all nations. Praise of God in these psalms is very explicit.

The Gospel text for today is a continuation of last Sunday's passage of the vine and the branches. These verses emphasize that the love that exists between the Father and the Son is the same love that must characterize the relationships of Jesus' followers. This love is so foundational for Christians that we are commanded to love one another. The noun *friend*, which Jesus uses to describe his relationship with the disciples, is derived from the verb *to love*. Thus, the friendship identified in this Gospel emphasizes mutual self-giving. Such friendship is far more than a casual relationship with another person.

◆ The Scriptures give evidence of the tension that existed between Jews and Gentiles in the early Church. How does this tension relate to what it means to be a Christian in the twenty-first century?

◆ Read today's Responsorial Psalm. Reflect on the ways that God has been revealed in your life. Take time to journal about your specific experiences of God.

◆ Whom do you know who exemplifies the kind of love that is in today's Gospel reading?

READING I *Acts 1:1–11*

In the first book, Theophilus, I dealt with all that Jesus did and taught until the day he was taken up, after giving instructions through the Holy Spirit to the apostles whom he had chosen. He presented himself alive to them by many proofs after he had suffered, appearing to them during forty days and speaking about the kingdom of God. While meeting with them, he enjoined them not to depart from Jerusalem, but to wait for "the promise of the Father about which you have heard me speak; for John baptized with water, but in a few days you will be baptized with the Holy Spirit."

When they had gathered together they asked him, "Lord, are you at this time going to restore the kingdom to Israel?" He answered them, "It is not for you to know the times or seasons that the Father has established by his own authority. But you will receive power when the Holy Spirit comes upon you, and you will be my witnesses in Jerusalem, throughout Judea and Samaria, and to the ends of the earth." When he had said this, as they were looking on, he was lifted up, and a cloud took him from their sight. While they were looking intently at the sky as he was going, suddenly two men dressed in white garments stood beside them. They said, "Men of Galilee, why are you standing there looking at the sky? This Jesus who has been taken up from you into heaven will return in the same way as you have seen him going into heaven."

RESPONSORIAL PSALM
Psalm 47:2–3, 6–7, 8–9 (6)

R. God mounts his throne to shouts of joy:
>> a blare of trumpets for the Lord.
> or: Alleluia.

All you peoples, clap your hands,
> shout to God with cries of gladness.
For the LORD, the Most High, the awesome,
> is the great king over all the earth. R.

God mounts his throne amid shouts of joy;
> the LORD, amid trumpet blasts.
Sing praise to God, sing praise;
> sing praise to our king, sing praise. R.

For king of all the earth is God;
> sing hymns of praise.
God reigns over the nations,
> God sits upon his holy throne. R.

READING II *Ephesians 4:1–13*

Shorter: Ephesians 4:1–7, 11–13
Alternate: Ephesians 1:17–23

Brothers and sisters, I, a prisoner for the Lord, urge you to live in a manner worthy of the call you have received, with all humility and gentleness, with patience, bearing with one another through love, striving to preserve the unity of the spirit through the bond of peace: one body and one Spirit, as you were also called to the one hope of your call; one Lord, one faith, one baptism; one God and Father of all, who is over all and through all and in all.

But grace was given to each of us according to the measure of Christ's gift. Therefore, it says: *He ascended on high and took prisoners captive; he gave gifts to men.* What does "he ascended" mean except that he also descended into the lower regions of the earth? The one who descended is also the one who ascended far above all the heavens, that he might fill all things.

And he gave some as apostles, others as prophets, others as evangelists, others as pastors and teachers, to equip the holy ones for the work of ministry, for building up the body of Christ, until we all attain to the unity of faith and knowledge of the Son of God, to mature manhood, to the extent of the full stature of Christ.

GOSPEL *Mark 16:15–20*

Jesus said to his disciples: "Go into the whole world and proclaim the gospel to every creature. Whoever believes and is baptized will be saved; whoever does not believe will be condemned. These signs will accompany those who believe: in my name they will drive out demons, they will speak new languages. They will pick up serpents with their hands, and if they drink any deadly thing, it will not harm them. They will lay hands on the sick, and they will recover."

So then the Lord Jesus, after he spoke to them, was taken up into heaven and took his seat at the right hand of God. But they went forth and preached everywhere, while the Lord worked with them and confirmed the word through accompanying signs.

Practice of Faith

As Jesus prepares to leave his followers for the final time, he declares them the heirs to his mission on earth. In his name they will work, and from heaven he will work with them. For those who mourn Jesus, departed now forever from his earthly life, he is present still—in his Church. What's more, he has given grace to this Church, gifting each member appropriately for their undertaking. Remember on this Ascension that Christ's followers are called in a special way to make the Church present and active; we are uniquely fitted for our task by Christ himself. ◆ Identify a place or circumstance where Christ's work can continue through you. ◆ *Lumen gentium*, a document from the Second Vatican Council, reminds us that the laity are called to make the world holy in ways that only the laity can. What is your gift, given to you by God, to be used in the service of the world? ◆ Consider whether the Lord is speaking to you through signs you have not yet understood.

Download more questions and activities for families, Christian initiation groups, and other adult groups at http://www.ltp.org/ahw.

Scripture Insights

On this Solemnity of the Ascension, commemorating the days after Jesus' first appearance to his disciples, some of our Scripture readings are from the Letter to the Ephesians and the Gospel of Mark, works that we have not heard for some time.

The familiar reading from the opening verses of the Acts of the Apostles speaks of the coming of the Holy Spirit and Jesus' ascent into heaven. Jesus promises that when the Spirit comes, the disciples will be his "witnesses in Jerusalem, throughout Judea and Samaria, and to the ends of the earth."

Once again, our Responsorial Psalm proclaims God's kingship over all the earth. On a feast such as this, the proclamation that "God reigns" seems most fitting.

In today's Second Reading from the Letter to the Ephesians, we hear exhortations on how to live as faithful followers of Jesus. If we are true to our call, we will be humble, gentle, patient, and loving, and we will pursue unity within the community. While the words of this letter are lovely, they are not all that easy to live.

From the Gospel of Mark, we hear a commission not unlike what we heard in our First Reading from the Acts of the Apostles, the good news of our Lord Jesus Christ must be shared with all peoples! While this portion of Mark is believed to have been a late addition to the earlier text, it is recognized as the canonical ending of this Gospel.

◆ What is most challenging in the reading from Ephesians? How do you find the text consoling?

◆ What do you think it means to "Go into the whole world and proclaim the gospel to every creature"? How do you announce the good news of Jesus Christ to people?

◆ How have you experienced God working in you and through you? Can you rejoice in being an instrument of God's love, despite the pain that this may cause you?

May 16, 2021 SEVENTH SUNDAY OF EASTER

READING I *Acts 1:15–17, 20a, 20c–26*

Peter stood up in the midst of the brothers—there was a group of about one hundred and twenty persons in the one place—. He said, "My brothers, the Scripture had to be fulfilled which the Holy Spirit spoke beforehand through the mouth of David, concerning Judas, who was the guide for those who arrested Jesus. He was numbered among us and was allotted a share in this ministry.

"For it is written in the Book of Psalms: *May another take his office.*

"Therefore, it is necessary that one of the men who accompanied us the whole time the Lord Jesus came and went among us, beginning from the baptism of John until the day on which he was taken up from us, become with us a witness to his resurrection." So they proposed two, Judas called Barsabbas, who was also known as Justus, and Matthias. Then they prayed, "You, Lord, who know the hearts of all, show which one of these two you have chosen to take the place in this apostolic ministry from which Judas turned away to go to his own place." Then they gave lots to them, and the lot fell upon Matthias, and he was counted with the eleven apostles.

RESPONSORIAL PSALM
Psalm 103:1–2, 11–12, 19–20 (19a)

R. The Lord has set his throne in heaven.
   or: Alleluia.

Bless the LORD, O my soul;
   and all my being, bless his holy name.
Bless the LORD, O my soul,
   and forget not all his benefits. R.

For as the heavens are high above the earth,
   so surpassing is his kindness toward those
         who fear him.
As far as the east is from the west,
   so far has he put our transgressions
         from us. R.

The LORD has established his throne in heaven,
   and his kingdom rules over all.
Bless the LORD, all you his angels,
   you mighty in strength,
         who do his bidding. R.

READING II *1 John 4:11–16*

Beloved, if God so loved us, we also must love one another. No one has ever seen God. Yet, if we love one another, God remains in us, and his love is brought to perfection in us.

This is how we know that we remain in him and he in us, that he has given us of his Spirit. Moreover, we have seen and testify that the Father sent his Son as savior of the world. Whoever acknowledges that Jesus is the Son of God, God remains in him and he in God. We have come to know and to believe in the love God has for us.

God is love, and whoever remains in love remains in God and God in him.

GOSPEL *John 17:11b–19*

Lifting up his eyes to heaven, Jesus prayed, saying: "Holy Father, keep them in your name that you have given me, so that they may be one just as we are one. When I was with them I protected them in your name that you gave me, and I guarded them, and none of them was lost except the son of destruction, in order that the Scripture might be fulfilled. But now I am coming to you. I speak this in the world so that they may share my joy completely. I gave them your word, and the world hated them, because they do not belong to the world any more than I belong to the world. I do not ask that you take them out of the world but that you keep them from the evil one. They do not belong to the world any more than I belong to the world. Consecrate them in the truth. Your word is truth. As you sent me into the world, so I sent them into the world. And I consecrate myself for them, so that they also may be consecrated in truth."

Practice of Faith

In the Gospel for this Sunday, Jesus wants the best for us and prays to our Father on our behalf. He wants us to be one with God just as he is. He wants us to be detached from the evils in this world and to be totally connected or consecrated in truth. How do your everyday activities help you to lean toward a holier life? What can you do to avoid sin or at least to ease away from potentially destructive tendencies? ◆ When you watch television programs or movies, become more aware of your program choices. Aim for those that steer you toward goodness, truth, or beauty. Are you viewing shows that have violent or sexually explicit themes that may influence you or family members in a negative way? ◆ Slowly read John 17:11b–19 and savor the intimate prayer that Jesus has with the Father. ◆ Consider journaling a prayer similar to the one in today's Gospel about your needs or desires.

Download more questions and activities for families, Christian initiation groups, and other adult groups at http://www.ltp.org/ahw.

Scripture Insights

The First Reading and the Gospel focus on the betrayal of Judas, which Jesus and Peter describe as a fulfillment of Scripture. While Jesus is silent on which Scripture is fulfilled, Peter points to Psalm 109:8 ("May another take his office") and Psalm 69:26 ("Make their camp desolate, / with none to dwell in their tents"). For Peter, Judas has done the unimaginable: turned away from the ministry he had once received.

In the Gospel, Judas is one of the disciples whom the Father gave to Jesus and whom Jesus guarded, but he is also "lost." How could the Good Shepherd lose one of his sheep? Judas is literally called the "son of destruction" (translated "the one destined to be lost"), a phrase used in 2 Thessalonians 2:3, in parallel to "the lawless one," whose coming reveals the working of Satan (2 Thessalonians 2:9). Satan had infiltrated the heart of Judas (John 6:70; 13:2, 27). He was not merely lost—he was snatched away.

Jesus' plea to the Father to "keep them [his disciples] from the evil one" thus takes on more urgency. Because Christ prayed for all his future disciples (John 17:20), we know that we too are included in his prayer and likewise receive the gift of the Spirit as described in the Second Reading. This brings us back to the Acts of the Apostles. Choosing an Apostle by lot might seem that the disciples were leaving it to chance. In the first-century Church, however, using lots indicated utter reliance on God's power and the guidance of the Holy Spirit.

◆ Why do you think that Judas' replacement needs to be a witness to the ministry of Jesus from his baptism until his Ascension?

◆ What might it mean for Christians not to belong to the world but to be sent into the world?

◆ How do you see God's love being brought to perfection in you and in the Church?

READING I *Acts 2:1–11*

When the time for Pentecost was fulfilled, they were all in one place together. And suddenly there came from the sky a noise like a strong driving wind, and it filled the entire house in which they were. Then there appeared to them tongues as of fire, which parted and came to rest on each one of them. And they were all filled with the Holy Spirit and began to speak in different tongues, as the Spirit enabled them to proclaim.

Now there were devout Jews from every nation under heaven staying in Jerusalem. At this sound, they gathered in a large crowd, but they were confused because each one heard them speaking in his own language. They were astounded, and in amazement they asked, "Are not all these people who are speaking Galileans? Then how does each of us hear them in his native language? We are Parthians, Medes, and Elamites, inhabitants of Mesopotamia, Judea and Cappadocia, Pontus and Asia, Phrygia and Pamphylia, Egypt and the districts of Libya near Cyrene, as well as travelers from Rome, both Jews and converts to Judaism, Cretans and Arabs, yet we hear them speaking in our own tongues of the mighty acts of God."

RESPONSORIAL PSALM *Psalm 104:1, 24, 29–30, 31, 34 (see 30)*

R. Lord, send out your Spirit, and renew the
      face of the earth.
  or: Alleluia.

Bless the LORD, O my soul!
  O LORD, my God, you are great indeed!
How manifold are your works, O LORD!
  The earth is full of your creatures. R.

If you take away their breath, they perish
  and return to their dust.
When you send forth your spirit, they are created,
  and you renew the face of the earth. R.

May the glory of the LORD endure forever;
  may the LORD be glad in his works!
Pleasing to him be my theme;
  I will be glad in the LORD. R.

READING II *Galatians 5:16–25*

Alternate: 1 Corinthians 12:3b–7, 12–13

Brothers and sisters, live by the Spirit and you will certainly not gratify the desire of the flesh. For the flesh has desires against the Spirit, and the Spirit against the flesh; these are opposed to each other, so that you may not do what you want. But if you are guided by the Spirit, you are not under the law. Now the works of the flesh are obvious: immorality, impurity, lust, idolatry, sorcery, hatreds, rivalry, jealousy, outbursts of fury, acts of selfishness, dissensions, factions, occasions of envy, drinking bouts, orgies, and the like. I warn you, as I warned you before, that those who do such things will not inherit the kingdom of God. In contrast, the fruit of the Spirit is love, joy, peace, patience, kindness, generosity, faithfulness, gentleness, self-control. Against such there is no law. Now those who belong to Christ Jesus have crucified their flesh with its passions and desires. If we live in the Spirit, let us also follow the Spirit.

GOSPEL *John 15:26–27; 16:12–15*

Alternate: John 20:19–23

Jesus said to his disciples: "When the Advocate comes whom I will send you from the Father, the Spirit of truth that proceeds from the Father, he will testify to me. And you also testify, because you have been with me from the beginning.

"I have much more to tell you, but you cannot bear it now. But when he comes, the Spirit of truth, he will guide you to all truth. He will not speak on his own, but he will speak what he hears, and will declare to you the things that are coming. He will glorify me, because he will take from what is mine and declare it to you. Everything that the Father has is mine; for this reason I told you that he will take from what is mine and declare it to you."

Practice of Hope

The birthday of the Church is something to celebrate, especially in a secular world desperate for more believers of Jesus to become a bolder presence. In the reading from Acts, we hear of God's Spirit filling the believers with the power to speak different languages. Devout Jews from many regions who were in Jerusalem at the time were amazed that they could understand this group that had gathered. We too can allow ourselves to be filled with God's Spirit so that our daily actions flow with divine messages. ◆ Experiment with some translation apps to explore how your voice—your messages of hope—can be relayed to non-English-speaking friends in other countries. ◆ Reflect on Pope Francis' statement in *Amoris laetitia* "The church is a family of families, constantly enriched by the lives of all those domestic churches" (87). Consider how the practice of faith in your home can enrich the Church.

Download more questions and activities for families, Christian initiation groups, and other adult groups at http://www.ltp.org/ahw.

Scripture Insights

In these readings, the Holy Spirit is the actor, the subject, the doer of all the verbs. The hymn "Veni, Sancte Spiritus" asks the Spirit to shine, fill, heal, renew, wash, bend, melt, warm, guide, and give joy. In Acts 2, the disciples are first passive recipients of the Spirit's power; the tongues of fire were perceived by them, and they were filled. Only after the Spirit empowers them do they begin to speak. Paul declares that the Galatians are led by either the Spirit or the law. In John 15 and 16, the Spirit is the active subject of all the verbs: testify, guide, speak, glorify, take, declare. The disciples' role? To listen and to be led.

Letting ourselves be led isn't easy. We're taught to forge our own paths. These readings call us to learn to be led, to become sensitive to the guiding nudges of the Spirit. This does not mean that Christians remain passive. In Acts as in John, the disciples of Jesus are commissioned to bear witness to the Good News in their preaching, healing, and teaching. But the Spirit's power is the source of ours.

The Spirit's work is primary, and ours is secondary. The Christian's job is to bear fruit: love, joy, peace, patience, kindness, generosity, faithfulness, gentleness, and self-control. These virtues may not come naturally to us; some of them might take hard work. As Paul graphically says, we must crucify our sinful desires first. Pentecost teaches that the fruit of the Spirit is finally the result of the Spirit's cultivation of the soil of our hearts rather than our striving. We prepare the soil; the Spirit grows the seed.

◆ How might you cultivate the soil of your heart so that the Spirit can grow fruit in your life?

◆ Read "Veni, Sancte Spiritus." Which of the roles and gifts of the Spirit do you most need today?

◆ What step can you take to "crucify" your sinful desires and turn toward the freedom of the Spirit?

Ordinary Time, Summer

Prayer before Reading the Word

God, sower of the seed,
we marvel at how your Word accomplishes
the purpose for which you sent it forth:
how few of the seeds you sow take root,
yet how spectacular their abundant yield.
Make us good soil, ready to receive what you sow,
that we may hear the Word and understand it,
bear fruit and yield a hundredfold.
We ask this through our Lord Jesus Christ,
        your Son,
who lives and reigns with you
in the unity of the Holy Spirit,
one God, for ever and ever. Amen.

Prayer after Reading the Word

To us, sinners and yet disciples,
O Lord of the harvest,
you entrust a share in the mission of Jesus,
who sent the Twelve to proclaim the Good News
and to bear witness without fear.
With your love forever sheltering and
        surrounding us,
may we proclaim from the housetops
the Gospel we have heard
and acknowledge openly before all
the one whom we confess as Lord,
Jesus Christ, your Son, who lives and reigns
        with you
in the unity of the Holy Spirit,
one God, for ever and ever. Amen.

May 24: *Genesis 3:9–15, 20 or Acts 1:12–14/John 19:25–34*
May 25: *Sirach 35:1–12; Mark 10:28–31*
May 26: *Sirach 36:1, 4–5a, 10–17; Mark 10:32–45*
May 27: *Sirach 42:15–25; Mark 10:46–52*
May 28: *Sirach 44:1, 9–13; Mark 11:11–26*
May 29: *Sirach 51:12cd–20; Mark 11:27–33*

May 31: Feast of the Visitation of the Blessed Virgin Mary
   Zephaniah 3:14–18a or Romans 12:9–16; Luke 1:39–56
June 1: *Tobit 2:9–14; Mark 12:13–17*
June 2: *Tobit 3:1–11a, 16–17a; Mark 12:18–27*
June 3: *Tobit 6:10–11; 7:1bcde, 9–17; 8:4–9a; Mark 12:28–34*
June 4: *Tobit 11:5–17; Mark 12:35–37*
June 5: *Tobit 12:1, 5–15, 20; Mark 12:38–44*

June 7: *2 Corinthians 1:1–7; Matthew 5:1–12*
June 8: *2 Corinthians 1:18–22; Matthew 5:13–16*
June 9: *2 Corinthians 3:4–11; Matthew 5:17–19*
June 10: *2 Corinthians 3:15—4:1, 3–6; Matthew 5:20–26*
June 11: Solemnity of the Most Sacred Heart of Jesus
   Hosea 11:1, 3–4, 8c–9; Ephesians 3:8–12, 14–19;
   John 19:31–37
June 12: *2 Corinthians 5:14–21; Luke 2:41–51*

June 14: *2 Corinthians 6:1–10; Matthew 5:38–42*
June 15: *2 Corinthians 8:1–9; Matthew 5:43–48*
June 16: *2 Corinthians 9:6–11; Matthew 6:1–6, 16–18*
June 17: *2 Corinthians 11:1–11; Matthew 6:7–15*
June 18: *2 Corinthians 11:18, 21–30; Matthew 6:19–23*
June 19: *2 Corinthians 12:1–10; Matthew 6:24–34*

June 21: *Genesis 12:1–9; Matthew 7:1–5*
June 22: *Genesis 13:2, 5–18; Matthew 7:6, 12–14*
June 23: *Genesis 15:1–12, 17–18; Matthew 7:15–20*
June 24: Solemnity of the Nativity of John the Baptist
   Isaiah 49:1–6; Acts 13:22–26; Luke 1:57–66, 80
June 25: *Genesis 17:1, 9–10, 15–22; Matthew 8:1–4*
June 26: *Genesis 18:1–15; Matthew 8:5–17*

June 28: *Genesis 18:16–33; Matthew 8:18–22*
June 29: Solemnity of Sts. Peter and Paul, Apostles
   Acts 12:1–11; 2 Timothy 4:6–8, 17–18; Matthew
   16:13–19
June 30: *Genesis 21:5, 8–20a; Matthew 8:28–34*
July 1: *Genesis 22:1b–19; Matthew 9:1–8*
July 2: *Genesis 23:1–4, 19; 24:1–8, 62–67; Matthew 9:9–13*
July 3: Feast of St. Thomas the Apostle
   Ephesians 2:19–22; John 20:24–29

July 5: *Genesis 28:10–22a; Matthew 9:18–26*
July 6: *Genesis 32:23–33; Matthew 9:32–38*
July 7: *Genesis 41:55–57; 42:5–7a, 17–24a; Matthew 10:1–7*
July 8: *Genesis 44:18–21, 23b–29; 45:1–5; Matthew 10:7–15*
July 9: *Genesis 46:1–7, 28–30; Matthew 10:16–23*
Jul 10: *Genesis 49:29–32; 50:15–26a; Matthew 10:24–33*

July 12: *Exodus 1:8–14, 22; Matthew 10:34—11:1*
July 13: *Exodus 2:1–15a; Matthew 11:20–24*

July 14: *Exodus 3:1–6, 9–12; Matthew 11:25–27*
July 15: *Exodus 3:13–20; Matthew 11:28–30*
July 16: *Exodus 11:10—12:14; Matthew 12:1–8*
July 17: *Exodus 12:37–42; Matthew 12:14–21*

July 19: *Exodus 14:5–18; Matthew 12:38–42*
July 20: *Exodus 14:21—15:1; Matthew 12:46–50*
July 21: *Exodus 16:1–5, 9–15; Matthew 13:1–9*
July 22: Feast of St. Mary Magdalene
   Song of Songs 3:1–4b or 2 Corinthians 5:14–17;
   John 20:1–2, 11–18
July 23: *Exodus 20:1–17; Matthew 13:18–23*
July 24: *Exodus 24:3–8; Matthew 13:24–30*

July 26: *Exodus 32:15–24, 30–34; Matthew 13:31–35*
July 27: *Exodus 33:7–11; 34:5b–9, 28; Matthew 13:36–43*
July 28: *Exodus 34:29–35; Matthew 13:44–46*
July 29: *Exodus 40:16–21, 34–38; John 11:19–27*
   or Luke 10:38–42
July 30: *Leviticus 23:1, 4–11, 15–16, 27, 34b–37;*
   Matthew 13:54–58
July 31: *Leviticus 25:1, 8–17; Matthew 14:1–12*

August 2: *Numbers 11:4b–15; Matthew 14:13–21*
August 3: *Numbers 12:1–13; Matthew 14:22–36*
   or Matthew 15:1–2, 10–14
August 4: *Numbers 13:1–2, 25—14:1, 26a–29a, 34–35;*
   Matthew 15:21–28
August 5: *Numbers 20:1–13; Matthew 16:13–23*
Aug 6: Feast of the Transfiguration of the Lord
   Daniel 7:9–10, 13–14; 2 Peter 1:16–19; Mark 9:2–10
August 7: *Deuteronomy 6:4–13; Matthew 17:14–20*

August 9: *Deuteronomy 10:12–22; Matthew 17:22–27*
August 10: Feast of St. Lawrence, Deacon and Martyr
   2 Corinthians 9:6–10; John 12:24–26
August 11: *Deuteronomy 34:1–12; Matthew 18:15–20*
August 12: *Joshua 3:7–10a, 11, 13–17; Matthew 18:21—19:1*
August 13: *Joshua 24:1–13; Matthew 19:3–12*
August 14: *Joshua 24:14–29; Matthew 19:13–15*

August 16: *Judges 2:11–19; Matthew 19:16–22*
August 17: *Judges 6:11–24a; Matthew 19:23–30*
August 18: *Judges 9:6–15; Matthew 20:1–16*
August 19: *Judges 11:29–39a; Matthew 22:1–14*
August 20: *Ruth 1:1, 3–6, 14b–16, 22; Matthew 22:34–40*
August 21: *Ruth 2:1–3, 8–11; 4:13–17; Matthew 23:1–12*

August 23: *1 Thessalonians 1:1–5, 8b–10; Matthew 23:13–22*
August 24: Feast of St. Bartholomew, Apostle
   Revelation 21:9b–14; John 1:45–51
August 25: *1 Thessalonians 2:9–13; Matthew 23:27–32*
August 26: *1 Thessalonians 3:7–13; Matthew 24:42–51*
August 27: *1 Thessalonians 4:1–8; Matthew 25:1–13*
August 28: *1 Thessalonians 4:9–11; Matthew 25:14–30*

Reading I
Deuteronomy 4:32–34, 39–40

Moses said to the people: "Ask now of the days of old, before your time, ever since God created man upon the earth; ask from one end of the sky to the other: Did anything so great ever happen before? Was it ever heard of? Did a people ever hear the voice of God speaking from the midst of fire, as you did, and live? Or did any god venture to go and take a nation for himself from the midst of another nation, by testings, by signs and wonders, by war, with strong hand and outstretched arm, and by great terrors, all of which the Lord, your God, did for you in Egypt before your very eyes? This is why you must now know, and fix in your heart, that the Lord is God in the heavens above and on earth below, and that there is no other. You must keep his statutes and commandments that I enjoin on you today, that you and your children after you may prosper, and that you may have long life on the land which the Lord, your God, is giving you forever."

Responsorial Psalm *Psalm 33:4–5, 6, 9, 18–19, 20, 22 (12b)*

R. Blessed the people the Lord has chosen to be his own.

Upright is the word of the Lord,
   and all his works are trustworthy.
He loves justice and right;
    of the kindness of the Lord the earth
      is full. R.

By the word of the Lord the heavens were made;
   by the breath of his mouth all their host.
For he spoke, and it was made;
   he commanded, and it stood forth. R.

See, the eyes of the Lord are upon those who
      fear him,
   upon those who hope for his kindness,
to deliver them from death
   and preserve them in spite of famine. R.

Our soul waits for the Lord,
   who is our help and our shield.
May your kindness, O Lord, be upon us
   who have put our hope in you. R.

Reading II *Romans 8:14–17*

Brothers and sisters: Those who are led by the Spirit of God are sons of God. For you did not receive a spirit of slavery to fall back into fear, but you received a Spirit of adoption, through whom we cry, "Abba, Father!" The Spirit himself bears witness with our spirit that we are children of God, and if children, then heirs, heirs of God and joint heirs with Christ, if only we suffer with him so that we may also be glorified with him.

Gospel *Matthew 28:16–20*

The eleven disciples went to Galilee, to the mountain to which Jesus had ordered them. When they all saw him, they worshiped, but they doubted. Then Jesus approached and said to them, "All power in heaven and on earth has been given to me. Go, therefore, and make disciples of all nations, baptizing them in the name of the Father, and of the Son, and of the Holy Spirit, teaching them to observe all that I have commanded you. And behold, I am with you always, until the end of the age."

Practice of Hope

In Matthew's Gospel account, Jesus authorizes his disciples to baptize in the name of the Father, Son, and Holy Spirit and promises that he would be with his friends always, "until the end of the age." He reminds them that "all power in heaven and on earth has been given to me." We can be assured of God's presence as we experience all the good things that happen in our lives. When we observe a change of heart, a child's growth, and the seasons changing, we are witnesses to God's continual presence. ◆ At this point in your day, take a few minutes to recognize several beautiful, God-filled moments. ◆ Since the Trinity shows the loving relationship among Father, Son, and Holy Spirit, consider how each aspect of this divine relationship affects you in prayer. ◆ Call, text, or email a friend or family member whom you do not see often to remind him or her how much you value your relationship.

Download more questions and activities for families, Christian initiation groups, and other adult groups at http://www.ltp.org/ahw.

Scripture Insights

The Great Commission, when Jesus sent the disciples to baptize, contains one of the first direct references to the Trinity in Scripture. Although it took the Church several hundred more years to describe fully the relationships among Father, Son, and Spirit, the truth of God's nature as Three-in-One is seeded throughout Scripture. While the Great Commission points forward to the doctrine of the Trinity, it also gestures back to Old Testament promises.

The command to make disciples "of all nations" hints at God's promise to bless all the nations through Abraham (Genesis 18:18; 22:18). Christ's claim that all authority in heaven and on earth had been given to him echoes Moses' declaration in the First Reading that the God of Israel alone reigns over the heavens and earth "and that there is no other." Now there is one, who is mysteriously not other at all, but the very same God in the flesh. The God of Israel shares authority with Christ the Son, who promises the disciples that he will be with them (fulfilling the title *Emmanuel*, God-with-us) until the completion of the age.

The Apostle Paul shows us how Christ remains present with his followers in the present age: through the Holy Spirit, who bears witness that God has adopted us as children and that we are heirs with Christ. Paul uses the word *with* four times in Romans 8:16–17: the Spirit bears witness "with our spirit"; "believers are joint heirs with Christ"; "we suffer with him [Christ]"; and "we may also be glorified with him." Christ not only promises to be with his followers but also calls them into loving union—with one another and with the Trinity.

◆ The Gospel reading reports that all the disciples worshiped but some of them also doubted. Is it possible to worship and doubt at the same time?

◆ The Psalm focuses attention on God's kindness. Where do you see God's kindness at work today?

◆ Why do you think God describes the Exodus as his greatest act since creation itself (Deuteronomy 4:32–34)?

READING I *Exodus 24:3–8*

When Moses came to the people and related all the words and ordinances of the LORD, they all answered with one voice, "We will do everything that the LORD has told us." Moses then wrote down all the words of the LORD and, rising early the next day, he erected at the foot of the mountain an altar and twelve pillars for the twelve tribes of Israel. Then, having sent certain young men of the Israelites to offer holocausts and sacrifice young bulls as peace offerings to the LORD, Moses took half of the blood and put it in large bowls; the other half he splashed on the altar. Taking the book of the covenant, he read it aloud to the people, who answered, "All that the LORD has said, we will heed and do." Then he took the blood and sprinkled it on the people, saying, "This is the blood of the covenant that the LORD has made with you in accordance with all these words of his."

RESPONSORIAL PSALM
Psalm 116:12–13, 15–16, 17–18 (13)

R. I will take the cup of salvation, and call on
      the name of the Lord.
  or: Alleluia.

How shall I make a return to the LORD
    for all the good he has done for me?
The cup of salvation I will take up,
    and I will call upon the name
        of the LORD. R.

Precious in the eyes of the LORD
    is the death of his faithful ones.
I am your servant, the son of your handmaid;
    you have loosed my bonds. R.

To you will I offer sacrifice of thanksgiving,
    and I will call upon the name of the LORD.
My vows to the LORD I will pay
    in the presence of all his people. R.

READING II *Hebrews 9:11–15*

Brothers and sisters: When Christ came as high priest of the good things that have come to be, passing through the greater and more perfect tabernacle not made by hands, that is, not belonging to this creation, he entered once for all into the sanctuary, not with the blood of goats and calves but with his own blood, thus obtaining eternal redemption. For if the blood of goats and bulls and the sprinkling of a heifer's ashes can sanctify those who are defiled so that their flesh is cleansed, how much more will the blood of Christ, who through the eternal Spirit offered himself unblemished to God, cleanse our consciences from dead works to worship the living God.

For this reason he is mediator of a new covenant: since a death has taken place for deliverance from transgressions under the first covenant, those who are called may receive the promised eternal inheritance.

GOSPEL *Mark 14:12–16, 22–26*

On the first day of the Feast of Unleavened Bread, when they sacrificed the Passover lamb, Jesus' disciples said to him, "Where do you want us to go and prepare for you to eat the Passover?" He sent two of his disciples and said to them, "Go into the city and a man will meet you, carrying a jar of water. Follow him. Wherever he enters, say to the master of the house, 'The Teacher says, "Where is my guest room where I may eat the Passover with my disciples?"' Then he will show you a large upper room furnished and ready. Make the preparations for us there." The disciples then went off, entered the city, and found it just as he had told them; and they prepared the Passover.

While they were eating, he took bread, said the blessing, broke it, gave it to them, and said, "Take it; this is my body." Then he took a cup, gave thanks, and gave it to them, and they all drank from it. He said to them, "This is my blood of the covenant, which will be shed for many. Amen, I say to you, I shall not drink again the fruit of the vine until the day when I drink it new in the kingdom of God." Then, after singing a hymn, they went out to the Mount of Olives.

Practice of Faith

Today's solemnity focuses on the Real Presence in the Eucharist: a reality for which we hunger and thirst. In a world in which people put up facades, honesty and permanence are desired. It can be easy to take for granted that bread and wine become the Body and Blood of Christ at each Mass. We also may overlook that Christ is present in the readings, the assembly, and the priest who presides at Mass. ♦ The next time you are at Mass, consider the four ways that Jesus is truly present at that banquet: in the Word, in the Eucharist, and within the assembly and the presider. Reflect on how privileged we are to participate in the Mass. ♦ Reflect on Jesus' words at the Last Supper regarding his presence in the bread and wine. ♦ Consider talking with someone who has left the practice of his or her Catholic faith about this Real Presence. Invite them to join you at Mass sometime.

Download more questions and activities for families, Christian initiation groups, and other adult groups at http://www.ltp.org/ahw.

Scripture Insights

The power of blood in the ancient world connects these readings. For the writers of the Old and the New Testaments, the life of every living creature was in its blood.

Exodus 24 describes the covenant with Israel, which extended the covenant made with Abraham and his descendants (Genesis 12—22). Whereas the Abrahamic covenant included blood only indirectly (Genesis 15:9–10; 17:9–14), in the Mosaic covenant, the blood of bulls is splashed on the altar and sprinkled on the people. The people offer bulls as "peace offerings" to God. After the destruction of the Temple, Israel wrestled with how to atone for their sins and reconcile with God apart from the offering of animal sacrifices. The psalmist's phrase "a sacrifice of thanksgiving" hints at this shift toward spiritual sacrifice.

Both the reading from Hebrews and Mark's Gospel account point to Jesus' Blood as true and lasting shalom. From the Blood come peace, wholeness, and a restored relationship between humanity and God. At the Last Supper, Christ is the mediator of a new covenant established by his Blood, which connects Jesus' sacrifice to the blood of the lambs sacrificed at Passover, the remembrance of God's redemption of Israel from slavery.

In Hebrews 9, the author argues "how much more" the Blood of Christ can do. He argues that if the blood of animals purified the flesh of those who had sinned, then how much more will the Blood of Christ purify consciences and free sinners for worship of the living God. The author accepts the necessity of death and blood to redeem humankind from transgressions, but the only death needed is that of Jesus, who offers his blood "once for all."

♦ Why does the author of Hebrews repeatedly refer to God as "the living God" (9:14; 3:12; 10:31; 12:22)?

♦ In societies without animal sacrifice, how might we fully grasp the meaning of Jesus' sacrifice as the end of all sacrifices?

♦ What does it mean to offer thanksgiving as a sacrifice?

June 13, 2021 ELEVENTH SUNDAY IN ORDINARY TIME

READING I *Ezekiel 17:22–24*

Thus says the Lord GOD:
I, too, will take from the crest of the cedar,
  from its topmost branches tear off a
    tender shoot,
and plant it on a high and lofty mountain;
  on the mountain heights of Israel I will
    plant it.
It shall put forth branches and bear fruit,
  and become a majestic cedar.
Birds of every kind shall dwell beneath it,
  every winged thing in the shade of
    its boughs.
And all the trees of the field shall know
  that I, the LORD,
bring low the high tree,
  lift high the lowly tree,
wither up the green tree,
  and make the withered tree bloom.
As I, the LORD, have spoken, so will I do.

RESPONSORIAL PSALM
Psalm 92:2–3, 13–14, 15–16 (see 2a)

R Lord, it is good to give thanks to you.

It is good to give thanks to the LORD,
  to sing praise to your name, Most High,
To proclaim your kindness at dawn
  and your faithfulness throughout
    the night. R.

The just one shall flourish like the palm tree,
  like a cedar of Lebanon shall he grow.
They that are planted in the house of the LORD
  shall flourish in the courts of our God. R.

They shall bear fruit even in old age;
  vigorous and sturdy shall they be,
declaring how just is the LORD,
  my rock, in whom there is no wrong. R.

READING II *2 Corinthians 5:6–10*

Brothers and sisters: We are always courageous, although we know that while we are at home in the body we are away from the Lord, for we walk by faith, not by sight. Yet we are courageous, and we would rather leave the body and go home to the Lord. Therefore, we aspire to please him, whether we are at home or away. For we must all appear before the judgment seat of Christ, so that each may receive recompense, according to what he did in the body, whether good or evil.

GOSPEL *Mark 4:26–34*

Jesus said to the crowds: "This is how it is with the kingdom of God; it is as if a man were to scatter seed on the land and would sleep and rise night and day and through it all the seed would sprout and grow, he knows not how. Of its own accord the land yields fruit, first the blade, then the ear, then the full grain in the ear. And when the grain is ripe, he wields the sickle at once, for the harvest has come."

He said, "To what shall we compare the kingdom of God, or what parable can we use for it? It is like a mustard seed that, when it is sown in the ground, is the smallest of all the seeds on the earth. But once it is sown, it springs up and becomes the largest of plants and puts forth large branches, so that the birds of the sky can dwell in its shade." With many such parables he spoke the word to them as they were able to understand it. Without parables he did not speak to them, but to his own disciples he explained everything in private.

Practice of Charity

Today's readings from Ezekiel and the evangelist Mark relate the power of God in our lives through nature. These readings help us to learn more about our role in God's world and God's desire that we build the kingdom here. As a practical application of growing more believers, we might consider getting our hands dirty in a community garden. What better place to learn about kingdom building than by working with others to grow vegetables that help feed families? Besides growing produce, we can witness God's creative growth among fellow gardeners. ◆ Check out the American Community Gardening Association's website to learn how to start or participate in a community garden. Resources are available at https://community garden.org. ◆ Work with parish administrators to see if your church grounds have areas in need of visual improvement or better maintenance. ◆ Gather family members and other churchgoers on occasion to beautify your parish to make it more inviting.

Download more questions and activities for families, Christian initiation groups, and other adult groups at http://www.ltp.org/ahw.

Scripture Insights

In Ezekiel 17:1–21, God tells Israel a parable about a shoot from a cedar tree and a seed that becomes a vine and then explains its meaning: while in exile in Babylon, Israel secretly sought help from Egypt, a deceitful move that provokes God's wrath (Israel was in Babylon as God's punishment for idolatry and unfaithfulness). But God promises to take a shoot from a cedar and plant it on Israel's heights. In other words, Israel does not need Egypt, because God's power will bring home and restore Israel. The Lord brings low; the Lord lifts high.

The parable of the mustard seed borrows imagery from Ezekiel 17. There, without the assistance of humans, a tree will grow from a shoot and will become a place under which birds take shelter. In Ezekiel, the tree is a cedar, whereas in Mark, Jesus describes a mustard tree, perhaps to emphasize its humble beginnings ("the smallest of all the seeds"). From a tiny, insignificant thing, the kingdom begins. As the Apostle Paul wrote, we plant our small seeds and water them, but God is responsible for the growth (1 Corinthians 3:6). The sower of the seed doesn't even know how it grows; his only job was to scatter it on the earth.

In the Second Reading, we hear, "we would rather leave the body and go home to the Lord." In 2 Corinthians 5, Paul tells us that we groan, longing to be clothed with our resurrection body (5:2; cf. Romans 8:22–23). Mark 4 calls us back to the truth that God gives the growth even to the seeds of these bodies and someday will flower them into resurrection trees. The Lord brings low; the Lord lifts high.

◆ What does it mean to "plant the seeds" of God's kingdom?

◆ Why do you think that God speaks in riddles and parables in both Ezekiel 17 and Mark 4?

◆ What do you need courage for today?

READING I *Job 38:1, 8–11*

The Lord addressed Job out of the storm and said:
Who shut within doors the sea,
    when it burst forth from the womb;
when I made the clouds its garment
    and thick darkness its swaddling bands?
When I set limits for it
    and fastened the bar of its door,
and said: Thus far shall you come but
        no farther,
    and here shall your proud waves be stilled!

RESPONSORIAL PSALM *Psalm 107:23–24, 25–26, 28–29, 30–31 (1b)*

R. Give thanks to the Lord, his love is everlasting.
or: Alleluia.

They who sailed the sea in ships,
    trading on the deep waters,
these saw the works of the LORD
    and his wonders in the abyss. R.

His command raised up a storm wind
    which tossed its waves on high.
They mounted up to heaven;
        they sank to the depths;
    their hearts melted away in their plight. R.

They cried to the LORD in their distress;
    from their straits he rescued them.
He hushed the storm to a gentle breeze,
    and the billows of the sea were stilled. R.

They rejoiced that they were calmed,
    and he brought them to their desired haven.
Let them give thanks to the LORD for his kindness
    and his wondrous deeds
        to the children of men. R.

READING II *2 Corinthians 5:14–17*

Brothers and sisters: The love of Christ impels us, once we have come to the conviction that one died for all; therefore, all have died. He indeed died for all, so that those who live might no longer live for themselves but for him who for their sake died and was raised.

Consequently, from now on we regard no one according to the flesh; even if we once knew Christ according to the flesh, yet now we know him so no longer. So whoever is in Christ is a new creation: the old things have passed away; behold, new things have come.

GOSPEL *Mark 4:35–41*

On that day, as evening drew on, Jesus said to his disciples: "Let us cross to the other side." Leaving the crowd, they took Jesus with them in the boat just as he was. And other boats were with him. A violent squall came up and waves were breaking over the boat, so that it was already filling up. Jesus was in the stern, asleep on a cushion. They woke him and said to him, "Teacher, do you not care that we are perishing?" He woke up, rebuked the wind, and said to the sea, "Quiet! Be still!" The wind ceased and there was great calm. Then he asked them, "Why are you terrified? Do you not yet have faith?" They were filled with great awe and said to one another, "Who then is this whom even wind and sea obey?"

Practice of Faith

The storms in our lives can be subtle when they form or they can rampage through our days as dramatically as what the evangelist Mark describes. As believers, we look to God to help calm these torments, yet we are reminded more often than not that good seems to emerge from the turbulence. While in the midst of a struggle, our challenge is to be patient and have faith in our Creator, who understands us and walks with us. After all, this is why God sent Jesus here. ◆ If you have ever kept a prayer journal, review some of the entries in months or years in which the storms of life were especially fierce. Say prayers of thanks for insights that you might be discovering since that time. ◆ If you haven't started a spiritual diary or sketchbook, consider doing so. Scripture passages such as today's might help you write or draw about issues you face.

Download more questions and activities for families, Christian initiation groups, and other adult groups at http://www.ltp.org/ahw.

Scripture Insights

In Job 38, the Lord declares his power to shut the sea's doors and still its proud waves. In Psalm 107, he raises up a windstorm so that the sailors cry to the Lord in their distress, and when he hushes the storm to a gentle breeze, the sailors rejoice and give thanks. Compare this to Mark 4, where the disciples "were filled with great awe" (more literally, they feared with a great fear) after Jesus stills their storm.

The disciples' terror is understandable. While the waves were crashing over their boat, their Lord and master slept peacefully in the stern. This is an evocative moment, echoing both Jonah (who also slept in a boat during a storm) and the God who neither slumbers nor sleeps (Psalm 121:4). When the disciples wake Jesus, their plaintive cry is a prayer to a God who appears to be asleep in a storm: "Do you not care that we are perishing?" Jesus commands the sea to be still and then turns from rebuking the waves to gently rebuking his disciples' lack of faith. He does not reveal his confidence that they will grow in faith. The disciples cannot yet answer the question "Who then is this?" It seems too wonderful and strange to be true, that their God might have just fallen asleep in the stern of their boat. By the end of Mark's account of the Gospel, their fear will turn to joy as they realize who has been accompanying them all this time.

The Apostle Paul summarizes the remarkable truth that took the disciples a little longer to grasp: whoever is in Christ is a new creation. The whole creation, wind and waves and all, has been remade by the Incarnation and Resurrection of Christ and awaits its final glorious redemption.

◆ Have you ever prayed, "Lord, don't you care that we are perishing?"

◆ What storm do you have in your life that you need Christ to calm for you?

◆ What does it mean to live not for ourselves but for Christ, who died for our sake and was raised (Second Reading)?

READING I *Wisdom 1:13–15; 2:23–24*

God did not make death,
> nor does he rejoice in the destruction of
> > the living.
For he fashioned all things that they might
> have being;
> and the creatures of the world
> are wholesome,
and there is not a destructive drug among them
> nor any domain of the netherworld on earth,
> for justice is undying.
For God formed man to be imperishable;
> the image of his own nature he made him.
But by the envy of the devil, death entered
> the world,
> and they who belong to his company
> experience it.

RESPONSORIAL PSALM
Psalm 30:2, 4, 5–6, 11, 12, 13 (2a)

R. I will praise you, Lord, for you have
> rescued me.

I will extol you, O LORD, for you drew me clear
> and did not let my enemies rejoice over me.
O LORD, you brought me up
> from the netherworld;
> you preserved me from among those going
> down into the pit. R.

Sing praise to the LORD, you his faithful ones,
> and give thanks to his holy name.
For his anger lasts but a moment;
> a lifetime, his good will.
At nightfall, weeping enters in,
> but with the dawn, rejoicing. R.

Hear, O LORD, and have pity on me;
> O LORD, be my helper.
You changed my mourning into dancing;
> O LORD, my God, forever will I give you
> thanks. R.

READING II *2 Corinthians 8:7, 9, 13–15*

Brothers and sisters: As you excel in every respect,
in faith, discourse, knowledge, all earnestness, and
in the love we have for you, may you excel in this
gracious act also.

For you know the gracious act of our Lord
Jesus Christ, that though he was rich, for your sake
he became poor, so that by his poverty you might
become rich. Not that others should have relief
while you are burdened, but that as a matter of
equality your abundance at the present time should
supply their needs, so that their abundance may
also supply your needs, that there may be equality.
As it is written: / *Whoever had much did not have
more, / and whoever had little did not have less.*

GOSPEL *Mark 5:21–43*

Shorter: Mark 5:21–24, 35b–43

When Jesus had crossed again in the boat to the
other side, a large crowd gathered around him, and
he stayed close to the sea. One of the synagogue
officials, named Jairus, came forward. Seeing
him he fell at his feet and pleaded earnestly with
him, saying, "My daughter is at the point of death.
Please, come lay your hands on her that she may
get well and live." He went off with him, and a
large crowd followed him and pressed upon him.

There was a woman afflicted with hemorrhages for twelve years. She had suffered greatly at
the hands of many doctors and had spent all that
she had. Yet she was not helped but only grew
worse. She had heard about Jesus and came up
behind him in the crowd and touched his cloak.
She said, "If I but touch his clothes, I shall be
cured." Immediately her flow of blood dried up.
She felt in her body that she was healed of her
affliction. Jesus, aware at once that power had gone
out from him, turned around in the crowd and
asked, "Who has touched my clothes?" But his
disciples said to Jesus, "You see how the crowd is
pressing upon you, and yet you ask, 'Who touched
me?'" And he looked around to see who had done
it. The woman, realizing what had happened to
her, approached in fear and trembling. She fell
down before Jesus and told him the whole truth.
He said to her, "Daughter, your faith has saved
you. Go in peace and be cured of your affliction."

While he was still speaking, people from the
synagogue official's house arrived and said, "Your

daughter has died; why trouble the teacher any longer?" Disregarding the message that was reported, Jesus said to the synagogue official, "Do not be afraid; just have faith." He did not allow anyone to accompany him inside except Peter, James, and John, the brother of James. When they arrived at the house of the synagogue official, he caught sight of a commotion, people weeping and wailing loudly. So he went in and said to them, "Why this commotion and weeping? The child is not dead but asleep." And they ridiculed him. Then he put them all out. He took along the child's father and mother and those who were with him and entered the room where the child was. He took the child by the hand and said to her, "*Talitha koum*," which means, "Little girl, I say to you, arise!" The girl, a child of twelve, arose immediately and walked around. At that they were utterly astounded. He gave strict orders that no one should know this and said that she should be given something to eat.

Practice of Charity

The continuing crisis in rising healthcare costs and lack of access can cause great concern to anyone with a serious illness. This is especially true for those who are impoverished. Fortunately, the efforts of organizations such as Catholic Relief Services (CRS), Doctors without Borders, and community health clinics for the poor are examples of God's healing Spirit alleviating those who suffer. God is at work in these doctors, nurses, and health professionals just as God healed the daughter of Jairus and the woman afflicted with hemorrhages, as described in today's Gospel. ◆ Check out the websites for these ministries to become more aware of their global reach. Perhaps your family can volunteer to support a local health clinic through raising funds or awareness. ◆ Prayer is a strong tool to help us become more compassionate toward our brothers and sisters who may be seriously ill. ◆ Explore the CRS website (www.crs.org /get-involved/parishioners) to discover the initiatives and prayer resources for learning about how to help others.

Download more questions and activities for families, Christian initiation groups, and other adult groups at http://www.ltp.org/ahw.

Scripture Insights

In the Gospel reading, the account of one miraculous healing interrupts another. Many details link the synagogue ruler Jairus and the unnamed woman: Twelve years are the length of her affliction and the age of Jairus' daughter. They both—Jairus and the woman—fall down at Jesus' feet, and they both believe that if Jesus simply touches the unwell body it will be healed. Jesus praises the woman for her faith and exhorts Jairus not to fear but to have faith. Other details separate them: Jairus is a powerful man, an official of the synagogue, and the woman who hemorrhages is a powerless woman who likely has been excluded from the synagogue because her affliction has made her ritually unclean. By healing both, Jesus symbolically heals all of Israel (if the number twelve is meant to resonate beyond itself), from the greatest to the least. The "raising" of Jairus' daughter also hints at the resurrection: as Wisdom reminds us, "God did not make death, / nor does he rejoice in the destruction of the living."

The Second Reading turns to Christian communities, with their mix of Jairuses and unnamed women. Paul urges his audience toward generosity for their impoverished brothers and sisters in Jerusalem: just as they abound in all other things, shouldn't they also abound in giving? Christ was rich but became poor so that they might become rich. Paul stops just short of instructing them to imitate this pattern fully, suggesting that their abundance could overflow enough to create equality.

◆ When did God change your mourning into dancing?

◆ What steps can be taken to ensure equality between a parish's rich and poor?

READING I *Ezekiel 2:2–5*

As the LORD spoke to me, the spirit entered into me and set me on my feet, and I heard the one who was speaking say to me: Son of man, I am sending you to the Israelites, rebels who have rebelled against me; they and their ancestors have revolted against me to this very day. Hard of face and obstinate of heart are they to whom I am sending you. But you shall say to them: Thus says the Lord GOD! And whether they heed or resist—for they are a rebellious house—they shall know that a prophet has been among them.

RESPONSORIAL PSALM
Psalm 123:1–2, 2, 3–4 (2cd)

R. Our eyes are fixed on the Lord, pleading for
　　　his mercy.

To you I lift up my eyes
　　who are enthroned in heaven —
as the eyes of servants
　　are on the hands of their masters. R.

As the eyes of a maid
　　are on the hands of her mistress,
so are our eyes on the LORD, our God,
　　till he have pity on us. R.

Have pity on us, O LORD, have pity on us,
　　for we are more than sated with contempt;
our souls are more than sated
　　with the mockery of the arrogant,
　　with the contempt of the proud. R.

READING II *2 Corinthians 12:7–10*

Brothers and sisters: That I, Paul, might not become too elated, because of the abundance of the revelations, a thorn in the flesh was given to me, an angel of Satan, to beat me, to keep me from being too elated. Three times I begged the Lord about this, that it might leave me, but he said to me, "My grace is sufficient for you, for power is made perfect in weakness." I will rather boast most gladly of my weaknesses, in order that the power of Christ may dwell with me. Therefore, I am content with weaknesses, insults, hardships, persecutions, and constraints, for the sake of Christ; for when I am weak, then I am strong.

GOSPEL *Mark 6:1–6*

Jesus departed from there and came to his native place, accompanied by his disciples. When the sabbath came he began to teach in the synagogue, and many who heard him were astonished. They said, "Where did this man get all this? What kind of wisdom has been given him? What mighty deeds are wrought by his hands! Is he not the carpenter, the son of Mary, and the brother of James and Joses and Judas and Simon? And are not his sisters here with us?" And they took offense at him. Jesus said to them, "A prophet is not without honor except in his native place and among his own kin and in his own house." So he was not able to perform any mighty deed there, apart from curing a few sick people by laying his hands on them. He was amazed at their lack of faith.

Practice of Charity

Perhaps you have heard of parents feeling dumbfounded after hearing glowing reports about their children from teachers and coaches. "Is this really my son/daughter or an imposter?" they ask. The children's behavior at home might be different most of the time. In Mark's Gospel, those in the Nazarene synagogue were astonished and angry upon hearing Jesus preach. They could not fathom that Jesus—someone from their village and raised by neighbors Mary and Joseph—had healed people and taught with such authority. ◆ Consider the blind spots that might be lurking in your personal life. ◆ In your prayer time, praise Jesus for who he is and ask him to heal aspects of your thoughts or behavior that keep you from seeing God's glorious deeds. ◆ Praise your spouse, family member, or friends for their loving ways. Recognize how their presence blesses you and do something that shows your love for them.

Download more questions and activities for families, Christian initiation groups, and other adult groups at http://www.ltp.org/ahw.

Scripture Insights

Paul explains that he was given a thorn in the flesh so that he "might not become too elated" over the abundance of his visions and divine revelations. The phrase "become elated" could also be "become conceited" or "start lording it over others." Christ specifically condemns lording any merit over others, urging his followers instead to become servants to one another (Matthew 20:25–28; Luke 22:24–27). Paul perceives that, paradoxically, his weaknesses allow the power of Christ to dwell in him and work through him.

The Gospel offers more thoughts on power, in a different key. The people of Jesus' hometown struggle to believe that the carpenter's son, who grew up as a normal boy in their midst, whose family was well known to them, can speak with such wisdom and perform such powerful deeds. Because of their lack of faith, Jesus is not able to do many powerful acts among them. He can only heal a few sick people who must have overcome their skepticism to trust their former neighbor. These acts portray power working not so much through weakness as through the familiar and the mundane (a small-town carpenter) and point to the counterintuitive way that power works in the kingdom.

Like the people of Nazareth, the people of Israel in Ezekiel's day were offered the chance to turn away from God's offer of salvation or to be forgiven and healed. The prophet Ezekiel, having caught a glimpse of God's glory, has fallen flat on his face. The spirit lifts him to his feet to receive his message for Israel: they are hard-hearted rebels, but they still have the chance to heed God's words rather than to resist—to turn and be healed—if only they will call on God to have pity on them, as in the Responsorial Psalm.

◆ How might God's power work through one of your weaknesses?

◆ Why were the Nazareth townspeople offended at the evidence of Jesus' wisdom and power?

◆ Where is God at work through the familiar and the mundane in your life?

READING I *Amos 7:12–15*

Amaziah, priest of Bethel, said to Amos, "Off with you, visionary, flee to the land of Judah! There earn your bread by prophesying, but never again prophesy in Bethel; for it is the king's sanctuary and a royal temple." Amos answered Amaziah, "I was no prophet, nor have I belonged to a company of prophets; I was a shepherd and a dresser of sycamores. The LORD took me from following the flock, and said to me, Go, prophesy to my people Israel."

RESPONSORIAL PSALM
Psalm 85:9–10, 11–12, 13–14 (8)

R. Lord, let us see your kindness, and grant us
your salvation.

I will hear what God proclaims;
the LORD—for he proclaims peace.
Near indeed is his salvation to those who fear him,
glory dwelling in our land. R.

Kindness and truth shall meet;
justice and peace shall kiss.
Truth shall spring out of the earth,
and justice shall look down from heaven. R.

The LORD himself will give his benefits;
our land shall yield its increase.
Justice shall walk before him,
and prepare the way of his steps. R.

READING II *Ephesians 1:3–14*

Shorter: Ephesians 1:3–10

Blessed be the God and Father of our Lord Jesus Christ, who has blessed us in Christ with every spiritual blessing in the heavens, as he chose us in him, before the foundation of the world, to be holy and without blemish before him. In love he destined us for adoption to himself through Jesus Christ, in accord with the favor of his will, for the praise of the glory of his grace that he granted us in the beloved. In him we have redemption by his blood, the forgiveness of transgressions, in accord with the riches of his grace that he lavished upon us. In all wisdom and insight, he has made known to us the mystery of his will in accord with his favor that he set forth in him as a plan for the fullness of times, to sum up all things in Christ, in heaven and on earth.

In him we were also chosen, destined in accord with the purpose of the One who accomplishes all things according to the intention of his will, so that we might exist for the praise of his glory, we who first hoped in Christ. In him you also, who have heard the word of truth, the gospel of your salvation, and have believed in him, were sealed with the promised Holy Spirit, which is the first installment of our inheritance toward redemption as God's possession, to the praise of his glory.

GOSPEL *Mark 6:7–13*

Jesus summoned the Twelve and began to send them out two by two and gave them authority over unclean spirits. He instructed them to take nothing for the journey but a walking stick—no food, no sack, no money in their belts. They were, however, to wear sandals but not a second tunic. He said to them, "Wherever you enter a house, stay there until you leave. Whatever place does not welcome you or listen to you, leave there and shake the dust off your feet in testimony against them." So they went off and preached repentance. The Twelve drove out many demons, and they anointed with oil many who were sick and cured them.

Practice of Faith

Most people seem to need so many things. They are sure to carry cellphones to connect with the world and one another as well as purses and wallets filled with a number of items. Jesus asked his closest friends to travel lightly as they evangelize: "no food, no sack, no money in their belts." How many items do you need when you leave the house for the day? Jesus asks us to live simply and not be dependent on useless things. ♦ Evaluate with your family which possessions are never used. Consider offering them to thrift shops, Goodwill, or Salvation Army stores that assist those in need. ♦ Think about your current amount of credit card debt. If unable to pay off your balance monthly, meet with a financial adviser to determine how to decrease your dependence on credit to make daily purchases. ♦ Pray over how much money is wasted needlessly because of unhealthy choices.

Download more questions and activities for families, Christian initiation groups, and other adult groups at http://www.ltp.org/ahw.

Scripture Insights

The common thread running through today's texts is the proclamation of God's will: through prophets and disciples, God calls for repentance and declares his steadfast love and salvation to all who will listen.

The prophet Amos had been a caretaker of sheep and sycamore trees. God plucked him out of Judah and sent him north to Israel. When Amos prophesies judgment against the king and people of Israel for their rebellion against God, the priest Amaziah wants Amos sent back to his homeland, Judah.

The psalmist eagerly waits for the proclamation of a different message—one of peace and salvation, where kindness meets truth, where justice and peace embrace. As a whole, Psalm 85 is a prayer for forgiveness and restoration ("Restore us once more, God our savior," verse 5). The psalmist is confident in God's steadfast love for Israel ("Near indeed is his salvation for those who fear him," verse 10).

In the Letter to the Ephesians today, the word *glory* is prominent. Paul repeats the phrase "for the praise of his [God's] glory" three times with slight variation ("for the praise of the glory of his grace" and "to the praise of his glory"). The Apostle Paul proclaims the mystery of God's will, decided before the foundation of the world, to sum up all things in Christ. The forgiveness promised to Israel in the Responsorial Psalm is offered to all who believed the Gospel and were thereby adopted into God's household.

The Gospel shows us the Twelve proclaiming the Gospel first to God's people Israel, that all might repent and participate in God's salvation through Christ. The disciples are given authority to drive out demons and power to heal bodily sicknesses, showing the wide reach of God's saving power against evil and death, sin and sickness, all to the praise of the glory of God's grace.

♦ Why did Jesus instruct the Twelve only to bring a staff for their journey to preach the Gospel?

♦ What does it mean that we "exist for the praise of his [God's] glory" (Ephesians 3:11)?

♦ When have you seen kindness and truth meet (Psalm 85:11)?

READING I *Jeremiah 23:1–6*

Woe to the shepherds who mislead and scatter the flock of my pasture, says the LORD. Therefore, thus says the LORD, the God of Israel, against the shepherds who shepherd my people: You have scattered my sheep and driven them away. You have not cared for them, but I will take care to punish your evil deeds. I myself will gather the remnant of my flock from all the lands to which I have driven them and bring them back to their meadow; there they shall increase and multiply. I will appoint shepherds for them who will shepherd them so that they need no longer fear and tremble; and none shall be missing, says the LORD.

Behold, the days are coming, says the LORD,
    when I will raise up a righteous shoot
        to David;
as king he shall reign and govern wisely,
    he shall do what is just and
        right in the land.
In his days Judah shall be saved,
    Israel shall dwell in security.
This is the name they give him:
    "The LORD our justice."

RESPONSORIAL PSALM
Psalm 23:1–3, 3–4, 5, 6 (1)

R. The Lord is my shepherd;
        there is nothing I shall want.

The LORD is my shepherd; I shall not want.
    In verdant pastures he gives me repose;
beside restful waters he leads me;
    he refreshes my soul. R.

He guides me in right paths
    for his name's sake.
Even though I walk in the dark valley
    I fear no evil; for you are at my side
with your rod and your staff
    that give me courage. R.

You spread the table before me
    in the sight of my foes;
you anoint my head with oil;
    my cup overflows. R.

Only goodness and kindness follow me
    all the days of my life;
and I shall dwell in the house of the LORD
    for years to come. R.

READING II *Ephesians 2:13–18*

Brothers and sisters: In Christ Jesus you who once were far off have become near by the blood of Christ.

For he is our peace, he who made both one and broke down the dividing wall of enmity, through his flesh, abolishing the law with its commandments and legal claims, that he might create in himself one new person in place of the two, thus establishing peace, and might reconcile both with God, in one body, through the cross, putting that enmity to death by it. He came and preached peace to you who were far off and peace to those who were near, for through him we both have access in one Spirit to the Father.

GOSPEL *Mark 6:30–34*

The apostles gathered together with Jesus and reported all they had done and taught. He said to them, "Come away by yourselves to a deserted place and rest a while." People were coming and going in great numbers, and they had no opportunity even to eat. So they went off in the boat by themselves to a deserted place. People saw them leaving and many came to know about it. They hastened there on foot from all the towns and arrived at the place before them.

When he disembarked and saw the vast crowd, his heart was moved with pity for them, for they were like sheep without a shepherd; and he began to teach them many things.

Practice of Faith

Allowing ourselves the time to be physically still and silent may seem like a luxury, but doing so is necessary in our efforts to engage more fully with our Creator. In today's Gospel, Jesus urges his Apostles, "Come away by yourselves to a deserted place and rest a while." Many of us have a constant need to connect with the news and with others and so are reluctant to set aside our phones, electronic games, and the internet. Since any meaningful relationship needs attention and nurturing, our most important one—with God—requires quiet reflection. ◆ Choose a day to lock your phone in a drawer for the evening. ◆ Check out resources that can lead you toward making a retreat, even for a short time in your home. ◆ Consider: www.ignatianspirituality.com; *Moment by Moment: A Retreat in Everyday Life*, by Carol Ann Smith; *Open the Door: A Journey to the True Self*, by Joyce Rupp; *The First Spiritual Exercises: Four Guided Retreats*, by Michael Hansen; and *Befriending Silence: Discovering the Gifts of Cistercian Spirituality*, by Carl McColman.

Download more questions and activities for families, Christian initiation groups, and other adult groups at http://www.ltp.org/ahw.

Scripture Insights

The prophet Jeremiah's cry, "Woe to the shepherds," is a judgment on Israel's leaders for misleading and scattering the sheep (the people of Israel) in their care. In Jeremiah and Psalm 23, God is the Good Shepherd who feeds his people, protects them, and does not lose one of them. Jeremiah points forward to Christ through his promise that God will "raise up a righteous shoot to David," a king who will govern with wisdom and justice.

When Jesus views the people as "sheep without a shepherd," he likewise condemns Israel's leaders for failing to care for, guide, and protect the people (Mark 6:34; cf. Jeremiah 50:6; Numbers 27:17; 2 Chronicles 18:16). The disciples have just returned from their mission to proclaim the Gospel and to heal. They have attracted so much attention that they don't even have time to eat, so Jesus tells them to come away to a quiet place to rest ("in verdant pastures he gives me repose"). The crowd discovers where the group has planned to retreat and arrives at their destination first. When Jesus sees the people, he is "moved with pity." The Greek word here means to be deeply moved, for one's insides to churn with emotion. Rather than escape the crowds, Jesus takes up the role of their shepherd and teaches them.

In Ephesians, Paul tells of how Christ has united the Israelites, who were heirs of the covenant, with the Gentiles, who were not. In the verse that precedes today's reading, Paul reminds his Gentile congregation in Ephesus that they once were "strangers to the covenants of promise, without hope and without God in the world" (Ephesians 2:12). They have now been brought near to God through Christ, whose death destroyed the barrier between Jew and Gentile and created one new humanity, at peace with God.

◆ Through what "dark valley" has God accompanied you (Psalm 23:4)?

◆ What other walls of enmity does Christ break down between people (Ephesians 2:14)?

◆ When moved with pity at the sight of the crowds, why is Jesus' first action to "teach them many things"?

111

July 25, 2021 SEVENTEENTH SUNDAY IN ORDINARY TIME

READING I *2 Kings 4:42–44*

A man came from Baal-shalishah bringing to Elisha, the man of God, twenty barley loaves made from the firstfruits, and fresh grain in the ear. Elisha said, "Give it to the people to eat." But his servant objected, "How can I set this before a hundred people?" Elisha insisted, "Give it to the people to eat. For thus says the LORD, 'They shall eat and there shall be some left over.'" And when they had eaten, there was some left over, as the LORD had said.

RESPONSORIAL PSALM *Psalm 145:10–11, 15–16, 17–18 (see 16)*

R. The hand of the Lord feeds us;
  he answers all our needs.

Let all your works give you thanks, O LORD,
  and let your faithful ones bless you.
Let them discourse of the glory of your kingdom
  and speak of your might. R.

The eyes of all look hopefully to you,
  and you give them their food in due season;
you open your hand
  and satisfy the desire of every living thing. R.

The LORD is just in all his ways
  and holy in all his works.
The LORD is near to all who call upon him,
  to all who call upon him in truth. R.

READING II *Ephesians 4:1–6*

Brothers and sisters: I, a prisoner for the Lord, urge you to live in a manner worthy of the call you have received, with all humility and gentleness, with patience, bearing with one another through love, striving to preserve the unity of the spirit through the bond of peace: one body and one Spirit, as you were also called to the one hope of your call; one Lord, one faith, one baptism; one God and Father of all, who is over all and through all and in all.

GOSPEL *John 6:1–15*

Jesus went across the Sea of Galilee. A large crowd followed him, because they saw the signs he was performing on the sick. Jesus went up on the mountain, and there he sat down with his disciples. The Jewish feast of Passover was near. When Jesus raised his eyes and saw that a large crowd was coming to him, he said to Philip, "Where can we buy enough food for them to eat?" He said this to test him, because he himself knew what he was going to do. Philip answered him, "Two hundred days' wages worth of food would not be enough for each of them to have a little." One of his disciples, Andrew, the brother of Simon Peter, said to him, "There is a boy here who has five barley loaves and two fish; but what good are these for so many?" Jesus said, "Have the people recline." Now there was a great deal of grass in that place. So the men reclined, about five thousand in number. Then Jesus took the loaves, gave thanks, and distributed them to those who were reclining, and also as much of the fish as they wanted. When they had had their fill, he said to his disciples, "Gather the fragments left over, so that nothing will be wasted." So they collected them, and filled twelve wicker baskets with fragments from the five barley loaves that had been more than they could eat. When the people saw the sign he had done, they said, "This is truly the Prophet, the one who is to come into the world." Since Jesus knew that they were going to come and carry him off to make him king, he withdrew again to the mountain alone.

Practice of Charity

Many cities and towns offer a food pantry, sometimes with a place where free hot meals are served. Volunteering to help at a community soup kitchen can be a humbling learning experience for people who have never worried about their next meal. Working at these centers of hope also can help us become more aware of the challenges of the working poor and to apply the principles of Catholic Social Teaching and justice. ◆ Become familiar with a food pantry or center where hot meals are served and check how you could volunteer there. ◆ Learn more about how current national issues are affecting the quality of life for the impoverished who are food insecure. A good resource is the Human Life and Dignity section of the United States Conference of Catholic Bishops' website: www.usccb.org. ◆ Set aside time to examine ways in which you live out humility and gentleness. How can you grow in those virtues?

Download more questions and activities for families, Christian initiation groups, and other adult groups at http://www.ltp.org/ahw.

Scripture Insights

The theme of today's texts is apparent in the refrain from the Responsorial Psalm: "The hand of the Lord feeds us; he answers all our needs."

In the reading from the Second Book of Kings, the prophet Elisha uses twenty barley loaves to feed a hundred people, despite the doubts of his servant. The prophet knows that it will be more than enough: "For thus says the LORD, 'They shall eat and there shall be some left over.'" Against this background, we read from John of the miracle of the feeding of the five thousand with five barley loaves and two fish. This is one of the few miracles all four evangelists record in the Gospels.

The disciples Philip and Andrew, like Elisha's servant, are doubtful that the meager amount will be enough. Elisha had twenty loaves; they only have five. Still, after everyone eats and is satisfied, twelve baskets are filled with the leftovers. The number *twelve* signifies the fullness of Israel: God has enough—more than enough—to satisfy the desires of all his people. The miraculous loaves also point beyond themselves to the true bread: Jesus, the bread from heaven, who feeds his people with his body.

Several numbers are prominent in the accounts of the miraculous meals (twenty, five, five thousand, twelve), but only the number *one* is noted in the Letter to the Ephesians. We read of one body of Christ, one Spirit, one hope, one Lord, one faith, one baptism, one God. The oneness of the saints points to the Bread of Life: the Body of Christ is Jesus' flesh and blood, the bread and wine of the Eucharist, and the united Christians who partake of the bread. The Ephesians have been called to "the riches of [God's] glory in his inheritance among the holy ones" (1:18), and the Apostle Paul urges them to be worthy of that calling through bearing patiently with one another in love.

◆ Where in your life do you see a scarcity that God might be planning to turn into abundance?

◆ Why is unity among Christians important to Paul?

◆ With whom do you need to bear patiently with love today?

READING I *Exodus 16:2–4, 12–15*

The whole Israelite community grumbled against Moses and Aaron. The Israelites said to them, "Would that we had died at the LORD's hand in the land of Egypt, as we sat by our fleshpots and ate our fill of bread! But you had to lead us into this desert to make the whole community die of famine!"

Then the LORD said to Moses, "I will now rain down bread from heaven for you. Each day the people are to go out and gather their daily portion; thus will I test them, to see whether they follow my instructions or not.

"I have heard the grumbling of the Israelites. Tell them: In the evening twilight you shall eat flesh, and in the morning you shall have your fill of bread, so that you may know that I, the LORD, am your God."

In the evening quail came up and covered the camp. In the morning a dew lay all about the camp, and when the dew evaporated, there on the surface of the desert were fine flakes like hoarfrost on the ground. On seeing it, the Israelites asked one another, "What is this?" for they did not know what it was. But Moses told them, "This is the bread that the LORD has given you to eat."

RESPONSORIAL PSALM
Psalm 78:3–4, 23–24, 25, 54 (24b)

R. The Lord gave them bread from heaven.

What we have heard and know,
    and what our fathers have declared to us,
we will declare to the generation to come
    the glorious deeds of the LORD
        and his strength
    and the wonders that he wrought. R.

He commanded the skies above
    and opened the doors of heaven;
he rained manna upon them for food
    and gave them heavenly bread. R.

Man ate the bread of angels,
    food he sent them in abundance.
And he brought them to his holy land,
to the mountains his right hand
    had won. R.

READING II *Ephesians 4:17, 20–24*

Brothers and sisters: I declare and testify in the Lord that you must no longer live as the Gentiles do, in the futility of their minds; that is not how you learned Christ, assuming that you have heard of him and were taught in him, as truth is in Jesus, that you should put away the old self of your former way of life, corrupted through deceitful desires, and be renewed in the spirit of your minds, and put on the new self, created in God's way in righteousness and holiness of truth.

GOSPEL *John 6:24–35*

When the crowd saw that neither Jesus nor his disciples were there, they themselves got into boats and came to Capernaum looking for Jesus. And when they found him across the sea they said to him, "Rabbi, when did you get here?" Jesus answered them and said, "Amen, amen, I say to you, you are looking for me not because you saw signs but because you ate the loaves and were filled. Do not work for food that perishes but for the food that endures for eternal life, which the Son of Man will give you. For on him the Father, God, has set his seal." So they said to him, "What can we do to accomplish the works of God?" Jesus answered and said to them, "This is the work of God, that you believe in the one he sent." So they said to him, "What sign can you do, that we may see and believe in you? What can you do? Our ancestors ate manna in the desert, as it is written: *He gave them bread from heaven to eat.*" So Jesus said to them, "Amen, amen, I say to you, it was not Moses who gave the bread from heaven; my Father gives you the true bread from heaven. For the bread of God is that which comes down from heaven and gives life to the world."

So they said to him, "Sir, give us this bread always." Jesus said to them, "I am the bread of life; whoever comes to me will never hunger, and whoever believes in me will never thirst."

Practice of Faith

In this Gospel, Jesus reminds us that his bread is what truly sustains us for eternal life. How often do you make yourself available to God during the day? ◆ Consider whether you can sometimes participate at a Mass by your home early in the day or near your workplace at noon. If that is not an option, try to find time to pause during the day to give thanks for the gift of our faith. ◆ Consider looking into retreat options to devote time to what feeds you. Even if your time apart from regular duties might be a few hours or one day, you will be able to allow our Creator's love for you to permeate your conscience even more. ◆ If you're not already spending an hour regularly at Eucharistic adoration, consider trying this traditional prayer practice. Even stopping for ten to fifteen minutes at a parish chapel that offers perpetual adoration might give a boost to your spiritual life.

Download more questions and activities for families, Christian initiation groups, and other adult groups at http://www.ltp.org/ahw.

Scripture Insights

In Exodus 16, the Israelites grumble against Moses and Aaron (and God) for leading them out of the abundance of Egypt into the starvation of the desert. In response, God sends them a daily portion of manna, testing whether they will trust God to continue giving them what they need. When the Israelites hedge their bets and try to save a little for the next day, the manna spoils.

The Swedish word *lagom* means "enough" or "just the right amount." It is a word of abundance, not a word of scarcity. It indicates a way of living in the world without anxiety, trusting that one has what one needs and does not need to grasp for more. Today's Responsorial Psalm declares that God sent the Israelites food "in abundance" (Psalm 78:25): God's "enough" is true abundance. It is the same logic behind the prayer to give us "our daily bread." We ask God to give us what we need for today and trust that God will do the same tomorrow.

The Gospel tells us that what God ultimately gives us is God's own self: God's Son, sent into the world not to condemn it but to save it; God's body, broken on the cross and offered as true food to a hungry world; God's heart, broken for us, so that we might never hunger again (John 6:35).

It's a paradox that "enough" means "more than you will ever need." To grasp this requires one to be "renewed in the spirit" of the mind, as Paul writes to the Ephesians. The old self—who Christians were prior to Christ—was corrupted by "deceitful desires." It's human nature to desire more, and more, and more. To trust God's loving provision requires a new self, re-created in Christ's truth. God provides that re-creation, too.

◆ Is it a challenge to trust that God always gives us enough?

◆ When has God given to you in abundance?

◆ What can you do today to put away the old self and put on the new self?

Reading I *1 Kings 19:4–8*

Elijah went a day's journey into the desert, until he came to a broom tree and sat beneath it. He prayed for death, saying: "This is enough, O Lord! Take my life, for I am no better than my fathers." He lay down and fell asleep under the broom tree, but then an angel touched him and ordered him to get up and eat. Elijah looked and there at his head was a hearth cake and a jug of water. After he ate and drank, he lay down again, but the angel of the Lord came back a second time, touched him, and ordered, "Get up and eat, else the journey will be too long for you!" He got up, ate, and drank; then strengthened by that food, he walked forty days and forty nights to the mountain of God, Horeb.

Responsorial Psalm
Psalm 34:2–3, 4–5, 6–7, 8–9 (9a)

R. Taste and see the goodness of the Lord.

I will bless the Lord at all times;
    his praise shall be ever in my mouth.
Let my soul glory in the Lord;
    the lowly will hear me and be glad. R.

Glorify the Lord with me,
    let us together extol his name.
I sought the Lord, and he answered me
    and delivered me from all my fears. R.

Look to him that you may be radiant with joy,
    and your faces may not blush with shame.
When the afflicted man called out,
        the Lord heard,
    and from all his distress he saved him. R.

The angel of the Lord encamps
    around those who fear him and delivers them.
Taste and see how good the Lord is;
    blessed the man who takes refuge in him. R.

Reading II *Ephesians 4:30—5:2*

Brothers and sisters: Do not grieve the Holy Spirit of God, with which you were sealed for the day of redemption. All bitterness, fury, anger, shouting, and reviling must be removed from you, along with all malice. And be kind to one another, compassionate, forgiving one another as God has forgiven you in Christ.

So be imitators of God, as beloved children, and live in love, as Christ loved us and handed himself over for us as a sacrificial offering to God for a fragrant aroma.

Gospel *John 6:41–51*

The Jews murmured about Jesus because he said, "I am the bread that came down from heaven," and they said, "Is this not Jesus, the son of Joseph? Do we not know his father and mother? Then how can he say, 'I have come down from heaven'?" Jesus answered and said to them, "Stop murmuring among yourselves. No one can come to me unless the Father who sent me draw him, and I will raise him on the last day. It is written in the prophets: *They shall all be taught by God.* Everyone who listens to my Father and learns from him comes to me. Not that anyone has seen the Father except the one who is from God; he has seen the Father. Amen, amen, I say to you, whoever believes has eternal life. I am the bread of life. Your ancestors ate the manna in the desert, but they died; this is the bread that comes down from heaven so that one may eat it and not die. I am the living bread that came down from heaven; whoever eats this bread will live forever; and the bread that I will give is my flesh for the life of the world."

Practice of Hope

Our family and friends who live the most ordinary lives may be models of the Christ-centered life. The Jews murmured about Jesus, who grew up in their community, disbelieving that he could be the "living bread." The Second Vatican Council's *Dogmatic Constitution on the Church* points out in paragraph 10 that, as baptized persons, we have the responsibility to witness Christ to the world through our faith-filled actions and prayer. In essence, we need to be living bread for this troubled world. ◆ Try praying through the news as you watch and listen to accounts of suffering. ◆ Become more aware of brothers and sisters in every country who struggle for basic necessities. Encourage family members to pray so that your prayers of hope help form the people you love. ◆ Bake a dessert or cook a meal for someone in your neighborhood who may be suffering, and prayerfully become "living bread" for others.

Download more questions and activities for families, Christian initiation groups, and other adult groups at http://www.ltp.org/ahw.

Scripture Insights

Paul continues his instructions in Ephesians about living in the Spirit and not in the grip of anger and malice. The passive verb "be removed" (4:31) suggests that the Spirit does the removing, but the Ephesians must allow the Spirit room to work, by striving to imitate God's ungrudging forgiveness.

Just prior to today's reading from the First Book of Kings, Elijah killed the prophets of Baal, and Queen Jezebel swore to kill him in retaliation. He flees to the desert and is so disheartened that he prays for death. The prophet Jonah also sat down under a tree in the desert and wished to die. Jonah struggled with God's extravagant mercy; Elijah, with the depths of Israel's idolatry. Elijah's forty-day journey to the mountain of God foreshadows other long walks in the wilderness: Israel's forty years of wandering, and Jesus' forty days of fasting before facing the devil's temptations. Elijah, like Jesus, receives help from an angel, who strengthens him: "The angel of the Lord encamps around those who fear him and delivers them" (Psalm 34:8).

In the Gospel, Jesus' encounter with the Jews recalls Moses' interaction with the Hebrews he led out of Egypt. Here, the Jews are "murmuring" or complaining about Jesus just as the Israelites murmured about Moses. Understandably, they are unsettled by Jesus' words: Jesus claims not only to have descended from heaven but also that whoever eats his living bread will never die and that the bread he offers the world is his flesh. To Jesus' fellow Jews, these claims must have seemed shocking, even blasphemous. After all, they know his parents; he is from Nazareth, not heaven! The rest of the Gospel unfolds the audacious claim that Jesus has seen the Father, despite Scripture's insistence that nobody can see God and live (Exodus 33:20).

◆ Is there anything on Paul's list (bitterness, fury, anger, shouting, reviling, malice) you need to ask God's Spirit to remove?

◆ How does God deliver you from your fears (Psalm 34)?

◆ How has the Father drawn you to Jesus (John 6:44)?

READING I *Revelation 11:19a; 12:1–6a, 10ab*

God's temple in heaven was opened, and the ark of his covenant could be seen in the temple.

A great sign appeared in the sky, a woman clothed with the sun, with the moon under her feet, and on her head a crown of twelve stars. She was with child and wailed aloud in pain as she labored to give birth. Then another sign appeared in the sky; it was a huge red dragon, with seven heads and ten horns, and on its heads were seven diadems. Its tail swept away a third of the stars in the sky and hurled them down to the earth. Then the dragon stood before the woman about to give birth, to devour her child when she gave birth. She gave birth to a son, a male child, destined to rule all the nations with an iron rod. Her child was caught up to God and his throne. The woman herself fled into the desert where she had a place prepared by God.

Then I heard a loud voice in heaven say:

"Now have salvation and power come,
    and the Kingdom of our God
    and the authority of his Anointed One."

READING II *1 Corinthians 15:20–27*

Brothers and sisters: Christ has been raised from the dead, the firstfruits of those who have fallen asleep. For since death came through man, the resurrection of the dead came also through man. For just as in Adam all die, so too in Christ shall all be brought to life, but each one in proper order: Christ the firstfruits; then, at his coming, those who belong to Christ; then comes the end, when he hands over the Kingdom to his God and Father, when he has destroyed every sovereignty and every authority and power. For he must reign until he has put all his enemies under his feet. The last enemy to be destroyed is death, for "he subjected everything under his feet."

GOSPEL *Luke 1:39–56*

Mary set out and traveled to the hill country in haste to a town of Judah, where she entered the house of Zechariah and greeted Elizabeth. When Elizabeth heard Mary's greeting, the infant leaped in her womb, and Elizabeth, filled with the Holy Spirit, cried out in a loud voice and said, "Blessed are you among women, and blessed is the fruit of your womb. And how does this happen to me, that the mother of my Lord should come to me? For at the moment the sound of your greeting reached my ears, the infant in my womb leaped for joy. Blessed are you who believed that what was spoken to you by the Lord would be fulfilled."

And Mary said:

"My soul proclaims the greatness of the Lord;
    my spirit rejoices in God my Savior
    for he has looked with favor on his
        lowly servant.
From this day all generations will call
        me blessed:
    the Almighty has done great things for me
    and holy is his Name.
    He has mercy on those who fear him
    in every generation.
He has shown the strength of his arm,
    and has scattered the proud in their conceit.
He has cast down the mighty from
        their thrones,
    and has lifted up the lowly.
He has filled the hungry with good things,
    and the rich he has sent away empty.
He has come to the help of his servant Israel
    for he has remembered his promise of mercy,
    the promise he made to our fathers,
    to Abraham and his children for ever."

Mary remained with her about three months and then returned to her home.

Practice of Faith

Grace is a word that many find difficult to define. We sense grace personified in the Blessed Virgin Mary. This extraordinary woman agreed to the angel's divine request even though she was barely a teenager. Today's Gospel from Luke tells of Mary's travels to her cousin Elizabeth, where she will find comfort and support. Upon seeing Mary, Elizabeth declares that Mary and the baby in her womb are "blessed." ◆ In your prayer time, recall moments when you have felt especially blessed. Think about the circumstances surrounding these times and how these might have included unexpected challenges. ◆ Try to make the Magnificat part of your daily prayer. ◆ Meditate on Mary's words of faith in the Magnificat.

Download more questions and activities for families, Christian initiation groups, and other adult groups at http://www.ltp.org/ahw.

Scripture Insights

The Book of Revelation reveals the hidden heavenly drama behind the scenes of Jesus' humble birth. In John's vision, Mary is a glorious woman clothed with the sun, wearing a crown of twelve stars representing the twelve tribes of Israel. A great dragon, a symbol for God's adversary, Satan, crouches before her, waiting to devour her child as soon as he is born. At the moment of his birth, the baby is "caught up to God and his throne," a dramatic representation of God's protection of the newborn Jesus. The woman flees to the wilderness—a retelling of the Holy Family's flight into Egypt to find safety from the murderous King Herod. In Revelation as in the Gospel, Rome's earthly rulers (Herod, Caesar) are aligned with God's ancient adversary.

Mary knows that the child in her womb will defeat both of these mighty powers—arrogant, earthly oppressors and the spiritual forces of darkness. Her song of praise to God, the Magnificat, declares that the mighty ones (Herod, Caesar) will be toppled from their thrones and that the lowly and humble ones (like Mary) will be lifted high.

In First Corinthians, Paul joins his voice to Mary's when he writes that the Christ who once came in lowly weakness as a child will return in glory to destroy every ruler and authority and power, in heaven and on earth, including Satan and the death that he wields. Paul writes his letter to the Christians in Corinth a couple of decades after the death and Resurrection of Jesus. Caesar still rules securely on his throne; the emerging Christian faith is a tiny movement taking root in the Mediterranean basin. But Paul knows the truth that Mary and John saw: Christ already reigns over Caesar and Satan—and his kingdom will have no end.

◆ In what ways do you see Christ's victory over evil even now, while the powerful are still on their thrones?

◆ Why is death the last enemy that Christ destroys (Second Reading)?

◆ How can we imitate Mary's humble trust that God fulfills all of his promises?

READING I *Joshua 24:1–2a, 15–17, 18b*

Joshua gathered together all the tribes of Israel at Shechem, summoning their elders, their leaders, their judges, and their officers. When they stood in ranks before God, Joshua addressed all the people: "If it does not please you to serve the LORD, decide today whom you will serve, the gods your fathers served beyond the River or the gods of the Amorites in whose country you are now dwelling. As for me and my household, we will serve the LORD."

But the people answered, "Far be it from us to forsake the LORD for the service of other gods. For it was the LORD, our God, who brought us and our fathers up out of the land of Egypt, out of a state of slavery. He performed those great miracles before our very eyes and protected us along our entire journey and among the peoples through whom we passed. Therefore we also will serve the LORD, for he is our God."

RESPONSORIAL PSALM *Psalm 34:2–3, 16–17, 18–19, 20–21 (9a)*

R. Taste and see the goodness of the Lord.

I will bless the LORD at all times;
  his praise shall be ever in my mouth.
Let my soul glory in the LORD;
  the lowly will hear me and be glad. R.

The LORD has eyes for the just,
  and ears for their cry.
The LORD confronts the evildoers,
  to destroy remembrance
    of them from the earth. R.

When the just cry out, the LORD hears them,
  and from all their distress
    he rescues them.
The LORD is close to the brokenhearted;
  and those who are crushed
    in spirit he saves. R.

Many are the troubles of the just one,
  but out of them all the LORD delivers him;
he watches over all his bones;
  not one of them shall be broken. R.

READING II *Ephesians 5:21–32*

Shorter: Ephesians 5:2a, 25–32

Brothers and sisters: Be subordinate to one another out of reverence for Christ. Wives should be subordinate to their husbands as to the Lord. For the husband is head of his wife just as Christ is head of the church, he himself the savior of the body. As the church is subordinate to Christ, so wives should be subordinate to their husbands in everything. Husbands, love your wives, even as Christ loved the church and handed himself over for her to sanctify her, cleansing her by the bath of water with the word, that he might present to himself the church in splendor, without spot or wrinkle or any such thing, that she might be holy and without blemish. So also husbands should love their wives as their own bodies. He who loves his wife loves himself. For no one hates his own flesh but rather nourishes and cherishes it, even as Christ does the church, because we are members of his body.

For this reason a man shall leave his father
    and his mother
  and be joined to his wife,
  and the two shall become one flesh.

This is a great mystery, but I speak in reference to Christ and the church.

GOSPEL *John 6:60–69*

Many of Jesus' disciples who were listening said, "This saying is hard; who can accept it?" Since Jesus knew that his disciples were murmuring about this, he said to them, "Does this shock you? What if you were to see the Son of Man ascending to where he was before? It is the spirit that gives life, while the flesh is of no avail. The words I have spoken to you are Spirit and life. But there are some of you who do not believe." Jesus knew from the beginning the ones who would not believe and the one who would betray him. And he said, "For this reason I have told you that no one can come to me unless it is granted him by my Father."

As a result of this, many of his disciples returned to their former way of life and no longer accompanied him. Jesus then said to the Twelve, "Do you also want to leave?" Simon Peter answered him, "Master, to whom shall we go? You have the words of eternal life. We have come to believe and are convinced that you are the Holy One of God."

Practice of Faith

In today's Gospel, Jesus asks his disciples, "What if you were to see the Son of Man ascending to where he was before? It is the spirit that gives life, while the flesh is of no avail. The words I have spoken to you are Spirit and life." Several of Jesus' friends left him at that point because they weren't committed to this truth. God is faithful to us; we must live out our faith authentically and fully. ◆ Reflect on the level to which you are "all in" with your commitment to Christ. Are you satisfied with this level of commitment? ◆ What other people, efforts, or organizations do you devote time and energy to? Evaluate whether your enthusiasm for these is greater or less than your commitment to Jesus. ◆ What steps can you take to increase your commitment to your faith?

Download more questions and activities for families, Christian initiation groups, and other adult groups at http://www.ltp.org/ahw.

Scripture Insights

Joshua gives the Israelites a choice. Which god(s) will they serve? "Serve nobody" is not an option. They will serve this god or that. The people choose the God who rescued them from slavery in Egypt; they choose the One who heard their cries when they were brokenhearted and saved them when they were crushed in spirit (Psalm 34:18–19).

The Second Reading and the Gospel explore the Body of Christ first as the Church and then as the bread of the Eucharist. Paul instructs all Christians, men and women, to submit to one another out of reverence for Christ. His specific instructions for marriages lead Paul into the heart of the passage, a lengthy meditation on Christ's self-giving love for the Church. Even the mystery of two becoming one in the union of bodies becomes for Paul the greater mystery of Christ's union with his Church as his own body.

In John 6, the Jewish leaders have murmured or complained about Jesus' teaching that he is the bread from heaven, and now the disciples do too. The saying that they must eat Jesus' flesh is so shocking that some of Jesus' disciples turn aside and go back to their old lives. Jesus asks the Twelve, his closest friends, if they also want to go away. For once, Simon Peter gets it right. In one of the most poignant lines in the Gospel, he states, "To whom shall we go? You have the words of eternal life."

Where else can they go? What other gods could they serve now? They have tasted and seen the truth, that Jesus is the bread from heaven, the Holy One of God, the only one who can satisfy their longings. Like the people of Israel who chose to follow their God even into the wilderness, the disciples have nowhere else to go and will follow Jesus to the end.

◆ Are there sayings of Jesus that you find hard to accept?

◆ When have you felt God near to you when you were brokenhearted?

◆ What does it mean for Christians to be subordinate to one another?

121

READING I *Deuteronomy 4:1–2, 6–8*

Moses said to the people: "Now, Israel, hear the statutes and decrees which I am teaching you to observe, that you may live, and may enter in and take possession of the land which the LORD, the God of your fathers, is giving you. In your observance of the commandments of the LORD, your God, which I enjoin upon you, you shall not add to what I command you nor subtract from it. Observe them carefully, for thus will you give evidence of your wisdom and intelligence to the nations, who will hear of all these statutes and say, 'This great nation is truly a wise and intelligent people.' For what great nation is there that has gods so close to it as the LORD, our God, is to us whenever we call upon him? Or what great nation has statutes and decrees that are as just as this whole law which I am setting before you today?"

RESPONSORIAL PSALM
Psalm 15:2–3, 3–4, 4–5 (1a)

R. The one who does justice will live in the presence of the Lord.

Whoever walks blamelessly and does justice;
   who thinks the truth in his heart
   and slanders not with his tongue. R.

Who harms not his fellow man,
   nor takes up a reproach against his neighbor;
by whom the reprobate is despised,
   while he honors those who fear the LORD. R.

Who lends not his money at usury
   and accepts no bribe against the innocent.
Whoever does these things
   shall never be disturbed. R.

READING II
James 1:17–18, 21b–22, 27

Dearest brothers and sisters: All good giving and every perfect gift is from above, coming down from the Father of lights, with whom there is no alteration or shadow caused by change. He willed to give us birth by the word of truth that we may be a kind of firstfruits of his creatures.

Humbly welcome the word that has been planted in you and is able to save your souls.

Be doers of the word and not hearers only, deluding yourselves.

Religion that is pure and undefiled before God and the Father is this: to care for orphans and widows in their affliction and to keep oneself unstained by the world.

GOSPEL *Mark 7:1–8, 14–15, 21–23*

When the Pharisees with some scribes who had come from Jerusalem gathered around Jesus, they observed that some of his disciples ate their meals with unclean, that is, unwashed, hands.—For the Pharisees and, in fact, all Jews, do not eat without carefully washing their hands, keeping the tradition of the elders. And on coming from the marketplace they do not eat without purifying themselves. And there are many other things that they have traditionally observed, the purification of cups and jugs and kettles and beds.—So the Pharisees and scribes questioned him, "Why do your disciples not follow the tradition of the elders but instead eat a meal with unclean hands?" He responded, "Well did Isaiah prophesy about you hypocrites, as it is written:

This people honors me with their lips,
   but their hearts are far from me;
in vain do they worship me,
   teaching as doctrines human precepts.

You disregard God's commandment but cling to human tradition." He summoned the crowd again and said to them, "Hear me, all of you, and understand. Nothing that enters one from outside can defile that person; but the things that come out from within are what defile.

"From within people, from their hearts, come evil thoughts, unchastity, theft, murder, adultery, greed, malice, deceit, licentiousness, envy, blasphemy, arrogance, folly. All these evils come from within and they defile."

Practice of Charity

The Second Reading and the Gospel touch on the essence of Jesus' teaching to care for the marginalized. Pope Francis echoes this teaching when he urges his brother priests to go out as shepherds where there is suffering and brokenness so that they have the "odor of the sheep." All of us are called to be "doers of the word and not hearers only" and to care for the most vulnerable in our midst. ◆ Talk to the staff at your parish or a community administrator about helping out someone who is struggling to obtain adequate food or shelter. ◆ While grocery shopping, purchase additional canned goods to donate to the local food pantry. ◆ Discover how your local St. Vincent de Paul Society helps those in need. Determine if you can volunteer in one of their programs.

Download more questions and activities for families, Christian initiation groups, and other adult groups at http://www.ltp.org/ahw.

Scripture Insights

All of today's readings illuminate God's call to wholehearted obedience. Deuteronomy 4 names two purposes of God's holy law: one purpose faces inward, intended for the flourishing of Israel; one purpose faces outward, intended for witness to the world. For Israel, God gave the law "that you may live." As the psalmist writes, whoever follows the law will live well: in peace, without disturbance. The law is not to restrict followers but to set them free for a life of true abundance. As for the world, the law was given to Israel so that they could bear witness that their God's wisdom and kindness surpass all other nations' gods. The law illuminated the Israelites so that they might shine brightly, drawing other nations to Israel's God.

James picks up on the theme of fruitful obedience and applies it to Christians. He uses three metaphors to show how intertwined our lives are with God's "word of truth" (that is, the Scripture, or God's law): we are the infant children of the Word; we are like the first figs blossoming on the Word's tree; and we are the soil in which the Word is planted. Our lives are bound up with God's Word in such a way that to hear the Word without living it out would be to turn away from our parent, to wither on the tree, or to dry up and crack as desert soil.

Finally, Mark's Gospel warns that obedience to the law must be deeper than mere observance. Our obedience should be inward, coming from hearts turned toward God. Mark warns, rather literally, against paying "lip service" to the law without loving God with the heart. The purpose of God's holy law is inner transformation leading to abundant life.

◆ Does the honor that you give God come from your heart?

◆ Can our observance of God's holy law today serve as a witness that draws outsiders closer to God?

◆ How are you a "doer of the word"?

Ordinary Time, Autumn

Prayer before Reading the Word

In humility and service, O God,
your Son came among us
to form a community of disciples
who have one Father in heaven,
and one teacher, the Messiah.
Let your Spirit make our hearts
docile to the challenge of your Word,
and let the same mind be in us
that was in Christ Jesus.
We ask this through our Lord Jesus Christ,
            your Son,
who lives and reigns with you
in the unity of the Holy Spirit,
one God, for ever and ever. Amen.

Prayer after Reading the Word

To the last as to the first, O God,
you are generous and more than just,
for as high as the heavens are above the earth,
so high are your ways above our ways
and your thoughts above our thoughts.
Open our hearts to the wisdom of your Son,
fix in our minds his sound teaching,
that, without concern for the cost of discipleship,
we may work without ceasing
for the coming of your Kingdom.
We ask this through our Lord Jesus Christ,
            your Son,
who lives and reigns with you
in the unity of the Holy Spirit,
one God, for ever and ever. Amen.

Weekday Readings

August 30: *1 Thessalonians 4:13–18 Luke 4:16–30*
August 31: *1 Thessalonians 5:1–6, 9–11; Luke 4:31–37*
September 1: *Colossians 1:1–8; Luke 4:38–44*
September 2: *Colossians 1:9–14; Luke 5:1–11*
September 3: *Colossians 1:15–20; Luke 5:33–39*
September 4: *Colossians 1:21–23; Luke 6:1–5*

September 6: *Colossians 1:24—2:3; Luke 6:6–11*
September 7: *Colossians 2:6–15; Luke 6:12–19*
**September 8: Feast of the Nativity of
the Blessed Virgin Mary
Micah 5:1–4a or Romans 8:28–30;
Matthew 1:1–16, 18–23**
September 9: *Colossians 3:12–17; Luke 6:27–38*
September 10: *1 Timothy 1:1–2, 12–14; Luke 6:39–42*
September 11: *1 Timothy 1:15–17; Luke 6:43–49*

September 13: *1 Timothy 2:1–8; Luke 7:1–10*
**September 14: Feast of the Exaltation of the Holy Cross
Numbers 21:4b–9; Philippians 2:6–11; John 3:13–17**
September 15: *1 Timothy 3:14–16; John 19:25–27
or Luke 2:33–35*
September 16: *1 Timothy 4:12–16; Luke 7:36–50*
September 17: *1 Timothy 6:2c–12; Luke 8:1–3*
September 18: *1 Timothy 6:13–16; Luke 8:4–15*

September 20: *Ezra 1:1–6; Luke 8:16–18*
September 21: *Ephesians 4:1–7, 11–13; Matthew 9:9–13*
September 22: *Ezra 9:5–9; Luke 9:1–6*
September 23: *Haggai 1:1–8; Luke 9:7–9*
September 24: *Haggai 2:1–9; Luke 9:18–22*
September 25: *Zechariah 2:5–9, 14–15a; Luke 9:43b–45*

September 27: *Zechariah 8:1–8; Luke 9:46–50*
September 28: *Zechariah 8:20–23; Luke 9:51–56*
September 29: *Daniel 7:9–10, 13–14 or Revelation 12:7–12a;
John 1:47–51*
September 30: *Nehemiah 8:1–4a, 5–6, 7b–12; Luke 10:1–12*
October 1: *Baruch 1:15–22; Luke 10:13–16*
October 2: *Baruch 4:5–12, 27–29; Matthew 18:1–5, 10*

October 4: *Jonah 1:1—2:2, 11; Luke 10:25–37*
October 5: *Jonah 3:1–10; Luke 10:38–42*
October 6: *Jonah 4:1–11; Luke 11:1–4*
October 7: *Malachi 3:13–20b; Luke 11:5–13*
October 8: *Joel 1:13–15; 2:1–2; Luke 11:15–26*
October 9: *Joel 4:12–21; Luke 11:27–28*

October 11: *Romans 1:1–7; Luke 11:29–32*
October 12: *Romans 1:16–25; Luke 11:37–41*
October 13: *Romans 2:1–11; Luke 11:42–46*
October 14: *Romans 3:21–30; Luke 11:47–54*
October 15: *Romans 4:1–8; Luke 12:1–7*
October 16: *Romans 4:13, 16–18; Luke 12:8–12*

**October 18: Feast of St. Luke, Evangelist
2 Timothy 4:10–17b; Luke 10:1–9**
October 19: *Romans 5:12, 15b, 17–19, 20b–21; Luke 12:35–38*
October 20: *Romans 6:12–18; Luke 12:39–48*
October 21: *Romans 6:19–23; Luke 12:49–53*
October 22: *Romans 7:18–25a; Luke 12:54–59*
October 23: *Romans 8:1–11; Luke 13:1–9*

October 25: *Romans 8:12–17; Luke 13:10–17*
October 26: *Romans 8:18–25; Luke 13:18–21*
October 27: *Romans 8:26–30; Luke 13:22–30*
**October 28: Feast of Sts. Simon and Jude, Apostles
Ephesians 2:19–22; Luke 6:12–16**
October 29: *Romans 9:1–5; Luke 14:1–6*
October 30: *Romans 11:1–2a, 11–12, 25–29; Luke 14:1, 7–11*

**November 1: Solemnity of All Saints
Revelation 7:2–4, 9–14; 1 John 3:1–3; Matthew 5:1–12a**
**November 2: Commemoration of All the Faithful
Departed (All Souls' Day)
Wisdom 3:1–9; Romans 5:5–11 or Romans 6:3–9;
John 6:37–40**
November 3: *Romans 13:8–10; Luke 14:25–33*
November 4: *Romans 14:7–12; Luke 15:1–10*
November 5: *Romans 15:14–21; Luke 16:1–8*
November 6: *Romans 16:3–9, 16, 22–27; Luke 16:9–15*

November 8: *Wisdom 1:1–7; Luke 17:1–6*
**November 9: Feast of the Dedication
of the Lateran Basilica
Ezekiel 47:1–2, 8–9, 12; 1 Corinthians 3:9c–11, 16–17;
John 2:13–22**
November 10: *Wisdom 6:1–11; Luke 17:11–19*
November 11: *Wisdom 7:22b—8:1; Luke 17:20–25*
November 12: *Wisdom 13:1–9; Luke 17:26–37*
November 13: *Wisdom 18:14–16; 19:6–9; Luke 18:1–8*

November 15: *1 Maccabees 1:10–15, 41–43, 54–57, 62–63;
Luke 18:35–43*
November 16: *2 Maccabees 6:18–31; Luke 19:1–1*
November 17: *2 Maccabees 7:1, 20–31; Luke 19:11–28*
November 18: *1 Maccabees 2:15–29; Luke 19:41–44*
November 19: *1 Maccabees 4:36–37, 52–59/Luke 19:45–48*
November 20: *1 Maccabees 6:1–13; Luke 20:27–40*

November 22: *Daniel 1:1–6, 8–20; Luke 21:1–4*
November 23: *Daniel 2:31–45; Luke 21:5–11*
November 24: *Daniel 5:1–6, 13–14, 16–17, 23–28;
Luke 21:12–19*
November 25: *Daniel 6:12–28; Luke 21:20–28*
November 26: *Daniel 7:2–14; Luke 21:29–33*
November 27: *Daniel 7:15–27; Luke 21:34–36*

September 5, 2021

READING I *Isaiah 35:4–7a*

Thus says the LORD:
Say to those whose hearts are frightened:
    Be strong, fear not!
Here is your God,
    he comes with vindication;
with divine recompense
    he comes to save you.
Then will the eyes of the blind be opened,
    the ears of the deaf be cleared;
then will the lame leap like a stag,
    then the tongue of the mute will sing.
Streams will burst forth in the desert,
    and rivers in the steppe.
The burning sands will become pools,
    and the thirsty ground, springs of water.

RESPONSORIAL PSALM
Psalm 146:6–7, 8–9, 9–10 (1b)

R. Praise the Lord, my soul!
    or: Alleluia.

The God of Jacob keeps faith forever,
    secures justice for the oppressed,
    gives food to the hungry.
The LORD sets captives free. R.

The LORD gives sight to the blind;
    the LORD raises up those who were
        bowed down.
The LORD loves the just;
    the LORD protects strangers. R.

The fatherless and the widow the LORD sustains,
    but the way of the wicked he thwarts.
The LORD shall reign forever;
    your God, O Zion, through all generations.
        Alleluia. R.

READING II *James 2:1–5*

My brothers and sisters, show no partiality as you adhere to the faith in our glorious Lord Jesus Christ. For if a man with gold rings and fine clothes comes into your assembly, and a poor person in shabby clothes also comes in, and you pay attention to the one wearing the fine clothes and say, "Sit here, please," while you say to the poor one, "Stand there," or "Sit at my feet," have you not made distinctions among yourselves and become judges with evil designs?

Listen, my beloved brothers and sisters. Did not God choose those who are poor in the world to be rich in faith and heirs of the kingdom that he promised to those who love him?

GOSPEL *Mark 7:31–37*

Again Jesus left the district of Tyre and went by way of Sidon to the Sea of Galilee, into the district of the Decapolis. And people brought to him a deaf man who had a speech impediment and begged him to lay his hand on him. He took him off by himself away from the crowd. He put his finger into the man's ears and, spitting, touched his tongue; then he looked up to heaven and groaned, and said to him, *"Ephphatha!"*—that is, "Be opened!"—And immediately the man's ears were opened, his speech impediment was removed, and he spoke plainly. He ordered them not to tell anyone. But the more he ordered them not to, the more they proclaimed it. They were exceedingly astonished and they said, "He has done all things well. He makes the deaf hear and the mute speak."

Practice of Hope

Many people prefer to stay within their comfort zone and avoid trying new activities. They may attribute their reluctance to traveling to new places and participating in the unfamiliar to being shy or a past failure. In today's Gospel, Jesus traveled to regions where many residents might have believed in more than one god, according to scholars. In the district of Decapolis, Jesus healed a man who was deaf and had a speech impediment. Even though Jesus ordered people not to tell anyone, news spread throughout the region. ◆ Consider what you perceive as obstacles that keep you from leaving your comfort zone to do God's work. How do you avoid listening to the sounds of potential ministry needs in your midst? ◆ Choose one activity that is out of your routine that might take you to a new space of spiritual growth. ◆ Consider writing a note of encouragement or calling a distant relative to open up possibilities for healing in your life.

Download more questions and activities for families, Christian initiation groups, and other adult groups at http://www.ltp.org/ahw.

Scripture Insights

In the Gospel reading, people marvel when Jesus heals a man who can neither hear nor speak, opening his ears and loosing his tongue. Their astonishment is appropriate, since Jesus is fulfilling what the prophet Isaiah foretold: "Then will . . . the ears of the deaf be cleared, . . . then the tongue of the mute will sing" (Isaiah 35:5, 6). The key to understanding the amazement in the Gospel is in Isaiah's word "then." When will these things happen? When God comes with vindication and divine recompense to save his people Israel. When they see those signs—the blind see, the deaf hear, the mute speak—they will know, "Here is your God!"

Mark's Gospel shows Jesus performing these signs and declares, "Here is your God!" Mark places Jesus in the role of Yhwh, the Savior of Israel. But there's more. The healing occurs in the region known as the Decapolis—ten Roman cities originally settled by Greeks. It's unclear whether the man that Jesus healed is a Jew or a Greek, but Jesus' healing ministry in the Decapolis region hints at his mission to save not only Israel but the world.

Psalm 146 and the Letter of James remind us who the deaf and mute symbolize not only in Israel's economy but within God's purposes. The deaf and mute are the oppressed and vulnerable, the poor and hungry, the outcast and ignored. These are the bowed-down ones, and God promises to be faithful to them, to secure justice for them, to raise them up, to sustain them, and to protect them (Psalm 146:6b, 7, 8, 9). James draws on this deep biblical tradition to remind his hearers not to show partiality to the rich over the poor, since God chose the poor of the world to be rich in faith (James 2:5).

◆ Are there any ways that our churches favor those who are rich in resources over those with fewer resources?

◆ How can we apply the truth that God favors the vulnerable in our settings today?

◆ When have you felt God raise you up when you were bowed down?

September 12, 2021

TWENTY-FOURTH SUNDAY IN ORDINARY TIME

READING I *Isaiah 50:4c–9a*

The Lord GOD opens my ear that I may hear;
and I have not rebelled,
have not turned back.
I gave my back to those who beat me,
my cheeks to those who
plucked my beard;
my face I did not shield
from buffets and spitting.

The Lord GOD is my help,
therefore I am not disgraced;
I have set my face like flint,
knowing that I shall not be put to shame.
He is near who upholds my right;
if anyone wishes to oppose me,
let us appear together.
Who disputes my right?
Let that man confront me.
See, the Lord GOD is my help;
who will prove me wrong?

RESPONSORIAL PSALM
Psalm 116:1–2, 3–4, 5–6, 8–9 (9)

R. I will walk before the Lord,
in the land of the living.
or: Alleluia.

I love the LORD because he has heard
my voice in supplication,
because he has inclined his ear to me
the day I called. R.

The cords of death encompassed me;
the snares of the netherworld seized upon me;
I fell into distress and sorrow,
and I called upon the name of the LORD,
"O LORD, save my life!" R.

Gracious is the LORD and just;
yes, our God is merciful.
The LORD keeps the little ones;
I was brought low, and he saved me. R.

For he has freed my soul from death,
my eyes from tears, my feet from stumbling.
I shall walk before the LORD
in the land of the living. R.

READING II *James 2:14–18*

What good is it, my brothers and sisters, if some-one says he has faith but does not have works? Can that faith save him? If a brother or sister has noth-ing to wear and has no food for the day, and one of you says to them, "Go in peace, keep warm, and eat well," but you do not give them the necessities of the body, what good is it? So also faith of itself, if it does not have works, is dead.

Indeed someone might say, "You have faith and I have works." Demonstrate your faith to me without works, and I will demonstrate my faith to you from my works.

GOSPEL *Mark 8:27–35*

Jesus and his disciples set out for the villages of Caesarea Philippi. Along the way he asked his disciples, "Who do people say that I am?" They said in reply, "John the Baptist, others Elijah, still others one of the prophets." And he asked them, "But who do you say that I am?" Peter said to him in reply, "You are the Christ." Then he warned them not to tell anyone about him.

He began to teach them that the Son of Man must suffer greatly and be rejected by the elders, the chief priests, and the scribes, and be killed, and rise after three days. He spoke this openly. Then Peter took him aside and began to rebuke him. At this he turned around and, looking at his disciples, rebuked Peter and said, "Get behind me, Satan. You are thinking not as God does, but as human beings do."

He summoned the crowd with his disciples and said to them, "Whoever wishes to come after me must deny himself, take up his cross, and fol-low me. For whoever wishes to save his life will lose it, but whoever loses his life for my sake and that of the gospel will save it."

Practice of Charity

The message Jesus gave to his disciples and the crowd was a difficult one. Jesus calls his followers to deny themselves and follow him. No one wants to think about losing their life, but Jesus challenges us to accept the suffering that may occur when we live as Christians. In a society filled with convenience and comfort, we are called to be countercultural and actively pursue pathways that resist greed, selfishness, and excessiveness. ◆ Open a closet or look in several drawers at home that contain items or clothing that haven't been used for a while (or probably won't be utilized). Consider donating them to a needy family or to organizations that repurpose items. ◆ Donate accumulated change to a charity of your choice. Spare change that accumulates in dressers, drawers, and jars can yield a large donation. ◆ Examine your actions during the past week. How was your faith reflected in your works?

Download more questions and activities for families, Christian initiation groups, and other adult groups at http://www.ltp.org/ahw.

Scripture Insights

In the First Reading, we hear that the Lord God opens Isaiah's ears to hear God's Word. In the Psalm, God hears the cries of his people. Isaiah's declaration, "The Lord God is my help," finds expression in the psalmist's plea ("O Lord, save my life!") and his praise that God heard and saved him when he cried out.

Continuing last week's discussion, the Second Reading focuses on how the poorest members of the assembly are to be treated. It would do a person no good to be wished peace and warmth but not be fed or receive proper clothing. James emphasizes the need to demonstrate faith through action. In this case, he means the concrete actions of caring for the bodily needs of brothers and sisters who are hungry or need clothing. "The Lord keeps the little ones" (Psalm 116:6), and so must the follower of Christ.

The Gospel shows Peter at his best and at his worst in swift succession. First, Peter has a flash of insight; he recognizes and confesses Jesus as the Christ, sent from God to save the people. But then he rebukes Jesus, horrified at the thought that the Messiah (and his friend and Lord) must suffer and die. He is certain that the Messiah triumphs and is exalted to David's throne, not nailed to a Roman cross. Jesus sternly corrects Peter: the temptation to avoid the path of suffering and death is from Satan. The path to glory and exaltation leads through the cross, not around it. Like the prophet Isaiah, who refused to defend himself against his tormentors but cast all his hopes onto God, Jesus knows that whoever loses his life for the sake of the Gospel will save it. Like the psalmist, Jesus trusts that God will save him even from death and that he will "walk before the Lord in the land of the living" (Psalm 116:9).

◆ What kind of works are the best demonstration of our faith?

◆ Why does God use suffering, weakness, and death to achieve salvation?

◆ Do you trust that God will free us from death and bring us to new life at the resurrection?

READING I *Wisdom 2:12, 17–20*

The wicked say:
Let us beset the just one, because
    he is obnoxious to us;
  he sets himself against our doings,
reproaches us for transgressions of the law
  and charges us with violations
    of our training.
Let us see whether his words be true;
  let us find out what will happen to him.
For if the just one be the son
    of God, God will defend him
and deliver him from the hand of his foes.
With revilement and torture let us put the
    just one to the test
  that we may have proof of his gentleness
and try his patience.
Let us condemn him to a shameful death;
  for according to his own words,
    God will take care of him.

RESPONSORIAL PSALM
Psalm 54:3–4, 5, 6–8 (6b)

R. The Lord upholds my life.

O God, by your name save me,
  and by your might defend my cause.
O God, hear my prayer;
  hearken to the words of my mouth. R.

For the haughty have risen up against me,
  the ruthless seek my life;
they set not God before their eyes. R.

Behold, God is my helper;
  the Lord sustains my life.
Freely will I offer you sacrifice;
  I will praise your name, O LORD, for its
    goodness. R.

READING II *James 3:16—4:3*

Beloved: Where jealousy and selfish ambition exist, there is disorder and every foul practice. But the wisdom from above is first of all pure, then peaceable, gentle, compliant, full of mercy and good fruits, without inconstancy or insincerity. And the fruit of righteousness is sown in peace for those who cultivate peace.

Where do the wars and where do the conflicts among you come from? Is it not from your passions that make war within your members? You covet but do not possess. You kill and envy but you cannot obtain; you fight and wage war. You do not possess because you do not ask. You ask but do not receive, because you ask wrongly, to spend it on your passions.

GOSPEL *Mark 9:30–37*

Jesus and his disciples left from there and began a journey through Galilee, but he did not wish anyone to know about it. He was teaching his disciples and telling them, "The Son of Man is to be handed over to men and they will kill him, and three days after his death the Son of Man will rise." But they did not understand the saying, and they were afraid to question him.

They came to Capernaum and, once inside the house, he began to ask them, "What were you arguing about on the way?" But they remained silent. They had been discussing among themselves on the way who was the greatest. Then he sat down, called the Twelve, and said to them, "If anyone wishes to be first, he shall be the last of all and the servant of all." Taking a child, he placed it in their midst, and putting his arms around it, he said to them, "Whoever receives one child such as this in my name, receives me; and whoever receives me, receives not me but the One who sent me."

Practice of Hope

A desire to be recognized for our talents and contributions is common. In that regard, the disciples were no different from people today. In the Gospel, Jesus reminds us that leaders are servants. He highlights the presence of a child among them and says, "whoever receives me, receives not me but the One who sent me." ◆ How can you celebrate the people in your life who do less appreciated tasks, such as those who collect the garbage, drive a bus, deliver the mail, or cook and serve in restaurants and at home? Recognize these helpers who might seldom hear words of encouragement and gratitude. ◆ Offer to do tasks at home that others ordinarily perform. Simple acts of service bring to life Jesus' commandment to love each other. ◆ Reflect on the importance of being recognized. How can you learn to live with more humility?

Download more questions and activities for families, Christian initiation groups, and other adult groups at http://www.ltp.org/ahw.

Scripture Insights

Today we hear the psalmist cry out to God for defense against the haughty and ruthless who seek his life. Similarly, Wisdom displays a mocking test for "the just one" when transgressors of the law decide to torture and kill him; if he is truly just, then God will deliver and defend him. The psalmist provides the answer to the test: God heard and helped him. The Gospel reveals Jesus as the Just One, who was tortured and killed but then delivered by God from death.

Jesus predicts that he will be killed and rise again, but the disciples do not understand. The depth of their misunderstanding is revealed in what they discuss as they walk along the way: which of them is the greatest. Jesus must have been horrified. Have they learned nothing of his humble, gentle way? Have they not yet grasped that the path to greatness in the kingdom leads downward toward suffering, self-renunciation, and service, rather than upward toward good reputations and worldly glory? To teach them, he centers attention on a child, a person of the lowest social status in that society. But it is these—the lost and the least—who are counted great in God's economy.

James writes to Christians scattered throughout the Roman Empire, warning them against jealousy and selfish ambition. "Ask and it will be given to you," promised Jesus (Matthew 7:7). But James tells his listeners, "You ask but do not receive." Why? Because they ask God to assist them in their war against one another; they make requests out of ambitious desires rather than from peace, mercy, and gentleness. The tormenters in the Book of Wisdom look for proof of the just one's gentleness and patience. Gentleness, peace, patience, and endurance are among the marks of a righteous person, just as they marked Jesus himself (Matthew 11:29).

◆ Would you be willing to renounce your social status to serve God?

◆ Do you seek to be marked by gentleness, peace, and patience?

◆ How do your prayers extend past your desires to seek mercy for others?

September 26, 2021

READING I *Numbers 11:25–29*

The LORD came down in the cloud and spoke to Moses. Taking some of the spirit that was on Moses, the LORD bestowed it on the seventy elders; and as the spirit came to rest on them, they prophesied.

Now two men, one named Eldad and the other Medad, were not in the gathering but had been left in the camp. They too had been on the list, but had not gone out to the tent; yet the spirit came to rest on them also, and they prophesied in the camp. So, when a young man quickly told Moses, "Eldad and Medad are prophesying in the camp," Joshua, son of Nun, who from his youth had been Moses' aide, said, "Moses, my lord, stop them." But Moses answered him, "Are you jealous for my sake? Would that all the people of the LORD were prophets! Would that the LORD might bestow his spirit on them all!"

RESPONSORIAL PSALM
Psalm 19:8, 10, 12–13, 14 (9a)

R The precepts of the Lord give joy to the heart.

The law of the LORD is perfect,
    refreshing the soul;
the decree of the LORD is trustworthy,
    giving wisdom to the simple. R.

The fear of the LORD is pure,
    enduring forever;
the ordinances of the LORD are true,
    all of them just. R.

Though your servant is careful of them,
    very diligent in keeping them,
yet who can detect failings?
    Cleanse me from my unknown faults! R.

From wanton sin especially, restrain your servant;
    let it not rule over me.
Then shall I be blameless and innocent
    of serious sin. R.

READING II *James 5:1–6*

Come now, you rich, weep and wail over your impending miseries. Your wealth has rotted away, your clothes have become moth-eaten, your gold and silver have corroded, and that corrosion will be a testimony against you; it will devour your flesh like a fire. You have stored up treasure for the last days. Behold, the wages you withheld from the workers who harvested your fields are crying aloud; and the cries of the harvesters have reached the ears of the Lord of hosts. You have lived on earth in luxury and pleasure; you have fattened your hearts for the day of slaughter. You have condemned; you have murdered the righteous one; he offers you no resistance.

GOSPEL *Mark 9:38–43, 45, 47–48*

At that time, John said to Jesus, "Teacher, we saw someone driving out demons in your name, and we tried to prevent him because he does not follow us." Jesus replied, "Do not prevent him. There is no one who performs a mighty deed in my name who can at the same time speak ill of me. For whoever is not against us is for us. Anyone who gives you a cup of water to drink because you belong to Christ, amen, I say to you, will surely not lose his reward.

"Whoever causes one of these little ones who believe in me to sin, it would be better for him if a great millstone were put around his neck and he were thrown into the sea. If your hand causes you to sin, cut it off. It is better for you to enter into life maimed than with two hands to go into Gehenna, into the unquenchable fire. And if your foot causes you to sin, cut it off. It is better for you to enter into life crippled than with two feet to be thrown into Gehenna. And if your eye causes you to sin, pluck it out. Better for you to enter into the kingdom of God with one eye than with two eyes to be thrown into Gehenna, where 'their worm does not die, and the fire is not quenched.'"

Practice of Hope

Each of us has small habits that eventually may manifest into worse habits that are more difficult to change. With a priest or spiritual director, we may want to examine more serious sins and even small sins. Jesus teaches his disciples (and us) about the need to cut off vices or change sinful habits to be with him in the next life. ◆ Journal or prayerfully consider if you have tendencies that could potentially hurt yourself or others. For spiritual growth, talk with a spiritual adviser, counselor, or priest about serious sin. ◆ Be ready to celebrate a new healthy habit or activity that replaces the time, money, and other resources that had been used for old, harmful behavior. ◆ Share your spiritual progress with a close friend or family member to keep yourself accountable and healthy. You may make new friends in a support group who share similar challenges.

Download more questions and activities for families, Christian initiation groups, and other adult groups at http://www.ltp.org/ahw.

Scripture Insights

In the First Reading, we hear how the Lord provided Moses with assistance by bestowing some of the spirit that was on him onto seventy elders. This assistance relieved Moses of some of the burden of leading the people. When Moses' faithful assistant Joshua sees two people prophesying who weren't present at the official ceremony where God's spirit was bestowed, he demands that Moses stop them from prophesying. But Moses tells Joshua that he wishes all God's people would receive the Spirit and assume prophetic leadership.

Jesus' disciples echo Joshua's concerns. They see someone driving out demons in Jesus' name, and they try to stop him because he is not one of Jesus' disciples. But Jesus echoes Moses' reply. Nobody should be prevented from invoking the power of Jesus' name to drive out demons wherever they may be.

The next part of Jesus' instruction turns to the seriousness of either causing a "little one" to sin or allowing persistent sin in one's life to cause an eternal stumble. He tells them to take anything in their lives that causes them to sin—no matter how precious that thing may be—and to get rid of it so that it cannot lead them away from God. He might have told them to be like David, who in Psalm 19 searches himself carefully and asks God to cleanse him even from unknown faults.

James' hearers, on the other hand, have ignored Jesus' instructions. They have clung to their wealth, even though their gold has caused them to commit injustices: they have withheld wages and even committed murder. They should have cast aside their wealth lest it corrupt them and turn them away from God. Instead, James warns them that their condemnation is at hand.

◆ Where do you see God's Spirit at work in people outside of your faith community?

◆ What causes you to stumble and turn away from God?

◆ Can you identify at all with the psalmist, who notes that the law of the Lord refreshes the soul?

READING I   *Genesis 2:18–24*

The LORD God said: "It is not good for the man to be alone. I will make a suitable partner for him." So the LORD God formed out of the ground various wild animals and various birds of the air, and he brought them to the man to see what he would call them; whatever the man called each of them would be its name. The man gave names to all the cattle, all the birds of the air, and all wild animals; but none proved to be the suitable partner for the man.

So the LORD God cast a deep sleep on the man, and while he was asleep, he took out one of his ribs and closed up its place with flesh. The LORD God then built up into a woman the rib that he had taken from the man. When he brought her to the man, the man said:

"This one, at last, is bone of my bones
    and flesh of my flesh;
this one shall be called 'woman,'
    for out of 'her man' this one
        has been taken."

That is why a man leaves his father and mother and clings to his wife, and the two of them become one flesh.

RESPONSORIAL PSALM
Psalm 128:1–2, 3, 4–5, 6 (see 5)

R. May the Lord bless us all the days of our lives.

Blessed are you who fear the LORD,
    who walk in his ways!
For you shall eat the fruit of your handiwork;
    blessed shall you be, and favored. R.

Your wife shall be like a fruitful vine
    in the recesses of your home;
your children like olive plants
    around your table. R.

Behold, thus is the man blessed
    who fears the LORD.
The LORD bless you from Zion:
    may you see the prosperity of Jerusalem
    all the days of your life. R.

May you see your children's children.
    Peace be upon Israel! R.

READING II   *Hebrews 2:9–11*

Brothers and sisters: He "for a little while" was made "lower than the angels," that by the grace of God he might taste death for everyone.

For it was fitting that he, for whom and through whom all things exist, in bringing many children to glory, should make the leader to their salvation perfect through suffering. He who consecrates and those who are being consecrated all have one origin. Therefore, he is not ashamed to call them "brothers."

GOSPEL   *Mark 10:2–16*

Shorter: Mark 10:2–12

The Pharisees approached Jesus and asked, "Is it lawful for a husband to divorce his wife?" They were testing him. He said to them in reply, "What did Moses command you?" They replied, "Moses permitted a husband to write a bill of divorce and dismiss her." But Jesus told them, "Because of the hardness of your hearts he wrote you this commandment. But from the beginning of creation, *God made them male and female. For this reason a man shall leave his father and mother and be joined to his wife, and the two shall become one flesh.* So they are no longer two but one flesh. Therefore what God has joined together, no human being must separate." In the house the disciples again questioned Jesus about this. He said to them, "Whoever divorces his wife and marries another commits adultery against her; and if she divorces her husband and marries another, she commits adultery."

And people were bringing children to him that he might touch them, but the disciples rebuked them. When Jesus saw this he became indignant and said to them, "Let the children come to me; do not prevent them, for the kingdom of God belongs to such as these. Amen, I say to you, whoever does not accept the kingdom of God like a child will not enter it." Then he embraced them and blessed them, placing his hands on them.

Practice of Faith

In today's Gospel, Jesus talks about marriages that God has joined. Parishes and families can support and encourage couples to lovingly live out their marriage vows. Couples who are committed to each other should be honored and acknowledged. ◆ If you are a married couple, consider becoming involved in your diocesan marriage preparation program to help engaged people discern their vocation. ◆ Are there married couples who could use your help with childcare as they take a weekend getaway for renewal? Consider volunteering to allow them time alone. ◆ Work with your parish team on scheduling a renewal of vows for couples celebrating milestone anniversaries. These celebrations can take place at weekend liturgies.

Download more questions and activities for families, Christian initiation groups, and other adult groups at http://www.ltp.org/ahw.

Scripture Insights

The Gospel offers a difficult and countercultural teaching about marriage. The Pharisees, who are experts in God's law, test Jesus on a contested element of the law. Jewish teachers at the time agreed that the law made provisions for divorce but disagreed over what constituted appropriate grounds for divorce. Jesus concedes that the law does indeed allow for divorce under certain circumstances, but he suggests that this commandment was given not as a reflection of God's ultimate purpose but to make accommodations for human weakness. Jesus appeals to a more foundational principle. He points to what God originally intended for his created beings: that, as male and female, they would be joined in permanent union. Jesus quotes first from Genesis 1 ("God made them male and female"), the verse that also reveals the profound truth that both men and women are created in God's image (Genesis 1:27).

Jesus then quotes a verse from the second chapter of Genesis, in which husband and wife unite to become one flesh (Genesis 2:24). If the first chapter of Genesis concentrates on humanity's dignity and place within creation, the second chapter focuses on the harmonious suitability of the man and the woman, created to be in relation to one another. For Jesus, the creation accounts suggest that God's original intention was for the permanence of marriage.

The Second Reading focuses on a different kind of family relationship. The Letter from Hebrews states that Jesus was made "lower than the angels"—that is, he became human. But it was this very act that enabled him to lead all humanity into salvation, from death to glory. By taking on the mortal flesh of a human being, Jesus becomes a brother to all other human beings, both men and women. We are saved by a sibling.

◆ How can the Church accompany people who struggle in marriages that are filled with pain?

◆ How does your parish encourage and support families to bring up their children in the faith?

◆ Do you think of Jesus as a brother?

READING I *Wisdom 7:7–11*

I prayed, and prudence was given me;
> I pleaded, and the spirit of wisdom came
> > to me.
I preferred her to scepter and throne,
and deemed riches nothing in comparison
> > with her,
> nor did I liken any priceless gem to her;
because all gold, in view of her, is a little sand,
> and before her, silver is to be accounted mire.
Beyond health and comeliness I loved her,
and I chose to have her rather than the light,
> because the splendor of her
> > never yields to sleep.
Yet all good things together came
> > to me in her company,
> and countless riches at her hands.

RESPONSORIAL PSALM
Psalm 90:12–13, 14–15, 16–17 (14)

R. Fill us with your love, O Lord, and we will
> > sing for joy!

Teach us to number our days aright,
> that we may gain wisdom of heart.
Return, O LORD! How long?
> Have pity on your servants! R.

Fill us at daybreak with your kindness,
> that we may shout for joy
> > and gladness all our days.
Make us glad, for the days when you afflicted us,
> for the years when we saw evil. R.

Let your work be seen by your servants
> and your glory by their children;
and may the gracious care of the LORD our
> > God be ours;
> prosper the work of our hands for us!
> Prosper the work of our hands! R.

READING II *Hebrews 4:12–13*

Brothers and sisters: Indeed the word of God is living and effective, sharper than any two-edged sword, penetrating even between soul and spirit, joints and marrow, and able to discern reflections and thoughts of the heart. No creature is concealed from him, but everything is naked and exposed to the eyes of him to whom we must render an account.

GOSPEL *Mark 10:17–30*

Shorter: Mark 10:17–27

As Jesus was setting out on a journey, a man ran up, knelt down before him, and asked him, "Good teacher, what must I do to inherit eternal life?" Jesus answered him, "Why do you call me good? No one is good but God alone. You know the commandments: *You shall not kill; you shall not commit adultery; you shall not steal; you shall not bear false witness; you shall not defraud; honor your father and your mother.*" He replied and said to him, "Teacher, all of these I have observed from my youth." Jesus, looking at him, loved him and said to him, "You are lacking in one thing. Go, sell what you have, and give to the poor and you will have treasure in heaven; then come, follow me." At that statement his face fell, and he went away sad, for he had many possessions.

Jesus looked around and said to his disciples, "How hard it is for those who have wealth to enter the kingdom of God!" The disciples were amazed at his words. So Jesus again said to them in reply, "Children, how hard it is to enter the kingdom of God! It is easier for a camel to pass through the eye of a needle than for one who is rich to enter the kingdom of God." They were exceedingly astonished and said among themselves, "Then who can be saved?" Jesus looked at them and said, "For human beings it is impossible, but not for God. All things are possible for God." Peter began to say to him, "We have given up everything and followed you." Jesus said, "Amen, I say to you, there is no one who has given up house or brothers or sisters or mother or father or children or lands for my sake and for the sake of the gospel who will not receive a hundred times more now in this present age: houses and brothers and sisters and mothers and children and lands, with persecutions, and eternal life in the age to come."

Practice of Charity

Jesus reminds us in today's Gospel that possessions can envelop us so much that we lose sight of what is important. At first in the reading, it is easy to think Jesus is saying that the rich can never get to heaven; however, the message focuses more on what possesses or consumes our attention. Obsession with a particular perspective can keep us from considering others' views and harm our relationships. ◆ Assess how you spend the majority of your personal time. Do some activities overwhelm you or drain you of finances, emotional energy, or time with loved ones? Pray about how much you give of your time, talent, and treasure to our Creator. ◆ Rummage through a closet or drawer with items that you will never use. Donate clothing, items, or furniture to a charity or to friends and family who need them.

Download more questions and activities for families, Christian initiation groups, and other adult groups at http://www.ltp.org/ahw.

Scripture Insights

In the Gospel reading, a rich man believes he must do many things to inherit the kingdom of God and that he has done all of them. Jesus, however, teaches that only one thing is necessary: to follow Jesus. One cannot carry heavy baggage around while following Jesus. One must travel light. This is what the rich man cannot do. He wants to have his possessions (security, prestige) and have Jesus too.

Still, Jesus looks at the rich man and loves him. In Hebrews, the Word of God discerns the thoughts of the heart. The Word is both Scripture, through which God continues to speak, and Jesus Christ, the Word incarnate (as in John 1:14). No creature is concealed from Jesus; we are all exposed or laid bare to his eyes. But the eyes that fully see us look at us, and into us, with love.

The disciples are amazed. How could it be that a man who has faithfully kept God's commandments cannot enter the kingdom of heaven simply because he has many possessions that he doesn't want to give up? Peter protests that the disciples have done what the rich man could not; they have given up everything to follow Jesus. They preferred Jesus to all earthly riches (see Wisdom 7:8–10). Jesus reassures them that they will receive a hundredfold reward for their sacrifice. As in Wisdom, "all good things" come to the disciples in his company. The surprise is that they will receive it "in this present age"—perhaps through the fellowship and care of their new brothers and sisters in Christ (Acts 2:44–47; 4:32–35). The catch is buried quietly in the last line: "with persecutions." Following Jesus is an abundant, overflowing life, but not one free from suffering.

◆ What does it mean to "number our days aright," as the psalmist prays?

◆ Which of your possessions may be hindering your relationship with God or friends, family, or colleagues?

◆ How does the Word of God lay us bare before God (Second Reading)?

READING I *Isaiah 53:10–11*

The LORD was pleased
    to crush him in infirmity.

If he gives his life as an offering for sin,
    he shall see his descendants in a long life,
    and the will of the LORD shall
        be accomplished through him.

Because of his affliction
    he shall see the light in fullness of days;
through his suffering, my servant
        shall justify many,
    and their guilt he shall bear.

RESPONSORIAL PSALM
Psalm 33:4–5, 18–19, 20, 22 (22)

R. Lord, let your mercy be on us, as we place
    our trust in you.

Upright is the word of the LORD,
    and all his works are trustworthy.
He loves justice and right;
    of the kindness of the LORD
        the earth is full. R.

See, the eyes of the LORD are upon those who
        fear him,
    upon those who hope for his kindness;
to deliver them from death
    and preserve them in spite of famine. R.

Our soul waits for the LORD,
    who is our help and our shield.
May your kindness, O LORD, be upon us
    who have put our hope in you. R.

READING II *Hebrews 4:14–16*

Brothers and sisters: Since we have a great high priest who has passed through the heavens, Jesus, the Son of God, let us hold fast to our confession. For we do not have a high priest who is unable to sympathize with our weaknesses, but one who has similarly been tested in every way, yet without sin. So let us confidently approach the throne of grace to receive mercy and to find grace for timely help.

GOSPEL *Mark 10:35–45*

Shorter: Mark 10:42–45

James and John, the sons of Zebedee, came to Jesus and said to him, "Teacher, we want you to do for us whatever we ask of you." He replied, "What do you wish me to do for you?" They answered him, "Grant that in your glory we may sit one at your right and the other at your left." Jesus said to them, "You do not know what you are asking. Can you drink the cup that I drink or be baptized with the baptism with which I am baptized?" They said to him, "We can." Jesus said to them, "The cup that I drink, you will drink, and with the baptism with which I am baptized, you will be baptized; but to sit at my right or at my left is not mine to give but is for those for whom it has been prepared." When the ten heard this, they became indignant at James and John. Jesus summoned them and said to them, "You know that those who are recognized as rulers over the Gentiles lord it over them, and their great ones make their authority over them felt. But it shall not be so among you. Rather, whoever wishes to be great among you will be your servant; whoever wishes to be first among you will be the slave of all. For the Son of Man did not come to be served but to serve and to give his life as a ransom for many."

Practice of Hope

Customers who observe the chef or owner working alongside employees may sense that the quality of the food, product, or service is better. Good managers infuse a level of commitment to quality among staff so that patrons have reason to return. Jesus reiterates that true glory comes from being a servant for others. Many parents, teachers, military personnel, clergy, and women religious are often living examples of servant leadership. ◆ Write a note or purchase a gift of appreciation for someone who strives daily to serve others and is a model of excellence, often without being noticed. Encourage others as well to appreciate these helpers. ◆ Learn more about servant leadership, through the Greenleaf Center (www.greenleaf.org), which is located at Seton Hall University, South Orange, New Jersey. Discover how some companies and organizations are adopting this leadership style to enrich lives and build a society that is focused on compassion and justice. ◆ Reflect on how you might work on strengthening your practice of the servant aspect of leadership.

Download more questions and activities for families, Christian initiation groups, and other adult groups at http://www.ltp.org/ahw.

Scripture Insights

It is not surprising that the disciples were indignant at James and John. How bold to ask for seats of honor in heaven! If we are honest with ourselves, however, these disciples are asking for the same things most people desire. Perhaps they simply wish to be acknowledged for their dedication to Jesus.

Jesus does not scold James and John when they boldly tell him that they want him to do whatever they ask. Instead, he simply asks them what they wish to do. Of course, Jesus knows what they want. He is the high priest who sympathizes with our weaknesses and waits eagerly for us to approach his throne of grace for mercy and help. They ask Jesus to grant them—literally, give them—the two highest places of honor in the kingdom. Jesus replies that what he has to give is not what they expect.

Jesus gathers his disciples and tells them how they will be different from all other people. Instead of lording prestige over one another, they will lower themselves. The highest place of honor is not next to the king at the banquet table but on the floor with the lowest servants, kneeling to wash the dirty feet of the guests.

What Jesus has to give them turns out to be himself. He "did not come to be served but to serve and to give his life as a ransom for many." This fulfills Isaiah's prophecy that "through his suffering, my servant shall justify many."

Three times the psalmist praises the "kindness," or the loving faithfulness, of the Lord (Psalm 33:5, 18, 22). Instead of lording power over humankind, or rejecting us when we request selfish things, God stoops down to give us his life.

◆ What would you like to ask of Christ?

◆ Do you feel able to approach God's throne to request mercy?

◆ How can you serve someone today?

READING I *Jeremiah 31:7–9*

Thus says the LORD:
Shout with joy for Jacob,
    exult at the head of the nations;
    proclaim your praise and say:
The LORD has delivered his people,
    the remnant of Israel.
Behold, I will bring them back
    from the land of the north;
I will gather them from the ends of the world,
    with the blind and the lame in their midst,
the mothers and those with child;
    they shall return as an immense throng.
They departed in tears,
    but I will console them and guide them;
I will lead them to brooks of water,
    on a level road, so that none shall stumble.
For I am a father to Israel,
    Ephraim is my first-born.

RESPONSORIAL PSALM
Psalm 126:1–2, 2–3, 4–5, 6 (3)

R. The Lord has done great things for us; we are
    filled with joy.

When the LORD brought back the captives of Zion,
    we were like men dreaming.
Then our mouth was filled with laughter,
    and our tongue with rejoicing. R.

Then they said among the nations,
    "The LORD has done great things for them."
The LORD has done great things for us;
    we are glad indeed. R.

Restore our fortunes, O LORD,
    like the torrents in the southern desert.
Those that sow in tears
    shall reap rejoicing. R.

Although they go forth weeping,
    carrying the seed to be sown,
they shall come back rejoicing,
    carrying their sheaves. R.

READING II *Hebrews 5:1–6*

Brothers and sisters: Every high priest is taken from among men and made their representative before God, to offer gifts and sacrifices for sins. He is able to deal patiently with the ignorant and erring, for he himself is beset by weakness and so, for this reason, must make sin offerings for himself as well as for the people. No one takes this honor upon himself but only when called by God, just as Aaron was. In the same way, it was not Christ who glorified himself in becoming high priest, but rather the one who said to him:
    You are my son:
        this day I have begotten you;
just as he says in another place:
    You are a priest forever
        according to the order of Melchizedek.

GOSPEL *Mark 10:46–52*

As Jesus was leaving Jericho with his disciples and a sizable crowd, Bartimaeus, a blind man, the son of Timaeus, sat by the roadside begging. On hearing that it was Jesus of Nazareth, he began to cry out and say, "Jesus, son of David, have pity on me." And many rebuked him, telling him to be silent. But he kept calling out all the more, "Son of David, have pity on me." Jesus stopped and said, "Call him." So they called the blind man, saying to him, "Take courage; get up, Jesus is calling you." He threw aside his cloak, sprang up, and came to Jesus. Jesus said to him in reply, "What do you want me to do for you?" The blind man replied to him, "Master, I want to see." Jesus told him, "Go your way; your faith has saved you." Immediately he received his sight and followed him on the way.

Practice of Faith

A blind man named Bartimaeus cried out to Jesus as he was leaving Jericho. The blind man wanted to be able to "see." Some people may seem to have it all but may be blind in some areas of their life or may struggle with their faith. By sharing how God's Spirit works in our lives, we can become a spiritual gateway to others. ◆ Tell friends and family about your prayer practices to help them cultivate a deeper trust in Christ. ◆ Be encouraged by others' witness of prayer. Although some people may discourage you as you pray more and trust in our Creator (as the crowd initially did in this Gospel), be heartened by those who help clear a path for your future spiritual discoveries and insight.

Download more questions and activities for families, Christian initiation groups, and other adult groups at http://www.ltp.org/ahw.

Scripture Insights

The readings this week show life with God as a journey along "the way." In the Old Testament readings, "the way" is a journey home from exile in Babylon. God gathers his displaced people and brings them back to the land of Israel. It's a familiar road. The Jews first walked it weeping after Israel's defeat by Babylon. Now it is a path of joy and laughter as they set their hearts toward home.

As the Gospel reading indicates, early Christians sometimes referred to the lifelong journey of following Jesus as "the way." After the blind beggar Bartimaeus receives his sight again, he follows Jesus "on the way."

When Jesus asks, "What do you want me to do for you?" Bartimaeus has a simple answer: "I want to see." In Scripture, sight often has a double meaning. It means to see with one's physical eyes, but it also means to see with the heart and the mind—to perceive or understand. Bartimaeus receives both kinds of sight. He is no longer physically blind and does not need to beg on the side of the road anymore. But he also sees correctly that Jesus is the Son of God.

Just before Jesus heals Bartimaeus, he tells him, "Go your way; your faith has saved you." The word for "heal" and "save" are the same, and Jesus has done both: healed Bartimaeus and saved him. Instead of following Jesus' instructions to "Go your way," Bartimaeus does the right thing—he goes Jesus' way instead, taking up the role of the disciple by following him.

This too is a way of rejoicing and not of tears, paved by the one who deals patiently with our ignorance and errors. It will have its shares of hardships and sorrows, but it is ultimately a way of deep joy that leads to our home with the Lord.

◆ Do you look to God to guide you and keep you from stumbling?

◆ Where in your life are you lacking sight? Would you like Christ to help you see?

◆ Has God ever filled your mouth with laughter after a time of sorrow (Psalm 126:2)?

READING I *Deuteronomy 6:2–6*

Moses spoke to the people, saying: "Fear the Lord, your God, and keep, throughout the days of your lives, all his statutes and commandments which I enjoin on you, and thus have long life. Hear then, Israel, and be careful to observe them, that you may grow and prosper the more, in keeping with the promise of the Lord, the God of your fathers, to give you a land flowing with milk and honey.

"Hear, O Israel! The Lord is our God, the Lord alone! Therefore, you shall love the Lord, your God, with all your heart, and with all your soul, and with all your strength. Take to heart these words which I enjoin on you today."

RESPONSORIAL PSALM *Psalm 18:2–3, 3–4, 47, 51 (2)*

R. I love you, Lord, my strength.

I love you, O Lord, my strength,
O Lord, my rock, my fortress,
my deliverer. R.

My God, my rock of refuge,
my shield, the horn of my salvation,
my stronghold!
Praised be the Lord, I exclaim,
and I am safe from my enemies. R.

The Lord lives! And blessed be my rock!
Extolled be God my savior,
you who gave great victories to your king
and showed kindness to your anointed. R.

READING II *Hebrews 7:23–28*

Brothers and sisters: The levitical priests were many because they were prevented by death from remaining in office, but Jesus, because he remains forever, has a priesthood that does not pass away. Therefore, he is always able to save those who approach God through him, since he lives forever to make intercession for them.

It was fitting that we should have such a high priest: holy, innocent, undefiled, separated from sinners, higher than the heavens. He has no need, as did the high priests, to offer sacrifice day after day, first for his own sins and then for those of the people; he did that once for all when he offered himself. For the law appoints men subject to weakness to be high priests, but the word of the oath, which was taken after the law, appoints a son, who has been made perfect forever.

GOSPEL *Mark 12:28b–34*

One of the scribes came to Jesus and asked him, "Which is the first of all the commandments?" Jesus replied, "The first is this: *Hear, O Israel! The Lord our God is Lord alone! You shall love the Lord your God with all your heart, with all your soul, with all your mind, and with all your strength.* The second is this: *You shall love your neighbor as yourself.* There is no other commandment greater than these." The scribe said to him, "Well said, teacher. You are right in saying, 'He is One and there is no other than he.' And 'to love him with all your heart, with all your understanding, with all your strength, and to love your neighbor as yourself' is worth more than all burnt offerings and sacrifices." And when Jesus saw that he answered with understanding, he said to him, "You are not far from the kingdom of God." And no one dared to ask him any more questions.

Practice of Charity

Daily global, national, and local news can be overwhelming, leaving people feeling powerless. What God asks of us is straightforward. As the Gospel states, we are to love God, with our heart, soul, mind, and all our strength, and love our neighbors as ourselves. This may be harder than it sounds, but when we love others through our actions and thoughts, we are doing what God requests. Kindness felt in the workplace, school, and at home can have a ripple effect, reaching many others and creating waves of grace. ◆ Be especially attentive this week to people you encounter who may need an encouraging word. ◆ Follow up the question of "How are you?" with more care and be open to establishing a deeper connection. ◆ Try to realize that prayer includes listening to God. Carve out some of your prayer time to just be quiet with God.

Download more questions and activities for families, Christian initiation groups, and other adult groups at http://www.ltp.org/ahw.

Scripture Insights

The scribes knew God's law. They loved God's law. When a scribe, then, asks Jesus which is the first or greatest of the commandments, he is testing the Lord. Jesus answers the query by naming the two "love commandments": love God and love your neighbor. The command itself explains how to love God—with all one's soul, mind, and strength. That is, with your entire being, from head to toe. The scribe agrees; Jesus has identified the heart of the law.

The psalmist provides another illustration of what it means to love God, by expressing that love in song, praising God as his deliverer and stronghold, his rock and salvation. Deuteronomy provides another example. To love God is to fear God—that is, to show appropriate reverence and awe toward the Creator of the universe. To love is also to obey, to honor only the Lord and no other gods.

While the reading from the Gospel of Mark portrays Jesus as the wisest of scribes, the Book of Hebrews reveals his identity as a high priest. Jesus is like the high priests because he offered a sacrifice that atoned for the sins of the people. But the Risen Christ is unlike them because he will never die; his priesthood endures forever. He is also unlike them because the other high priests had to continually offer sacrifices. Christ needed to offer only one sacrifice: himself. As both priest and sacrificial lamb, Christ made one perfect sacrifice on the cross, "once for all."

Despite this, Jesus' work as priest is not done. Although he no longer offers sacrifices to atone for sin, the author of Hebrews writes that "he lives forever to make intercession" for those who approach God through him. That is his priestly role now: when we come to Jesus, he intercedes with God on our behalf.

◆ What does it mean to love God with the heart and the mind?

◆ When the scribe asks Jesus which is the first of the commandments, why does Jesus name two?

◆ How would you like Jesus Christ to intercede with God for you?

READING I *1 Kings 17:10–16*

In those days, Elijah the prophet went to Zarephath. As he arrived at the entrance of the city, a widow was gathering sticks there; he called out to her, "Please bring me a small cupful of water to drink." She left to get it, and he called out after her, "Please bring along a bit of bread." She answered, "As the LORD, your God, lives, I have nothing baked; there is only a handful of flour in my jar and a little oil in my jug. Just now I was collecting a couple of sticks, to go in and prepare something for myself and my son; when we have eaten it, we shall die." Elijah said to her, "Do not be afraid. Go and do as you propose. But first make me a little cake and bring it to me. Then you can prepare something for yourself and your son. For the LORD, the God of Israel, says, 'The jar of flour shall not go empty, nor the jug of oil run dry, until the day when the LORD sends rain upon the earth.'" She left and did as Elijah had said. She was able to eat for a year, and he and her son as well; the jar of flour did not go empty, nor the jug of oil run dry, as the LORD had foretold through Elijah.

RESPONSORIAL PSALM
Psalm 146:7, 8–9, 9–10 (1b)

R. Praise the Lord, my soul!
   or: Alleluia.

The LORD keeps faith forever,
   secures justice for the oppressed,
   gives food to the hungry.
The LORD sets captives free. R.

The LORD gives sight to the blind;
   the LORD raises up those
         who were bowed down.
The LORD loves the just;
   the LORD protects strangers. R.

The fatherless and the widow he sustains,
   but the way of the wicked he thwarts.
The LORD shall reign forever;
   your God, O Zion, through all generations.
         Alleluia. R.

READING II *Hebrews 9:24–28*

Christ did not enter into a sanctuary made by hands, a copy of the true one, but heaven itself, that he might now appear before God on our behalf. Not that he might offer himself repeatedly, as the high priest enters each year into the sanctuary with blood that is not his own; if that were so, he would have had to suffer repeatedly from the foundation of the world. But now once for all he has appeared at the end of the ages to take away sin by his sacrifice. Just as it is appointed that human beings die once, and after this the judgment, so also Christ, offered once to take away the sins of many, will appear a second time, not to take away sin but to bring salvation to those who eagerly await him.

GOSPEL *Mark 12:38–44*

Shorter: Mark 12:41–44

In the course of his teaching Jesus said to the crowds, "Beware of the scribes, who like to go around in long robes and accept greetings in the marketplaces, seats of honor in synagogues, and places of honor at banquets. They devour the houses of widows and, as a pretext recite lengthy prayers. They will receive a very severe condemnation."

He sat down opposite the treasury and observed how the crowd put money into the treasury. Many rich people put in large sums. A poor widow also came and put in two small coins worth a few cents. Calling his disciples to himself, he said to them, "Amen, I say to you, this poor widow put in more than all the other contributors to the treasury. For they have all contributed from their surplus wealth, but she, from her poverty, has contributed all she had, her whole livelihood."

Practice of Charity

"Time is of the essence" is a phrase that resonates with many in this busy world. It is tempting to cringe when a person needs more of our time. Tasks, after all, need to be accomplished. For many, the way time is spent can mean more than any donation. In today's Gospel, a poor widow donated money from her meager savings. Jesus pointed out that she contributed from her poverty. ◆ Examine your calendar to set aside time for face-to-face conversations with people who are important to you. ◆ Consider the donations that you made to your parish and charities and determine whether you are giving only from your surplus. ◆ Look at your calendar and decide whether you have more time to spend on a worthy parish or community project.

Download more questions and activities for families, Christian initiation groups, and other adult groups at http://www.ltp.org/ahw.

Scripture Insights

Hebrews reminds us that the high priests in Israel enacted a ritual that echoed a heavenly one. Every year, they entered into a "copy" of heaven (that is, the inner sanctum of the Jerusalem temple) to make atonement for sins. Jesus perfects and completes this ritual. He enters into the true sanctuary—heaven itself—and "once for all" makes atonement for sins by his sacrifice, bearing not the blood of others but his own blood. When Christ appears to us again, it will be for the final salvation that we eagerly await, when "the LORD shall reign forever" (Psalm 146:10) in the new creation.

The Gospel reading contains a double-edged sword. Jesus observes people putting money into the temple treasury. Wealthy people put in a lot, but Jesus does not comment on that. A poor widow puts in two coins, and Jesus gathers his disciples to proclaim that the woman has contributed more than everyone else put together, because she gave out of her poverty.

On the one hand, this is a praiseworthy story of costly generosity. The woman in the Gospel is like the widow of Zarephath, who gave her last scrap of flour and oil to the prophet Elijah. That widow's flour and oil never ran out; as the psalmist writes, "The widow [God] sustains."

The psalmist also writes, "but the way of the wicked he thwarts." Just before Jesus observes the widow, he warns against the scribes, who "devour the houses of widows." Suddenly Jesus' observation that she gave "her whole livelihood" takes on a sharper note. Have the scribes, who were associated with the temple leadership, devoured her house? Jesus' story challenges us not only to admire the widow but to condemn those who failed to care for her in her poverty.

◆ Why does Elijah ask the widow to give him food even after the widow says that she only has enough food left for one small meal?

◆ Do you ever think of Christ as appearing before God on your behalf? Why would this be important to you?

◆ What does the Gospel reading teach about how to give?

READING I *Daniel 12:1–3*

In those days, I, Daniel,
heard this word of the Lord:
"At that time there shall arise
Michael, the great prince,
guardian of your people;
it shall be a time unsurpassed in distress
since nations began until that time.
At that time your people shall escape,
everyone who is found written in the book.

"Many of those who sleep in the dust of the
earth shall awake;
some shall live forever,
others shall be an everlasting horror
and disgrace.

"But the wise shall shine brightly
like the splendor of the firmament,
and those who lead the many to justice
shall be like the stars forever."

RESPONSORIAL PSALM
Psalm 16:5, 8, 9–10, 11 (1)

R. You are my inheritance, O Lord!

O LORD, my allotted portion and my cup,
you it is who hold fast my lot.
I set the LORD ever before me;
with him at my right hand
I shall not be disturbed. R.

Therefore my heart is glad and my soul rejoices,
my body, too, abides in confidence;
because you will not abandon my soul to the
netherworld,
nor will you suffer your faithful one to
undergo corruption. R.

You will show me the path to life,
fullness of joys in your presence,
the delights at your right hand forever. R.

READING II *Hebrews 10:11–14, 18*

Brothers and sisters: Every priest stands daily at his ministry, offering frequently those same sacrifices that can never take away sins. But this one offered one sacrifice for sins, and took his seat forever at the right hand of God; now he waits until his enemies are made his footstool. For by one offering he has made perfect forever those who are being consecrated.

Where there is forgiveness of these, there is no longer offering for sin.

GOSPEL *Mark 13:24–32*

Jesus said to his disciples: "In those days after
that tribulation
the sun will be darkened,
and the moon will not give its light,
and the stars will be falling from the sky,
and the powers in the heavens will
be shaken.

"And then they will see 'the Son of Man coming in the clouds' with great power and glory, and then he will send out the angels and gather his elect from the four winds, from the end of the earth to the end of the sky.

"Learn a lesson from the fig tree. When its branch becomes tender and sprouts leaves, you know that summer is near. In the same way, when you see these things happening, know that he is near, at the gates. Amen, I say to you, this generation will not pass away until all these things have taken place. Heaven and earth will pass away, but my words will not pass away.

"But of that day or hour, no one knows, neither the angels in heaven, nor the Son, but only the Father."

Practice of Hope

All of us are journeying through time together, even though we may live in different parts of the world. Most people experience the change of seasons. We know that eventually winter will arrive, followed by a slow transformation into spring. In the same way, each of us knows that we eventually pass from this worldly life to the next and that the aging process has seasons to discover and endure. Our faith in the life, death, and Resurrection of Jesus can be hopeful because we have his Word and God's promise of new life. ◆ Find some photographs of yourself when you were a child, then a teenager, and beyond. As you reflect on these images, think about all of the positive changes that have happened through the years; the occasions of new life that emerged in you over time. ◆ Journal about or ponder all the ways that the Holy Spirit works in your life today. ◆ Consider how God is thriving in the lives of your family members and friends.

Download more questions and activities for families, Christian initiation groups, and other adult groups at http://www.ltp.org/ahw.

Scripture Insights

The two Old Testament readings point to the joys of eternal life. The psalmist is confident that God will not abandon his soul to "the netherworld" but will show him "the path to life, fullness of joys in your presence." Daniel writes that after a time of tribulation, "Many of those who sleep in the dust of the earth shall awake"—some to life and some to everlasting disgrace. Those who have been wise and just "shall shine brightly like the splendor of the firmament."

In the Gospel, Jesus also refers to a time of tribulation and then the final judgment. He quotes from another portion of Daniel to promise that at the end of all things the Son of Man (Jesus himself) will "gather his elect . . . from the end of the earth to the end of the sky" (Mark 13:26–27; see Dan 7:13–14). He tells his disciples to be alert for the signs of the end, but he also discourages speculation by insisting that not even the Son knows the day or hour of the end—only the Father.

Hebrews continues its theme of Jesus' unique sacrifice. Unlike the sacrifices of the earthly priests, Jesus' sacrifice for sin was effective and does not need to be repeated. Seated at the right hand of God (the highest place of honor in heaven), Christ now waits, as we do, for the end, when all of his enemies (the enduring power of sin, evil, and death) will be defeated forever, and the faithful will be raised to everlasting life. In the Gospel, the stars fall from the sky; in Daniel, the just ones take the place of the stars, lighting up the new age with their radiance.

◆ Why do you think it is important that no one know the time of the Second Coming?

◆ What does it mean to say that the wise and the just will "be like the stars"?

◆ Like the psalmist, are you confident that God will not abandon your soul?

November 21, 2021   OUR LORD JESUS CHRIST, KING OF THE UNIVERSE

READING I *Daniel 7:13–14*

As the visions during the night continued, I saw
  one like a son of man coming,
    on the clouds of heaven;
when he reached the Ancient One
    and was presented before him,
the one like a Son of man received dominion,
      glory, and kingship;
  all peoples, nations,
      and languages serve him.
His dominion is an everlasting dominion
  that shall not be taken away,
  his kingship shall not be destroyed.

RESPONSORIAL PSALM
Psalm 93:1, 1–2, 5 (1a)

R. The Lord is king; he is robed in majesty.

The LORD is king, in splendor robed;
  robed is the LORD and girt about with
    strength. R.

And he has made the world firm,
  not to be moved.
Your throne stands firm from of old;
  from everlasting you are, O LORD. R.

Your decrees are worthy of trust indeed;
  holiness befits your house,
  O LORD, for length of days. R.

READING II *Revelation 1:5–8*

Jesus Christ is the faithful witness, the firstborn of the dead and ruler of the kings of the earth. To him who loves us and has freed us from our sins by his blood, who has made us into a kingdom, priests for his God and Father, to him be glory and power forever and ever. Amen.

  Behold, he is coming amid the clouds,
    and every eye will see him,
    even those who pierced him.
  All the peoples of the earth will lament him.
    Yes. Amen.

    "I am the Alpha and the Omega," says the Lord God, "the one who is and who was and who is to come, the almighty."

GOSPEL *John 18:33b–37*

Pilate said to Jesus, "Are you the King of the Jews?" Jesus answered, "Do you say this on your own or have others told you about me?" Pilate answered, "I am not a Jew, am I? Your own nation and the chief priests handed you over to me. What have you done?" Jesus answered, "My kingdom does not belong to this world. If my kingdom did belong to this world, my attendants would be fighting to keep me from being handed over to the Jews. But as it is, my kingdom is not here." So Pilate said to him, "Then you are a king?" Jesus answered, "You say I am a king. For this I was born and for this I came into the world, to testify to the truth. Everyone who belongs to the truth listens to my voice."

Practice of Faith

Jesus the Christ is celebrated as the true King in our celebration of Mass, but he did not reside in any castle or empire. Through God's gift of the Spirit, Jesus Christ rests inside each of us. Over this past liturgical year, we have heard many stories of Jesus' reign as the true servant leader who showed us how to live in simplicity and in connection with God. Jesus taught us how to pray and how to die to ourselves in the eternal hope of new life with our Creator. In this era of excess and publicity seeking, it is easy to forget that the strongest leaders serve others quietly. ◆ Consider the walls built in your neighborhood to keep out people whose presence might challenge your and your neighbors' way of life. Pray to understand what you can do to reach out to people and help your community serve the most vulnerable. ◆ Celebrate Jesus Christ as the king in your life by connecting with the Holy Spirit throughout the day. ◆ Ponder the image of king and determine your comfort level with this title given to Jesus.

Download more questions and activities for families, Christian initiation groups, and other adult groups at http://www.ltp.org/ahw.

Scripture Insights

"Are you the King of the Jews?" Pilate wants to know. If Jesus declares himself to be king of the Jews, then Pilate can execute him for sedition, for threatening Caesar's authority. Jesus' roundabout answer must have puzzled Pilate. Jesus, of course, is a king—not only of the Jews, but over the whole universe, even over Caesar. Pilate has simply misunderstood the nature of Jesus' kingship. He is not a king among other kings. Instead, Jesus is a king the way God is a king: "in splendor robed," the psalmist declares. Emperors and presidents come and go; Jesus' throne endures forever.

When the visionary John writes to the Christians of Asia Minor (Caesar's domain, remember), he tells them that Christ "has made us into a kingdom"—in other words, Jesus' kingdom consists of every person who "listens to [his] voice" (John 18:37). Revelation names the universal scope of Jesus' rule by identifying him as the exalted Son of Man in Daniel's vision who was given everlasting "dominion, glory, and kingship" over all the peoples and nations of the earth (Daniel 7:14; Revelation 1:6–7). When the author of Revelation declares that "all the peoples of the earth will lament him" or wail over him, he is borrowing from the prophet Zechariah, who prophesied that God would "pour out a spirit of compassion" on his people so that they would mourn for the one they had pierced as if weeping over a firstborn son or an only child (12:10).

In this way, Revelation suggests that the nations might do what Pilate and the high priests could not: recognize Jesus as the true king, the one who was and is and is to come, and bow before him in repentance.

◆ What does the suffering Jesus standing before Pilate teach you about kingship?

◆ What does it mean for you to belong to Jesus' kingdom? If you take this to heart, will it change the way that you live?

◆ How can you be a faithful witness for Jesus Christ and the kingdom?